RITE OUT OF TIME

A STUDY OF THE ANCIENT RITE OF CHURCHING AND ITS SURVIVAL IN THE TWENTIETH CENTURY

MARGARET HOULBROOKE

SHAUN TYAS
DONINGTON
2011

© Margaret Houlbrooke 2011

Published by

SHAUN TYAS
1 High Street
Donington
Lincolnshire
PE11 4TA

ISBN
978–1–907730–10–8

Printed and bound in Great Britain
by MPG Book Group, Bodmin and King's Lynn

CONTENTS

Acknowledgements	vi
Preface	vii
Introduction: Rites, Rituals and Purifications	1
1 History of the Churching Service: Custom and Liturgy	8
2 Churching in Three Counties: Written Records in Berkshire, Staffordshire and London	24
3 Women and the Decision to be Churched	46
4 'To What Extent is the Churching of Women still Maintained?' Clerical Replies to the Southwark Visitation of 1951	71
5 Churching Discovered through Personal Testimony	101
6 Out of Time: the Decline of Churching in the Twentieth Century	125
Conclusion	137
Appendix: Sources and Bibliography	139
Index	149

ACKNOWLEDGEMENTS

I want to thank Ralph Houlbrooke and Malcolm Hamilton for their wise advice, encouragement and patience as my study took shape. I am grateful to Margaret Lyle and Tom McBride for expertly and imaginatively giving graphic expression to my facts and figures. For permission to cite unpublished material my thanks go to Alan Bartlett, Richard Sykes and M. W. Staton.

I am grateful to all those who made this study possible: staff in the London Metropolitan Archives and County Record Offices in Reading, Stafford and Woking who helped me to penetrate the obscurities of parish maps and records; Sue Brown who drove me to my London parishes; and the many women and clergy who offered written and oral testimony on churching.

My thanks go too to those who have read chapters and offered advice and critcism: Mark Laynesmith, Joan Dils, Tony Corley, Claudine McCreadie, Lillian Waites and Hazel Morgan.

Greatest debts of thanks and gratitude are to Ralph, Tom and Sarah who kept me going, and unfailingly supported all that I was trying to do.

PREFACE

This book is about my search for an ancient ritual as it has survived into modern times: 'the form of thanksgiving which Christian women make after childbirth'. My interest in it arose during a discussion about the life and duty of the medieval wife which soon revealed to me churching's importance and long duration. In a very short time students, friends and readers of the *Church Times*, responding to my enquiries and a short questionaire about churching, gave me a fund of stories and recollections, some quite strange and unexpected, which were to become the starting-point of this research. They suggested that for new mothers this rite was not just a thanksgiving after childbirth, but also a compulsory ritual to bring about release from alleged shame and uncleanness. Exploring this apparent dual identity (thanksgiving *and* purification) was to lead me into the history of earliest church liturgy, which had to deal with such notions as the sin of Eve, Levitical prohibitions, and taboo associated with women entering sacred buildings. Looking at recent times, it brought up unexpected talk of superstition and evidence of the control of mothers during and after childbirth. There were some interesting encounters with members of the clergy who have undertaken churchings in the recent past.

In most histories this childbirth rite is placed firmly in the past. An early footprint is found in Bede's *History of the English Church*. Becky Lee demonstrated its significance to families in the middle ages. In two fascinating articles, Will Coster and David Cressy illustrated how it caused debate and confrontation in the early modern period. But a study by Donna Ray brought it from the eighteenth into the twentieth century, and two unpublished theses brought it firmly into the 1960s: one was based in southern Staffordshire, the other in an area of Newcastle.[1]

---

[1] Bede, *A History of the English Church and People*, tr. Leo Shirley Price (Harmondsworth, 1962); Becky Lee, 'Men's Recollections of a Women's Rite: Medieval English Men's Recollections Regarding the Rite of the Purification of Women after Childbirth', *Gender & History*, 14. 2 (August, 2002), pp. 224–41; Will Coster, 'Purity, Profanity and Puritanism: The Churching of Women 1500–1700', in *Women in the Church*, ed. W. Sheils and D. Wood, *Studies in Church History*, XXVII (Oxford, 1990), pp. 377–87; David Cressy, 'Purification, Thanksgiving and the Churching of Women in Post-Reformation England', *Past and Present*, 141 (1993), pp. 106–46; Donna E. Ray, 'A View from the Childwife's Pew: The Development of Rites around Childbirth in the Anglican Communion', *Anglican and Episcopal History*, LXIX. 4 (2000), pp. 443–73; Richard Sykes, 'Popular Religion in Dudley and the Gornals c. 1914–1965' (Unpub-

It became a matter of compelling interest to establish whether, and to what extent, this ancient ceremony really has been celebrated in the recent past. I began to search for written evidence, and found it in parish records all over the country, mostly in weekly registers and fee books. I chose three areas for particular scrutiny: the Archdeaconry of Old Berkshire in the diocese of Oxford; Stafford Archdeaconry in the diocese of Lichfield; and the dioceses of Middlesex and Southwark where they lie within the Metropolitan area of London. Added to this was the evidence of a visitation in the whole diocese of Southwark which told much about clerical attitudes to churching in 1951, a year at the very centre of my twentieth-century study.

Most other written records had petered out by then, but correspondence and oral testimony from contemporary parishioners and clergy who could remember churchings, both recent and long past, brought the study up to the end of the twentieth century. Nearly all participants confirmed that until the 1980s it was not unusual for a new mother to go for a churching, generally sent along by her own mother, sometimes propelled by her family's sanctions and reproaches.

How is it that this thanksgiving rite, with all it ambiguities, has remained popular for so long? Were women really willing to submit to it? And why, apparently, has it finally come to an end? The study was launched by these questions, and has attempted some answers in the following pages.

---

lished Ph.D. Thesis, University of Wolverhampton, 1999); M. W. Staton, 'The Rite of Churching: a Sociological Analysis, with Special Reference to an Urban Area in Newcastle-upon-Tyne' (Unpublished M. A. Thesis, University of Newcastle, 1980).

INTRODUCTION
RITES, RITUALS AND PURIFICATIONS

Most societies have developed some rite of passage following the pain and hazard of recent childbirth, to allow women to celebrate this important event and express relief that the time of danger and uncertainty is at an end. Its earliest known Christian form, the medieval 'blessing', set the stage for a public ritual during which the new mother would take her place under the church porch, to be joined there by the priest in prayers and psalms of thanksgiving for her safe delivery. This was followed by cleansing with holy water sprinkled from a spray of hyssop, before she was formally allowed to step inside the church, her first entry since the birth, to complete the celebration. As she left she was expected to make an offering to the priest, of the baby's linen chrisom, or a small sum of money. By these means (initial exclusion from the church, symbolic cleansing, and obligatory offering) what might have seemed a simple thanksgiving achieved the status of a purification rite, something designed both to ritualise the transition through which the mother had recently passed (conception, pregnancy and parturition), and also to prevent any associated 'impurity' or 'uncleanness' from adversely affecting those with whom she came into contact.

From its earliest years the Christian church adopted the notion that new mothers were in some way compromised by childbirth. Its early medieval penitentials forbade them to enter a church before thirty-three (or sixty-six) days had elapsed since the birth of a boy (or girl): only after this time might they leave their houses and go through the churching rite which gained them a return to full membership of the church's gatherings and services.[1] Versions of the ancient ceremony, with its combination of heartfelt thanks, precise timings and confining prohibitions, have remained in the liturgies of Western Christendom until almost the end of the twentieth century. This recollection, given in an interview in August, 2004, describes the start of a Roman Catholic churching in 1970:

> I went to our local church at home, where I knew the priest very well, and he met me at the door and he led me up the aisle ... And there were certain candles lit, I'm sure. And I held on to something, and I thought it was the lace at the bottom of his ... I think it was the stole that I held ... and the candle which I carried; we went to the altar rail, we prayed together; and I think

---

[1] See Ludwig Bieler (ed.), *The Irish Penitentials* (Dublin, 1963), pp. 93, 117, 181, 223.

it was supposed to be something quite joyful but I remember being a bit, you know, unnerved by it all, and of course, being a bright young thing at the time, thinking 'well I'm not unclean because I've had a baby – I'm absolutely marvellous because I've produced a child.'[2]

Rites of passage are found in all societies: exclusion and ceremonial at significant moments such as birth and naming, coming of age, betrothal, marriage, childbearing, and death. They are designed to confront common fear of real physical danger, and to allay superstitious dread of ill-luck, possibly some jealous working of an evil eye, that might threaten those connected to the event or its aftermath. One early attempt to explain this fear was made in 1904 by the social anthropologist Arnold Van Gennep:

> The person who must pass from one [state] to another is himself in danger and emanates danger to others. The danger is controlled by ritual which precisely separates him from his old status, segregates him for a time, and then publicly declares his entry into his new status ... The whole repertoire of ideas concerning pollution and purification are used to mark the gravity of the event.

More recently Mary Douglas has shown how this applies to a woman after childbirth. Birth, she says, is of its nature an uncontrolled event, dangerous and 'untidy'. Churching, a purification ceremony of thanksgiving and re-admission to the church, emphasised the restoration of safety, order and control. Until it had taken place, the new mother would be thought to remain 'polluted', carrying a threat of danger to her family and community.[3] The rite was believed to be of vital importance: a woman's safe passage from conception, through pregnancy to labour and birth, was so essential to society, and at the same time so fraught with danger to both mother and child that its purification ceremonies must, at all costs, take place.

Notions of 'pollution', 'uncleanness' and 'purification' have turned up frequently during this research: adopted in the church's early liturgies; disputed by reformers in the sixteenth and seventeenth centuries; still given endorsement by popular tradition in the nineteenth; and found repeated surprisingly often in the twentieth by clergy and women, though with diminishing evidence of real conviction or belief. Since their currency has survived, along with the traditions of ritual exclusion associated with them, it is important to examine in what exactly early purification ideas consisted, particularly where they were targeted at women in childbirth.

---

[2] Testimony given in Oxfordshire, November, 2004.
[3] Arnold Van Gennep, *The Rites of Passage* (London, 1909), pp. 41, 166; Mary Douglas, *Purity and Danger: an Analysis of the Concepts of Pollution and Taboo* (London, 1966), p. 94.

INTRODUCTION

In early Christian definition it is hard to escape the conclusion that female sexuality and its effects on male behaviour lie somewhere near the heart of this perception of 'pollution'. Why else was Eve's disobedience cursed with pain and travail in childbirth? For what other reason did the Decrees of Leviticus condemn newly-delivered women to weeks of exclusion? How else could St Paul justify his advice that women 'adorn themselves in modest apparel, with shamefacedness and sobriety', and conduct themselves 'in silence, with all subjection'? He explained:

> For Adam was first formed, then Eve. And Adam was not deceived, but the woman being deceived was in the transgression. Notwithstanding she shall be saved in childbearing, if they continue in faith and charity and holiness with sobriety.

This theme continues as some remarkably specific pointers are given in the Venerable Bede's account of the correspondence between Augustine of Canterbury and Pope Gregory I, soon after Augustine had been sent by the Roman church to England in A.D. 597 on a mission to the island's inhabitants, both Christian and Pagan. The new archbishop had asked the pope for advice about, among many things, matters of sex and marriage:

> May an expectant mother be baptized? How soon after childbirth may she enter church? ... How soon after childbirth may a husband have relations with his wife? And may a woman properly enter church at certain periods? And may she receive communion at these times? And may a man enter a church after relations with his wife before he has washed? Or receive the sacred mystery of Communion? These uncouth English people require guidance on all these matters.

Gregory's response was quite mild. He saw no problem about women entering a church either during menstruation or after giving birth, both being natural events. He wrote:

> Were a woman to enter church and return thanks in the very hour of her delivery, she would do nothing wrong.

But he supported Levitical rules that exclusion from church must follow episodes of intercourse which had led to conception and resulted in the travail of labour and birth. Later, referring to the narrative of the Fall in the Book of Genesis, he explained his view of the dangers of female sexuality:

> The fault lies in the bodily desires, not the pain of child-birth; the desire is in the bodily union, the pain is in the birth, so that Eve, the mother of us all, was told: 'In sorrow shalt thou bring forth children'.

If sexual intercourse was the major taboo, procreation must carry its stigma:

> We do not condemn marriage itself, but since lawful intercourse must be

accompanied by bodily pleasure, it is fitting to refrain from entering a holy place, since desire itself is not blameless. For even David, who said: *'Behold, I was conceived in iniquity, and in sin my mother brought me forth'*, was not himself born of any illicit union, but in lawful wedlock. But knowing himself to have been conceived in iniquity, he grieved that he had been born in sin.[4]

This is why instructions for both men and women concerning abstention, exclusion and penance were set out by Gregory and developed over the next three centuries in the penitentials of early church fathers such as, for instance, Augustine's successor at Canterbury, Theodore of Tarsus, and the Irish bishops Cummean, Finnian and Egbert. All insisted that, in the case of newly-delivered women, only after a given period of exclusion from church had been completed might re-admission to holy places, and partaking of Holy Communion, be permitted. As Rob Meens has written recently:

> One may conclude that Augustine's questions to Gregory the Great triggered a discussion about sexuality, human nature and impurity that lasted during the whole period we now call the Middle Ages. A tendency to regard women and men in certain bodily states as impure and to bar them from the holy, apparently persisted throughout the period.

Indeed Gerald Rouwhorst has explained that such rule-bound rites held political significance for the early church:

> Early Christians were in varied, cosmopolitan groups; they wanted to put social boundaries between genders (celibacy, virginity) and to distinguish themselves from non-Christians eg. Jews and pagans ... Christianity is the only 'place' which is pure from pollution and recalls the purity of the virginal mother of Jesus.[5]

Nevertheless childbirth purification rites were by no means a Christian monopoly. In *Miasma and Pollution* Robert Parker finds them being undertaken by contemporary late Hellenic communities which, to get rid of 'defilement' and appease the gods, observed a week of ceremonial processions, bathing of images, name-giving and final animal sacrifice, following a birth. The mother, still seen as 'pol-

---

[4] *The First Epistle of Paul the Apostle to Timothy*, Chapter 2, 9–15; Bede, *A History of the English Church and People*, tr. Leo Sherley-Price (Harmondsworth, 1962), pp. 76–80.

[5] Bieler, *The Irish Penitentials*, pp. 93, 117, 181, 223; R. Meens, 'Questioning Ritual Purity: The Influence of Gregory the Great's Answers to Augustine's Queries, about Childbirth, Menstruation and Sexuality', in *St Augustine and the Conversion of England*, ed. Richard Gameson (Stroud 1999), pp. 175–86; Idem, '"A relic of superstition": Bodily Impurity and the Church from Gregory the Great to the Twelfth-Century Decretists', in *Purity and Holiness: the Heritage of Leviticus*, eds M. J. H. M. Poorthus & J. Schwarz (Brill, 2000), Vol. II, pp. 281–95; G. Ruowhorst, 'Leviticus 12–15 in Early Christianity', Poorthus & Schwarz, p. 189.

INTRODUCTION

luting', would be confined and excluded for three days. And, still familiar in modern times, Jewish women faced elaborate regimes of abstention, seclusion and ritual baths before, during and after confinement.[6]

In fact there is little doubt that some of the Christian fear of 'ill-luck' associated with the unchurched had its origin in pagan superstition. This connection has never been entirely lost. When Augustine and other Christian missionaries discovered alien altars, relics and ceremonies in sixth- and seventh-century Britain, the Pope advised them not to destroy these 'ancient shrines', but rather to attempt to convert their worshippers, gradually integrating them into Roman Christian ritual. Many pagan beliefs and practices were never eliminated. In *Religion and the Decline of Magic* Keith Thomas cites belief that the sun and the moon, ghosts and fairies were still thought to affect women and their newborn babies in late seventeenth-century Suffolk and Yorkshire. Judith Okley has traced the purification ritual's traditional importance in gypsy culture; and from his work on nineteenth-century rural South Lindsey, where he found a vigorous churching tradition, James Obelkevich reckoned:

> Of all the rites this was the best integrated with its accompanying superstition, but, as in confirmation, the motives for participating in the rite owed nothing to Christianity and everything to superstition. Christianity provided the ritual, but paganism gave it its meaning.[7]

Behind most of these ceremonies lurked layers of misogyny. Discrimination against the female dates at least from Plato's thought about soul and body: that women, devoted to bodily preoccupations and the bearing of children, drag men down from developing the life of the soul; females live at the same inferior level as children, slaves and brutes, distracting and damaging to higher male pursuits. In *Man and the Natural World* Keith Thomas notes the survival of such attitudes to women during the early modern period:

> Over many centuries theologians had debated, half frivolously, half seriously, whether or not the female sex had souls ... even Puritan opponents

---

[6] Robert Parker, *Miasma: Pollution and Purification in Early Greek Religion* (Oxford, 1983), pp. 32–55; Richard and Eva Blum, *The Dangerous Hour: The Lore of Crisis and Mystery in Rural Greece* (London, 1970), pp. 11–20; Edward Shorter, *A History of Women's Bodies* (Harmondsworth, 1982), pp. 95–115;.Rachel Alder, 'Tumah and Tahara: Ends and Beginnings', in E. Koltun (ed.), *The Jewish Woman* (New York, 1976), pp. 63–71.

[7] S. D. Church, 'Paganism in Conversion-Age Anglo-Saxon England: the Evidence of Bede's *Ecclesiastical History* Reconsidered', *History*, 93, Issue 2, No. 310 (April, 2008), pp. 162–8; K. V. Thomas, *Religion and the Decline of Magic* (Harmondsworth, 1973), pp. 456–7; Judith Okley, 'Gipsy Women: Models in Conflict', in Ardener, Shirley (ed.), *Perceiving Women* (London, 1975), pp. 55–61; James Obelkevich, *Religion and Rural Society: South Lindsey 1825–1875* (Oxford, 1976), pp. 259, 271.

of the churching ceremony sometimes referring to the mother as a sow with her piglets following her.

Patricia Crawford suggests that the reprinting of the seventeenth-century work, the so-called *Aristotle's Master-Piece*, in the nineteenth century revived ancient ideas about women which included the emphasis on their need for cleansing, and may also have strengthened the belief that allegedly persisted until the 1880s that women's 'sensation of animal gratification' was an essential element in the successful conception of a child.[8]

Nineteenth- and twentieth-century society continued to need rituals through which to face the rigours of birth and death, and prevent unknowable ill-luck threatening future safety. And so this ancient childbirth rite of thanksgiving and purification, with its prayers and offerings, exclusions and re-admissions, has been celebrated in unbroken tradition until the third and even fourth quarter of the twentieth century.

Vivid examples of its continuation in recent decades are found in two unpublished works on popular belief well after the Second World War. Reference to purification was found to a surprising extent by M. W. Staton who completed in 1980 the fullest known study of recent churching practice, based on fieldwork in the Newcastle suburb of Byker. Among older women he discovered a widespread acknowledgement of what the ceremony implied:

> There was an underlying belief that the new mother was in some way unclean, barred from any other house in the community, and from attending any church service, including the baptism of her own child, until she had been through the ritual of churching.[9]

Younger mothers continued with the ceremony, having received the idea from their elders 'that having babies is a sin'. Staton comments that 'there are still fears and anxieties surrounding childbirth that are interpreted in the light of the supernatural':

> It is truly amazing that such views have persisted through the generations, probably from medieval days and earlier, despite the teaching of the church since the Reformation that churching is primarily an act of thanksgiving, not purification.

Ordained himself, he added:

---

[8] Thomas, *Man and the Natural World: Changing Attitudes in England, 1500–1800* (Harmondsworth, 1983), pp. 43–5; Patricia Crawford, 'Attitudes to Menstruation in Seventeenth-Century England', *Past & Present*, 91 (1975), pp. 47–73.

[9] M. W. Staton, 'The Rite of Churching: a Sociological Analysis, with Special Reference to an Urban Area in Newcastle-upon-Tyne' (Unpublished M. A. Thesis, University of Newcastle, 1980), p. 225.

INTRODUCTION

> Anglican clergy have been trying to stamp it out in many places. But it is still widely practised and accepted ... Women continue with these beliefs and prejudices.[10]

The second work is by Richard Sykes, who looked at churching among other rites of passage in his thesis: *Popular Religion in Dudley and the Gornals c.1914–1965*, completed in 1999. This also referred to widely-held notions of superstition and folk belief held in connection with thanksgiving in the churching service:

> The Christian act of thanksgiving and the folk belief in warding off ill-luck were regarded as complementary aspects of a single ritual attached to the rite of passage of birth.[11]

Like Staton he reported clerical impatience with such superstitious notions, quoting the Revd Peter Baker, vicar of St Luke's Church, Dudley who wrote emphatically in a parish magazine in the 1960s:

> I do not think it is right that a woman, the first day she is up, should come to church, this is merely a sop to superstition and the church should not be party to it ... Mothers you will NOT be unlucky ... the roof will NOT fall in if your shadow crosses someone else's doorstep. You are NOT impure. You CAN go out and about quite normally if you have not been churched within the shortest possible time after your confinement. There is nothing magical about this beautiful little service.

Other parish magazines, dated 1964, also condemned superstition about the ritual. But the clergy of Dudley were not all speaking with one voice. One Mrs Cash told Sykes that Fr Ferley of St Edmund's Church, Dudley, had warned her that after the birth of her son in 1951, 'she could not take communion until she had been churched since she remained until such a time unclean'.[12] More traces of these attitudes elsewhere in mid-century are found below in Southwark's parishes (Chapter Four) and widespread oral testimony (Chapter Five).

Staton's work in particular outlines quite starkly the survival of traditional assumptions about a woman's obligation to purge her shame after childbirth, and he shows how, even in the late twentieth century, new mothers responded to direction by family, church and neighbourhood to go along for a churching.

---

[10] *Ibid.*, pp. 263, 230, 264.
[11] Richard Sykes, 'Popular Religion in Dudley and the Gornals c. 1914–1965' (Unpublished Ph.D. Thesis, University of Wolverhampton, 1999), p. 180.
[12] *Ibid.*, pp. 182, 193.

CHAPTER ONE

HISTORY OF THE CHURCHING SERVICE: CUSTOM AND LITURGY

Evidence of the earliest childbirth purifications is scattered and obscure. Only in the Middle Ages can one begin to glimpse the new mother at the church porch, veiled and holding a lighted candle, her hand grasping the sleeve or stole of the priest, her gift (known in some early medieval penitentials as a 'shame offering') prepared. In attendance will be her women friends, perhaps also husband, family and neighbours. Charles Caspers writes that some of these occasions were so extravagant that municipal authorities tried to limit the numbers present, and see to it that only women were present.[1] Warned by custom and penitentials, the mother will not have crossed the threshold out of her own house until this moment of celebration.

'Blessing of a Woman' in the Missal of Sarum

A full picture of the ritual itself emerges in the twelfth century when missals began to publish liturgies of thanksgiving and re-admission, forerunners of the later churching service. Most widely used was the liturgy of Sarum.[2] Called in full *Blessing of a Woman after Childbirth Before the Church Porch*, this brief service is set out below:

Excluded from the church, because as yet unchurched, the new mother had to stay outside in the porch where the priest conducted most of the service. Prayers, responses and collect emphasised the recent rigours of 'the peril of childbirth'; cleansing was demonstrated with the sprinkling of holy water from a spray of hyssop; admission to the church completed the ritual. The theme of protection was underlined in Psalm 121, promising God's safe keeping from evil and danger, 'so that the sun shall not burn thee by day, nor the moon by night'; 'The Lord shall preserve thy going out and thy coming in'. Psalm 128 set out a more optimistic message for the new family, with its lines:

> Thy wife shall be like a fruitful vine by the sides of thine house:
> Thy children like olive plants round about thy table.

---

[1] Charles Caspers, 'Leviticus 12, Mary and Wax: Purification and Churching in Late Medieval Christianity', in Poorthus & Schwarz, *Purity and Holiness*, p. 300.

[2] Vernon Staley (ed.), *The Sarum Missal in English* (London, 1911), pp. 278–9.

HISTORY OF THE CHURCHING SERVICE

BLESSING OF A WOMAN AFTER CHILDBIRTH
BEFORE THE CHURCH PORCH
from the Sarum Missal

First the priest shall say these Psalms:

> I will lift up mine eyes etc.   (Ps. cxxi)
> Blessed are all they etc.   (Ps. cxxviii)
>   *with* Glory be to the Father etc.

Our Father, etc.
V And lead us not into temptation,
R But deliver us from evil.
V O Lord, save thine handmaiden,
R My God, who trusteth in thee.
V Send her help from thy holy place
R And defend her out of Sion.
V Be thou to her, O Lord, a strong tower.
R From the face of her enemy.
V Lord, hear my prayer,
R And let my prayer come unto thee.
V The Lord be with you.
R And with thy spirit.

Let us pray.

Collect

O God, who hast delivered this woman thy servant from the peril of Childbirth, and hast made her to be devoted to thy service; grant that when the course of this life hath been faithfully finished, she may obtain eternal life, and rest under the wings of thy mercy.
Through etc.

Then shall the woman be sprinkled with holy water by the priest, saying,

Thou shalt purge me, O Lord, with hyssop.

Then shall the priest lead her by the right hand into the church, saying,

Enter into the temple of God, that thou mayest have eternal life, and live for ever and ever.   Amen.

It seems that this medieval service of blessing was well-liked and widely used. Becky Lee conveyed its popularity in a recent article which set out to show how highly the churching rite was regarded among both wives and husbands. Lee agrees with Caspers that from the twelfth to the sixteenth centuries women would enjoy celebrating childbirth among their own friends, neighbours and relatives, often in costly and elaborate ceremonies; and she adds that for their husbands also churchings might have had a particular importance. On occasion they were invoked to provide crucial proof of paternity and age in inheritance suits: out of 1,019 such cases found in Chancery records, post-partum purification was mentioned 106 times. The impression given is of a popular and uncontentious ritual: 'public celebrations of paternity and lineage; an occasion of female social activity'.[3]

Purification, Thanksgiving and Churching in the Church of England from 1549

During the sixteenth century churching was to become one of the sources of dispute between conservative and reforming members of the church; its origin, name and true purpose were areas of disagreement which for the next two centuries were to focus particularly on the issue of purification.

Of the varied strands in Sarum's *Blessing of a Woman* the English Book of Common Prayer adopted the first for its title in 1549, calling the churching ceremony *The Order of the Purification of Women*. But three years later, as Protestant leaders began to denounce it as a 'Jewish' and 'popish' ceremonial, it was described in terms of its other two elements: *The Thanks Giving of Women after Child Birth, commonly called The Churching of Women*. Thereafter the word *purification* disappeared for good.[4] This 1552 title remained unchanged for the next 428 years in succeeding versions of the Book of Common Prayer in 1559, 1662 and 1928, until its alteration in the 1980 Alternative Worship Book into *Thanksgiving after the Birth of a Child*, and recent appearance as *Thanksgiving for a Child* in the Common Worship liturgy of the year 2000.[5]

Do the earlier alterations tell of refinements of the churching ceremony's scope? If purification was no longer to be included in its name, could this mean that it had been eased out of the way in which women after childbirth were regarded? The changes that took place during the reign of Edward VI between 1549 and 1552 certainly seem to suggest an attempt to alter the balance of the three elements in the service. In Cranmer's first Book of Common Prayer, though the structure of 'The Order of the Purification of Women' remained almost unchanged from the Sarum Missal's service, with Psalm 121, the responses, prayers and final Collect all being retained, some new ceremonial practices were introduced. Despite the suggestion in its new title that this service was intended to be about cleansing as well as thanksgiving, it actually lessened the Sarum emphasis on purification, in that no hyssop or sprinkling with holy water were mentioned and the woman was no longer told to wait in the porch outside the

---

[3] Becky Lee, 'Men's Recollections of a Women's Rite', pp. 224–41.
[4] E. C. S. Gibson, *The First and Second Prayer Books of Edward VI* (London & New York, 1910, pp. 278–9.
[5] *The Book of Common Prayer with the Additions and Deviations Proposed in 1928* (Oxford, 1928); *The Alternative Service Book 1980: Services Authorized for Use in the Church of England in Conjunction with the Book of Common Prayer* (London, 1980); *Common Worship Pastoral Services* (London, 2000).

church, but (as already in the York rite) might enter on her own, kneeling to wait for the priest at the rood screen 'nigh unto the quier doore'. In other words, the service could now be conducted entirely inside the church, even though the woman was still unchurched when it started. Nevertheless a new final instruction, *the woman that is purified must offer her Chrisom and other accustomed offering*, reminds us that this was still intended to be more than a simple thanksgiving.

Three years later, in the Second Edwardian prayer book, four further changes were made to the service. As Gibson says, 'to England's Protestant reformers the clear sacramental teaching and the ritual of the first book were now objectionable, and they never rested until they had secured the alteration of it'.[6] First, 'purification' was omitted from its title and from the sentence on offerings, which were now expected from 'the woman that comes to give her thanks', no longer from 'the woman that is purified'. Second, the woman was no longer left on the margin at the choir door; as rood screens were now being removed from all churches, she was to 'kneel down in some convenient place nigh unto the place where the table stands', a point somewhere in the centre of the church where communion had now come to be administered. Third, the former assumption in the opening prayer that the baby had already been baptised: 'Forasmuch as it hath pleased almighty God of his goodness to give you safe deliverance, and your child baptism...' was omitted; which may be part of the reason why, in the fourth change, there was no requirement to offer a chrisom, only 'other accustomed offerings' (a baby's chrisom would not have become available until after its baptism).

But Psalm 121 and the 1549 responses, prayers and final Collect were retained, and the service was to remain unaltered in Elizabeth's third edition of the prayer book in 1559. It appears as a welcome excuse for celebration in the descriptions of Britain (1577) and England (1587) by the Revd William Harrison, historian and topographer, writing about the diet of artificers and husbandmen. He referred to women's churching feasts:

> In feasting also this latter sort (I mean the husbandmen) do exceed after their manner, especially at bride-ales, purifications of women, and such odd meetings, where it is incredible to tell what meat is consumed and spent, each one bringing such a dish or so many with him as his wife and he do consult upon ...

He later singled out the popularity of saffron and 'the manifold use that it hath in the kitchen and pastry, also in our cakes at bride-ales and thanksgivings of women'.[7] But leading reformers disliked the whole ceremony throughout this time of change. Bishop Latimer protested:

> that the law was made unto the Jews, and not unto us; and that women lying

[6] Gibson, *First and Second Prayer Books*, pp. 428–9.
[7] Georges Edelen (ed.), William Harrison, *The Description of England: The Classic Con-*

> in childbed be not unclean before God; neither is purification used to that end, that it should cleanse from sin; but rather a civil and political law, made for natural honesty's sake.

Though the word 'purification' had disappeared as a title, they were sure that the idea of it still lay behind much popular practice, and the retaining of Psalm 121 in all three of these sixteenth-century churching services could be seen still to refer to the woman's alleged vulnerability to danger from sun and moon and 'all evil', and consequent need to be confined within her own threshold. Though not specifically required, veils and chrisoms were still in evidence, their use indeed sometimes enforced by local church courts in the face of some women's refusal to conform. To puritans such as politician Thomas Cartwright and separatist minister Henry Barrow, the whole ceremony was 'a mixed action of Judaism and popery':

> Why are women held in superstitious opinion, that this action is necessary? Why is it a statute and ordinance of their church? An especial part of their worship ... To conclude, why should such solemn, yea public thanks (to take it at the fairest they can make it) be given openly in the church more for the safe deliverance of those women, being (though a singular benefice of God) yet a thing natural, ordinary and common?

Barrow spoke of it further with undisguised distaste:

> The woman's monthly restraint and separation from your church, her coming after that just time wimpled, veiled, with her gossips and neighbours following her, her kneeling down before and offering unto the priest, the priest's churching, praying over her, blessing her from sun and moon, delivering her in the end to her former vocation, show somewhat beside giving of thanks.[8]

We learn from Donna Ray in her perceptive essay on churching: 'Some Puritan women simply refused to comply with the rite', and she describes Dorothy Hazzard, wife of a Puritan minister, offering her room to expectant mothers so that they could 'avoid churching by giving birth in her parish'.[9] Hostility reached a climax in 1645 as the churching service was abolished when the Directory of Public Worship replaced the Book of Common Prayer.

But many women continued to seek churching, even under the regime of the Interregnum. Its abolition had given offence: Horton Davies has described

---

temporary Account of Tudor Social Life (Washington and New York, 1968), pp. 131, 354.

[8] Cressy, 'Purification, Thanksgiving', p. 120; W. P. M. Kennedy, *Elizabethan Episcopal Administration*, Vol. I (London, 1924), p. 29; Coster, 'Purity, Profanity, and Puritanism' pp. 383–4; Cressy, 'Purification, thanksgiving', pp. 119–20; L. H. Carlson, *The Writings of Henry Barrow* (London, 1966), p. 77.

[9] Donna E. Ray, 'A View from the Childwife's Pew', pp. 452–9.

how Dr Henry Hammond in *A View of the New Directory* of 1645 led the Anglican criticism. He deplored:

> the absence of any thanksgiving after childbirth by which the *Directory* is effectively setting up "Schools of *ingratitude* in the church".[10]

David Cressy argues that the ceremony was still widely welcomed as a time to recognise and celebrate the mother's survival and achievement, just as Becky Lee had discovered it to be in earlier centuries. Neither the women nor their husbands and neighbours 'thought in terms of pollution or defilement'.[11]

At the Restoration the churching service was re-established almost intact as part of the course of reconciliation, though, significantly for the future, the Laudian canon that had made its use obligatory was discontinued.[12] In a new Preface the 1662 Book of Common Prayer outlined its aim to keep the old liturgy largely unchanged 'notwithstanding all the vain attempts and importunate assaults made against it by such men as are given to change'. Some ceremonies were to be put away, because 'the burden of them was intolerable', or 'they were so far abused partly by the superstitious blindness of the rude and unlearned'; while others would be kept

> for discipline and order ... they be neither dark nor dumb ceremonies, but are set forth that every man may understand what they do mean and to what use they do serve.[13]

Churching was probably valued as a useful ceremony that offered regular opportunities to establish good parish practice. It was reissued with only minor alterations. There was now little concern about its location in the church (no mention of choir door or table), but a stand was taken on one controversy: a rubric decreed for the first time that the woman seeking to be churched was to appear 'decently apparelled', suggesting, though not forcefully, that she ought to wear a veil. New Psalms, numbers 116 and 127 (one to be optional), appeared. They contain nothing about the sun and moon; but Psalm 116 emphasises other dangers in childbirth with its 'trouble and heaviness ... misery and tears'; and in Verse 3 appear shades of its violent reality:

> the snares of death compassed me round about: and the pains of hell gat hold upon me.

It was during the years following the Restoration that churches began to install churching pews, called sometimes 'the midwife's pew', 'the childwife's

[10] Horton Davies, *Worship and Theology in England from Andrewes to Baxter and Fox, 1603–1690* (Princeton, 1975), p. 421.
[11] Cressy, 'Purification, Thanksgiving', p. 119.
[12] I. M. Green, *The Re-establishment of the Church of England* (Oxford, 1978), p. 8.
[13] 'The Preface', *The Book of Common Prayer, 1662* (Cambridge, 1862), pp. 1–2.

pew', 'the churching seat' or even, as at Sedgfield, Durham, 'the sick-wife's stall'. These might be placed at the back of the church, or close to the pulpit in full view of all, replacing the mother's customary location at the altar rails or in the Lady Chapel. Donna Ray quotes a suggestion made in 1661 at the Savoy Conference:

> It is fit that the woman performing especial service of thanksgiving would have a special place for it, where she may be perspicuous to the whole congregation.

One old pew (Plate 1) which unfortunately has not survived, has been described at Romaldkirk, in Yorkshire: 'The churching pew is like a huge box, and must have made churching a very terrifying experience for the chief person concerned'.[14]

Popular response to liturgical change becomes hard to detect after 1662. Earlier, during the reformation period, new developments had been explained and endorsed by bishops and clergy, imposed through visitations, and in the last resort enforced by the church courts. These left records of protests and refusals by both conservatives determined to keep their traditional services, and reformers concerned to stamp out remaining errors, be they seen as popish, Jewish, or merely superstitious. But popular reaction left fewer traces at the end of the seventeenth century. Cressy points out that after 1662 most protest about churchings, as recorded in visitations, was in the form of abstention; by members of dissenting families, or occasionally by women put off by the journey to church, discrimination in pew allocation, or even a vicar's unsavoury reputation. He judges that the churching liturgy was now less vigorously imposed, and that anyone abstaining was increasingly unlikely to be pursued as a point of discipline.[15]

Restoration liturgy for the churching of women was to remain in the Book of Common Prayer for well over three hundred years. It may have fallen into abeyance in some places, but enough records have been found in fee books, churching registers and clergy diaries to suggest that women of all classes continued to be churched throughout the eighteenth and nineteenth centuries. The Revd James Woodforde's diary recorded churchings in Ardington (Berkshire) and Babcary (Somerset), before reaching his parsonage in Weston Longeville (Norfolk). Here he wrote of thirty churchings between 1776 and 1795, generally of 'a Woman', three times of named parishioners, the wives of John Reeves, Andrew Spragges and Mr Burnham. The ceremony only disappeared from the diary when Mr Corbould came to assist him. Perhaps he took over churching duties and chose to keep no records.[16] Woodforde's contemporary, the Revd William Holland,

---

[14] Ray, 'A View from the Childwife's Pew', p. 455; Coster, 'Purity, Profanity, and Puritanism', pp. 382–3; plans of churching pews taken from G. W. O. Addleshaw and Frederick Etchells, *The Architectural Setting of Anglican Worship* (London, 1948), pp. 85 and 94.

[15] Cressy, *'Purification, Thanksgiving'*, pp. 142–3.

[16] John Beresford (ed.), *The Diary of a Country Parson: The Reverend James Woodforde*

wrote in his journal of twenty-six churchings in Somerset around Asholt, Dodington and Overstowey from 1800 to 1816. He churched wives of substantial farmers (one 'very well and strong' after her fourteenth child) as well as villagers and the anonymous poor.[17]

It is mostly in the books of wealthy urban parishes that post-1662 churching records can be found, entered largely in order to register the payment of fees. Surviving in those of Holy Trinity, Clapham Common are an Account Book of Samuel Symonds, Lecturer, which included:

> An Account of the Hatbands, Gloves and Rings that I had given me at Funerals and Churchings since I came there in May 1689, and another Account of what I have received or hath been given me for churching gentlewomen at home in the parish of Clapham.

This showed that in 1691 he had been paid as much as 5s. each for churching Mrs Mansfield and Mrs Tylor. A Fee Book for St George's, Bloomsbury between 1765 and 1771 revealed that, in this wealthy parish, fees of never less than 2s., and often more were paid by the thirty-five women who were churched; and a Churching Register at St John the Baptist, New Windsor, listed around 2,460 churchings between 1789 and 1832, never naming the women, but rather their husbands, who, though often artisans and tradesmen, unfailingly paid 1s. In Wantage the Reverend William Butler made several diary entries between the 1850s and 1870s concerned with churching cases; once he refused to church a woman because she had married irregularly with her aunt's husband; on other occasions he turned away women whose babies had been born very soon after wedlock (in one case the day after). One woman who had been a dissenter was granted her churching: '& this may give us an opportunity to bring her to a better mind'. Also in Berkshire, volumes bound in fine white leather with brass fastenings were kept by St Andrew's, Sonning, in which, from 1830 to 1875, between carefully pencilled vertical lines, lists of figures identified the allocation of women's offerings: *Vicar 4d, Clerk 2d, Sexton 0d.*[18]

Large numbers of late eighteenth- and nineteenth-century London churchings were found in the parishes of St George the Martyr, Southwark, 1777–83; St

---

1758–1802 (Oxford, 1924), Vol. I, *1758–76*, pp. 28, 36, 44, 90, 191, 302, 336; Vol. II, *1782–87*, pp. 24, 80, 121, 207, 286, 311, 313, 320; Vol. III, *1788–92*, pp. 252, 258, 260, 263, 308, 313, 357, 386, 389; Vol. IV, *1793–96*, pp. 26, 93, 163, 178.

[17] Jack Ayres (ed.), *Paupers and Pig-Killers: the Diary of William Holland, a Somerset Parson 1799–1818* (Stroud, 1995), pp. 26, 27, 52, 77, 80, 95, 98, 117.

[18] LMA P95/TRI 1/88, Holy Trinity, Clapham, Account Book of Samuel Symonds, Lecturer 1688–89 (at the end of a Baptismal list of 1706); P82/GEO 1/73, St George, Bloomsbury, Rector's Fee Book, 1765-72; BRO D/P1491A/3 on MF8399, St John the Baptist, New Windsor, Register of Churchings and Fees, 1796-1832; D/P 143/28/1–3, Diary of William Butler; D/P113/1B/1, Register of Fees due to Vicar, Clerk and Sexton of the Parish of Sonning, 1832–50; 1B/2: Register of Fees 1851–88.

Leonards, Streatham, 1799–1806; St Dunstan and All Saints, Stepney, 1821–30; St Peter, Regent Square, 1829–41; St Stephens, Hammersmith, 1859–84; St Pauls, Clerkenwell, 1878–82; and Holy Trinity, Hoxton, 1888–91. In Hoxton seventy-six churchings were recorded in one year (1889); in Clerkenwell the vicar of St Pauls wrote out fifty-seven entries for 1872 with revealing personal comments on the churched mothers: 'nicely dressed', 'the godmother had a black eye', 'lost child 3 weeks ago, very melancholy', 'one of our nicest girls, yet fell: married in very poor position'.[19]

From the 1880s weekly registers of services began to be kept in most Church of England parishes. Of churching, Donna Ray suggests that by this time 'the rite was much reduced in its significance', as she had found an 1852 Book of Common Prayer containing only a rubric and prayer for its celebration. Yet other volumes for 1857 and 1862 have come to light which still have the 1662 service printed in full. Certainly detailed lists in Berkshire, London and Staffordshire show large numbers of churchings still taking place in the decades leading up to 1900 and far beyond. The ceremony was undertaken by women of all classes, rich and poor. Pat Jalland writes:

> Lavinia Talbot, Ivy Chamberlain, Mary Gladstone and others all mentioned being churched before the baptism ... The only vestige of the old idea of uncleanliness was to be found in the custom that a newly delivered mother could not attend a wedding before she was churched and hence purified. Lady Carrington, for example, in 1880, regretted that she could not attend her sister's wedding as it was only two weeks since the birth. 'It was very sad not being actually in the church'.[20]

From Churching to Thanksgiving in the Twentieth Century

If the churching rite had indeed been 'drifting down' and out of use by the twentieth century, it might be expected that it would have been abandoned, or at least considerably reduced, by the time that the Book of Common Prayer was revised in 1928. The revision's authors had after all acknowledged that they were accepting the need to come up to date:

> since 1662 there has been change almost beyond belief in the facts and modes of English life ... we dare not think that a Book of Common Prayer

[19] LMA P92/GEO/372, St George the Martyr, Southwark, Rector's Fee Book, 1777–83; P95/LEN/81–83, St Leonard, Streatham, Clerk's Register of Fees, 1787–1806; P93/DUN/208, St Dunstan and All Saints, Rector's Fee Book, 1821–30; P90/PET/1, St Peter, Regent Square, St Pancras (Camden), Register of Baptisms, 1829–41 (churchings inserted throughout); P80/STE/62, St Stephen, Hammersmith, Church Attendance Book, 1859–84 (a list of 428 churched women's names is in the back); P76/PAU2/37, St Paul, Clerkenwell, Register of Churchings 1878–82; P91/TRI/28, Holy Trinity, Hoxton, Register of Parish or Congregational Meetings, showing Expenses, &c., 1888–91.
[20] Pat Jalland, *Women, Marriage and Politics 1860–1914* (Oxford, 1988), pp. 157–8.

fitted for the seventeenth century can supply every want of the twentieth.[21]

But in fact the churching ceremony was left almost unchanged in 1928, presumably as a valued thanksgiving, and also something which would retain the adherence of parishioners loyal to old patterns of worship: it could be one way of meeting urgent concern about falling church attendance. Indeed the new book echoed much of the style and language of 1662, and the old churching ceremony underwent only a few amendments. Husbands were now invited to accompany their wives if they wished, and three new prayers appeared at the end. The first of these is a thanksgiving to be used if no communion is held; the second acknowledges the gift of a child; the last, which does not mention the child but contains the words: 'comfort this thy servant whose heart is sore smitten and oppressed' might have been devised for use after a stillbirth, or if the birth had not gone well. There was no word in 1928 about 'decent apparel', but the final rubric on offerings remained unchanged, and new mothers were still given the old warning that they must tender them before they might receive holy communion, just as in earlier forms. Though the Revised Prayer Book of 1928 was never legally adopted, it was published and its services were popular and widely used until 1980. During this period copies of the churching service were printed on cards and kept for convenience at the back of churches, often becoming battered and well-thumbed from frequent use. An example is illustrated in Plate 2.

The Church's commitment to churching and other ancient 'occasional' services (such as *Visitation of the Sick*; *Baptism of those of Riper Years*) might have appeared to be waning when in 1946 they were all simply left out of an inexpensive and convenient 'Sunday Service Book' produced during the regime of Archbishop Geoffrey Fisher. This compact green-covered volume was widely welcomed in Anglican parishes, and in some, such as Christ Church, Stone, has been found still in use beyond the end of the century.

But already profound changes to the rite of churching were being considered by a new Liturgical Commission. Set up in 1955, this body began to send out alternative forms of many services with the aim of eventually bringing the old Book of Common Prayer up to date. Churching had come to arouse increasing apprehension in one particular respect: was it being used as a replacement for the more important rite of baptism, introducing a newborn child to the church while allowing its christening to be delayed until adulthood? This problem was to trouble the Commission for nearly fifty years, as a leading member, David Hebblethwaite, explained, reviewing its work between 1984 and 2004:

> Thanksgiving for the Birth of a Child became more prominent than the other rites both because of the synodical process and also because of con-

---

[21] Preface, *The Book of Common Prayer with the Additions and Deviations Proposed in 1928* (Oxford, 1928), p. 1.

tinuing debate in the church (focussed in the Synod debates on Christian initiation in July 1991) whether thanksgiving could be perceived as an alternative to baptism for the 'less committed'.[22]

Despite these fears, thanksgiving after childbirth continued to be included in the 'Pastoral Rites package'. When the Alternative Service Book was introduced in 1980, intended to supplement (still not to supersede) the 1662 and 1928 books of common prayer, a simplified and re-worded ceremony was introduced in two new services: *Thanksgiving After the Birth of a Child*, and *Thanksgiving After Adoption*. They abandoned former references to the mother's pain and danger, and thanksgiving was almost the only topic of prayers, psalms and responses. Only in two of the nine final optional readings can any hint of purification and sequestration be found: one is from I Samuel 1: 20 ff., in which Hannah did not 'go about' until her new baby had been weaned; the other from the Gospel of St Luke 2, 22, 28a (28b–35) which mentions the days of purification of the Virgin Mary. But, shorn of its old, darker moments, this whole event was to be no longer confined to a personal encounter between woman and priest, as hitherto in twentieth-century churchings. In both of the new thanksgivings, parents, natural or adoptive, and any other children of the family, were invited to attend wherever possible. The service might take place at Holy Communion or Morning or Evening Prayer, or prior to a baptism, though emphatically not as its alternative.[23]

Abandonment of attitudes and ideas inherent in the old churching ceremony went a stage further in the final year of the twentieth century, following more Commission meetings, and among many negotiations with the House of Bishops and Synod over details of radical change, which produced the new 2000 liturgy of Common Worship. Continuing debates had resulted in many alternatives and options that were now offered in a whole series of services. The Revd Trevor Lloyd, Archdeacon of Barnstaple and consultant to the Liturgical Commission since 1981, wrote in 2001 of the changes that he had been trying out in his local church:

> The Common Worship service focusses not on the woman, but on the child. In theory at least the mother might have died in childbirth, but there could still be a thanksgiving for the arrival of the child ... And the child might have arrived not by birth but by adoption. The emphasis is on the child as part of the family, with prayers for mother, father and other children, even for grandparents and other relatives.

Changes in purpose, including the woman's re-incorporation, were discussed:

> Common Worship has one very flexible service which can be used at home, in hospital or at church. It does not start with the mediaeval question, 'How can we encourage and allow this woman back into our holy building?' but

[22] David Hebblethwaite, *Liturgical Revision in the Church of England 1984–2004: The working of the Liturgical Commission* (Cambridge, 2002), p. 7.
[23] *The Alternative Service Book 1980* (London, 1980), pp. 213–17.

with the more homely and contemporary question, 'Tell us how you feel about the arrival of this child, and we will see if we can express that in prayer and thanksgiving' ... One further point to note which follows naturally from the fact that this service is not about getting back into church, but an opportunity to give thanks in other locations too, is that there is no restriction about who may take this service.

Baptism remained quite a problem:

> There were some in the church who, though committed people of faith, did not want their child baptized, preferring for it to be the child's decision when older ... Those in the church who did not want a baptism were happy to have the Thanksgiving as a more immediate rite after birth, with the baptism following a little later as a bigger family occasion for them ... For some the service of Thanksgiving was actually all that they wanted and they decided not to go immediately on to baptism. They usually went away very appreciative of the service and became a warm 'fringe contact' to be kept in touch with and followed up as appropriate.[24]

And so Common Worship introduced a thanksgiving service which was to be centred almost exclusively on the child, whose name was affirmed. In a ceremony more simplified than that of 1980, the note of thanksgiving was all-pervading and the liturgy more inclusive, with additional prayers to bless the family, the parents and other relatives, midwives and health workers, adopted children and children with special needs. Only once was the mother's act of giving birth mentioned in the text of the service:

> May *N*, remembering no longer her anguish, trust you in all things. As she asks for all she would receive, may she discover that in you her joy is complete.

Birth was also mentioned four times among the fourteen suggested Bible readings: one (in a longer passage than that in the Alternative Service Book) from Luke, 2: 22–4 and 33–40; another from Luke, 1: 39–45 about the visit of Mary to Elizabeth who was unexpectedly with child; a third from the story of the Annunciation in Matthew, 1: 18–25. The reference to childbirth found in the fourth, taken from Psalm 139: 7–18, could be thought to contain a dark, troubled reflection on God's presence through a time of pain and vulnerability, unexpectedly returning to the much earlier liturgical mood:

> If I ascend into heaven you are there: if I make my bed in the grave you are there also ... If I say 'Surely the darkness will cover me: and the night will enclose me' ... You knew my soul and my bones were not hidden from you: when I was formed in secret and woven in the depths of the earth.

---

[24] *Common Worship*, 2000: *Pastoral Services*, pp. 15–17; Trevor Lloyd, *Thanksgiving for the Gift of a Child: A Commentary on the Common Worship Service* (Cambridge, 2001), pp. 5, 19;

The reading stopped before verse 19: 'If only you would slay the wicked, O God: if only the men of blood would depart from me!'; this might have indeed have cast an ancient and intriguing shadow over the joy and optimism being striven for in the rest of the service.[25]

Thus by the end of the twentieth century this rite of passage, originally a ceremony which celebrated the mother's personal achievement of childbirth, emphasised her physical and moral vulnerability, and restored her after a period of seclusion to communion with the church, had been given an entirely new Anglican form. Still expressing thanks and joy, but omitting practically all reference to sin and danger, it now tried to address what the 1980 Alternative Service Preface called 'rapid social and intellectual changes' in 'the religious life of the present generation'. Churching had begun by offering women protection from a decidedly stern view of their involvement in sin and disobedience. Michael Vasey of Cranmer Hall, Durham, in charge of drafting the portfolio of new rites and prayers, acknowledged that 'the old churching of women fulfilled an important social role in supporting women in the ambiguities of motherhood'; but these were to be given little more than a passing reference in the revised liturgy.[26] The purpose of the new services was now to include and retain contact with as many families as possible, lest they and their children melt away into a secular life in which organised religion might play no part.

Churching becomes Thanksgiving in the Wider World

Two other denominations within England have also transformed their childbirth services into simple thanksgivings. They, too, have been perturbed at the prospect of generations of children growing up unbaptised, and concerned to respond to recent and profound changes in family life. The Methodist Church first published its *Act of Thanksgiving on the Occasion of the Birth of a Child* in the 1936 Book of Offices, but forty years later withdrew the service for fear that it was being used to replace infant baptism by families and ministers of Anabaptist leanings. In 1999 it was revived. The Faith and Order Committee explained:

> Once-accepted patterns of family life are far less common than they were ... in a post-Christian age ... many families' hold on the faith and experience of Christian worship comes through the occasional offices of baptism, marriage and the funeral service.

And so they introduced *An Act of Thanksgiving after the Birth or Adoption of a Child* to offer families a chance to present children to the church in infancy, accepting that baptism might not come about until many years later:

---

[25] *Common Worship*, pp. 15–17.
[26] Michael Vasey, in Trevor Lloyd, *Thanksgiving for the Gift of a Child*, p. 7.

An Act of Thanksgiving serves to welcome the child into the local congregation. Some *parents* may have reservations about the Baptism of young children, while still desiring to give thanks for *their* child's arrival and to dedicate themselves for *their* new task.[27]

One mother remembers that Methodists once viewed their thanksgivings 'all in a spirit of purification'; while a minister has recalled that back in the 1960s they used to refer to them as 'churchings'. But such testimony is rare, and now only the new thanksgivings are spoken of.[28]

The Roman Catholic Church has also brought radical changes to its traditional Sarum-based rite. In Kevin C. Kearns' book on life in the tenements of Dublin, Irish Catholic women were still in the 1930s vigorously insisting that new mothers went for churching. He quotes the case of Mary, still unchurched, as she was peeling potatoes:

> And me aunt looked at me and says, Leave down them, you're tainted! You're tainted in the eyes of God ... She more or less said that I was with the devil ... You were tainted unless you got this candle and (renounced) the devil and all his works. And it made you a Catholic again.

The Liturgy Adviser for the diocese of Portsmouth has described how from 1969, following Vatican II, 'the old ritual of churching was dropped and tacked on to the end of baptism as a blessing'. This took place in the early 1970s. But in 1989 a new *Blessing of a Mother Before Childbirth and After Childbirth* was introduced, designed for mothers who have not attended their children's baptism, and to meet the needs of families whose children have been adopted or fostered.[29] In practice, frequency of Blessing services depended on area: in a brief survey of fifteen Catholic priests in the two dioceses of Birmingham and Portsmouth none could recall any performed during their own incumbencies; yet a woman who in 1970 had attended the traditional Sarum service in Liverpool remembers that 'everyone was churched in those days'; mothers said that they could not go out until they had been 'done'; an observation familiar to Anglicans at the time.[30]

The Baptist Church has never included churching among its practices, but has continued to hold to this day the ideas of Henry Barrow and Dorothy Hazzard that there could be no place for a ceremony that did not allow childbirth to be understood as 'natural, ordinary and common'. The son of a Baptist minister in Stafford, recalled his father's surprise when an Anglican vicar went out one

---

[27] 'Introduction to An Act of Thanksgiving after the Birth or Adoption of a Child', *Methodist Book of Orders* (1999), p. 399.
[28] Memories from Brierley Hill (Worcestershire) and Birmingham.
[29] K. C. Kearns, *Dublin Tenement Life: an Oral History* (Dublin, 1994), pp. 190–1; Recorded conversation, April 2005; *The Missal in Latin and English,* 3rd edn (London, 1989), pp. 79–84.
[30] Testimony given in Oxfordshire, January, 2005.

evening 'to do a churching' in the late 1950s. He said:

> Baptists do not need churching; they have a dedication and naming ceremony, and later the child may attend a 'believer's baptism' from the age of twelve. There is no book of services though there is one of hymns and readings.[31]

A search through the registers of Congregationalist churches in London, Berkshire and Staffordshire has discovered no thanksgiving records of any kind.

Revision of the 1662 liturgy was undertaken in world-wide Anglican or Episcopal churches, as churching was transformed into various forms of thanksgiving for the birth or adoption of a child. Within the British Isles, in 1984 the Church of Wales and in 1993 the Church of Ireland introduced their own revised thanksgiving services; though by 1980 the Scottish Episcopal Church, which had been using a slightly adapted 1662 rite, had dropped churching and thanksgiving altogether from its prayer book. Anglican communions throughout the world adopted their own new thanksgiving liturgies in the following chronological order: 1962 The Church of South India; 1978 & 1995 The Church of England in Australia; 1979 The American Episcopal Church; 1985 The Anglican Church of Canada; 1989, The Anglican Church in New Zealand; 1990 The Anglican Church of the Province of South Africa.

Donna E. Ray, who is the main source of information for these Anglican changes, has observed that only in New Zealand is attention still paid to the wellbeing of the mother. Its service has two prayers, one spoken by her: 'I thank you for sustaining me through the pain of labour', the other by the priest: 'We give you thanks that she has been brought safely through the time of pregnancy and labour'.[32]

Survival of Traditional Liturgy of Thanksgiving

Only in the Greek and Russian Orthodox Churches has the rite of thanksgiving remained unchanged. At least one book of commentary confirms that its liturgy means what is indicated by its titles and prayers. There are four services: *Prayers for a Woman on the First Day after Childbirth*; *At the Naming of the Child on the Eighth Day after his Birth*; *For a Woman on the Fortieth Day after Childbirth*; and eventually the child's baptism. Among the expressions of joy and blessing they contain several striking references to dark moments. The first prays for the woman's safety from 'the oppression of the devil', 'the evil eye', 'bodily uncleanness' and 'divers inward troubles'; the second refers to 'every evil snare of the enemy'; the third to 'sin and uncleanness' and 'the stains of her soul'. This third ceremony, closest to a churching, is conducted in the narthex of the church away from other worshippers, and followed by celebration among the whole congrega-

---

[31] Recorded conversation, April, 2005.
[32] Donna Ray, 'A View from the Childwife's Pew', pp. 465–9.

tion.³³ Priests reserve the right to omit the prayers that they consider unsuitable for modern use, and one was quite critical about the long survival of some Orthodox attitudes:

> I think there is a Greek popular culture that tends as it were to blame women; and lots of women, alas, accept that and so I don't like prayers which would, however indirectly, encourage that ... With the English sometimes I am a little selective in the prayers, and I leave out certain prefaces, and I might tell them that I am going to do that, unless they have any objection ... It seems to be very much bound up with a sort of purity idea; in the west there could be behind all this the influence of St Augustine and the view that all children are born in original sin, and are therefore, until baptised, objects of God's wrath and will go to Hell; I know the Roman Catholic Church doesn't teach that now but that was what St Augustine believed. Not because he was a cruel person, (he wasn't) but he was logical, and his view of original sin led him to that position. But in the Orthodox position we've never really gone along with the Augustinian view of original guilt, or only in a very modified way, but it's much more about purity.

Another was much more positive about the value of the service:

> Women do it as part of following a tradition. There is not a proper theology. It recognises and celebrates the importance of childbirth, and the role of women in human life. Ideas about impurity are not emphasised.³⁴

This is a service still popular with most women after childbirth in Orthodox churches in England. There must be some combination of the attraction of a historic rite and loyalty to the expatriate church, as women respond to the traditions handed down by their mothers, free from the doubts that those from a perhaps more individualistic English culture have said that they feel about the service.

Conclusion

Prayer Book prefaces have explained that, as 'the facts and modes of English life' have changed 'almost beyond belief', some ceremonies have had to 'be put away'. Yet published liturgy in the late twentieth century still includes some remnant of the churching rite. Its title and function may have been drastically simplified in three out of the four major churches, but it is still a rite of passage; new mothers are at the centre of a public thanksgiving, as the baby is welcomed into the church, amid hopes that a baptism will soon follow. Designed for the end of the twentieth century, the ritual is shorn of any remaining 'ambiguity', and notions of 'purification' in any sense have been almost entirely abandoned and consigned to folklore.

---

[33] Grove, R., 'Baby Dedication in Traditional Christianity: Eastern Orthodox "Churching" of Forty-Day-Olds', *Journal of Eucumenical Studies*, 27.1 (Winter 1990); Alexander Schmemann, *Of Water and the Spirit* (London, 1974), p. 131.
[34] Testimony given in Oxfordshire in 2004.

CHAPTER TWO
CHURCHING IN THREE COUNTIES: WRITTEN RECORDS IN BERKSHIRE, STAFFORDSHIRE AND LONDON

The churching service has undeniably remained in print in Church of England prayer books, but one is bound to ask how far it has had a real place in twentieth-century religious practice. Part of the answer lies in thousands of parish registers and vestry fee books where vicars, clerks and curates have recorded ceremonies. Such records are here investigated in three English counties to see what can be discovered about the popularity of the churching ritual, and the part played by clergy in its celebration.

Parish Records as Sources for the Study of Churching

The quest began among registers and vestry books in the counties of Berkshire, Staffordshire and Metropolitan London, all of which have well-kept and fully-catalogued parish records. It was important to find parishes with reasonably extensive churching material: fourteen were chosen for their detailed registers in Berkshire; ten were discovered in Staffordshire, and twelve in Metropolitan London. Most useful were the *registers of services* kept in every church. Acting occasionally as a diary of parish events, more often merely a list of dates, services, preachers and their texts, and tally of attendances and offerings, these had been launched in nearly all parishes by 1900. Notes of churchings were generally found inserted in margins or written into columns at the side of the page, often along with comments on the weather, or the destination of offerings. They followed a fairly standard format; generally a date, woman's name and clerical signature were found, with occasionally an additional address, occupation or fee.

Churching references were also found slipped into *preachers' books* and *vicars' fee books,* usually with only the scarcest accompanying details.[1] But by far the most informative records were found in ten dedicated *churching registers*; one was kept in Berkshire, two in Staffordshire, and seven in London. In their columns lay full ranges of names, dates, addresses, occupations and fees offered.[2] Examples of three from London parishes may be seen in Plate 3.

[1] For example, BRO D/P 157 1B1/2, St Peter's, Wootton, whose incumbents kept churching lists along with notes of baptism in the back pages of two preachers' books, 1903–10 and 1910–21.

[2] Churching Registers: in Berkshire, BRO D/P172B 1A/2, St Stephen, Reading 1919–42;

Elsewhere, if details were scarce, a parish's *baptismal registers* could be called upon to supply addresses and occupations of its churchgoing families, and numbers of babies christened in any particular year. These numbers could be set alongside those of the churching lists, allowing an estimate to be made of the proportion of new mothers choosing to be churched as well as having their babies baptised. A valuable addition to these sources is the 1901 Ordnance Survey, whose county maps have been scrutinised to establish the location of the church in each parish, be it among a maze of streets or huddle of village houses. They show where families lived: the density of urban terraces, isolation of scattered cottages and outlying farms, and exclusiveness of local mansions within their parks and woodlands. It becomes possible, then, to measure how much of a challenge was faced by newly-delivered women in the early years of the century as they journeyed to the churching service and back.

Together, these sources furnish some of the best evidence of churching in the first half of the twentieth century. Though spare and dry at first glance, they can be made to yield vivid pictures from the past. Named women can be glimpsed in their homes and families; addresses, occupations and fees suggest their class and social status. It becomes possible to know whether or not a new mother chose to be churched, to calculate how quickly she went for churching or baptism, and to envisage what travelling to church must have involved. In addition, the community in which she lived emerges: family members crop up as neighbours or occasionally acting as godparents; how much support for her may have come from insistent relatives, or pressure from a watchful street? Finally, the clergy with whom the women went through this intensely personal service have left their mark in registers and fee books, filled in with varying levels of efficiency.

'Churching Parishes' in the Three Counties

It is now time to introduce the churching parishes whose records form the heart of this chapter and the next. Maps 1–3 (Plates 4–6) will outline their location in each county, while tables I–III list their names, their size and nature, numbers of their recorded churchings, and the dates within which they have been studied. Here, order is significant: the lists are topped by parishes that churched most in relation to parish size (*average annual churchings per thousand*), and descend to those that churched least.

---

in Staffordshire, SRO D834/1/6/1, St Mary, Stafford, 1875–1905; D4242/5, Christ Church, Stone, 1861–84; in London, LMA P78/JNE/ 006, St John the Evangelist, Blackheath, 1926–56; P85/CTC2/ 20, Christ Church, North Brixton, 1907-1971; P78/EMM/1, Emmanuel, West Greenwich, 1888–1906; P80/PET/ 35/1, St Peter, Hammersmith, 1870–1944; P81/EMM/ 30, Emmanuel, West Hampstead, 1912–51; P83/PAU2/ 22/1, St Paul, Upper Holloway, 1870–1947; P89/ALS/ 95, All Souls, Langham Place, Marylebone, 1878–1904.

(a) *Churching in Fourteen Berkshire Parishes*

The map in plate 4 makes it clear that most of the ten churching parishes lie in the countryside of West Berkshire. Eight of them (the town of Wantage, and villages of Ardington and Lockinge, East Challow, Shrivenham and Shellingford) lie in the Vale of White Horse; West Ilsley on the Berkshire Downs.[3] These are regions of astonishing beauty, among the most striking in Southern Britain, the long chalk ridge of rolling downland giving way to winding lanes and shaded brooks in the deep, flat clay valley. Northwards the land rises and then falls away to the banks of the River Thames, which until 1974 was the northern boundary of the county of Berkshire. Everywhere in the landscape there are trees in sight; some outlined on the horizon in distant copses of beech and oak, others giving shade to roads and fields, and more again in the gardens and greens of the succession of small, quiet villages. William Cobbett greatly admired this harmonious country. Riding near Aldbourne in October 1826, he wrote:

> I love the Downs so much that, if I had to choose, I would live even here, and especially would farm here, rather than on the banks of the Wye in Herefordshire, in the Vale of Gloucester, of Worcester, or Evesham.[4]

This turns out to be a promising region for good churching records. Many of its parsons undertook the ceremony with considerable frequency and wrote of it fully and conscientiously in their registers. Away from the Vale and Downs, fewer churching records have survived, but good detail is also found in the villages of Radley and Wootton to the north, the hamlet of Newtown in the south-west, and the small town of Sandhurst far to the south-east, as well as in the parishes of St Mary and St Stephen in the town of Reading and St Catherine on the Bearwood estate nearby.

In Table I the duration of churching records in these Berkshire parishes varied from six years in East Challow to fifty in Shellingford. It will immediately be obvious that churchings were relatively low in all 'town' parishes apart from Wantage, whose high average numbers (13 per 1000) owed much to a series of powerful church leaders: early on the great William Butler, vicar from 1847 to 1880, and later two vigorous parsons, the Revds Thomas Archer-Houblon and Maurice Ponsonby. Assertively high church, actively concerned in the town's many institutions, and supported by sisters of neighbouring St Mary's Convent, they established churching as a regular and enduring routine which was to draw-in dozens of women to the church of SS Peter & Paul, centrally placed one side of the town's market square. Their huge, leather-bound registers of services breathe authority laced with confident familiarity; churched women's first names abound (Flossie

[3] Map adapted from J. Dils (ed.), *An Historical Atlas of Berkshire* (Berkshire Record Society, 1998), p. ix.
[4] William Cobbett, *Rural Rides* (Harmondsworth, 1975), p. 411.

Table I. Berkshire parishes listed to show total and annual average numbers per thousand of their population churched, in descending order of magnitude.

Parish	Nature	Pop	Dates recorded	Churchings years	Churchings total number	Averages per year	Averages per year per 1000
Wootton, St Peter	village	388	1890–1918	28	213	8	21
Ardington, Holy Trinity	estate village	433	1899–1911	12	80	7	16
Wantage, SS Peter & Paul	market town	4146	1898–1921	23	1200	52	13
Lockinge, All Saints	estate village	301	1927–1950	21	59	3	10
Shellingford, St. Faith	estate village	204	1888–1938	50	91	2	10
East Challow, St Nicholas	village	574	1901–1907	6	27	5	9
Shrivenham, St Andrew	large village	953	1907–1931	24	179	7	7
Radley, St.James	estate village	444	1898–1928	30	79	3	7
Bearwood, St Catherine	estate village	822	1899–1906	7	30	4	5
Reading, St Stephen	county town	5391	1919–1942	23	554	24	5
Sandhurst, St Michael	large village	2386	1905–1945	22	207	9	4
West Ilsley, All Saints	village	276	1902–1917	15	21	1	4
Reading, St Mary	county town	14811	1916–1921	6	179	30	0.2
Newtown, St Mary	hamlet	–	1902–1924	22	61	3	–

Population figures have been taken from the censuses of 1901, 1921 and 1931, whichever is closest to the main period of churching record in each parish.

and Annie, Phoebe, Mary and Elizabeth), clearly familiar to the clergy as again and again they came for the ceremony. When the baptisms came to be written in, friends and relations appeared as godparents, their first names also known and recorded. There is a moment of disappointment when Wantage's fine record comes to an end in 1921 after logging 1,200 churchings in twenty-three years.[5]

The two Reading parishes relied on contrasting populations for their churching record. St Mary the Virgin, the Civic Church, located in the heart of the town, drew its large congregations from a wide area and broad social range. Its tally of 179 churchings in six years from a population of 14,811, is not large, no more than an average of 0.2 per thousand per year. The society of St Stephen's church was quite different: it lay in a close-knit working-class area east of the town, most of its parishioners employed locally in factories and the railway, gasworks and prison. Yet it boasted the only dedicated churching register in the county, fully and meticulously kept, which tells of 554 women churched in twenty-three years, almost all offering a fee of one shilling. Though its average per annum (twenty-four) is but four-fifths of that of St Mary (thirty), its population is only two-fifths the size, and so its annual average (of five per thousand) is many times greater. This is the first of several indications that churching levels tend to be high in poorer, disadvantaged parishes: St Stephen's figures will be compared with others in the Potteries and Black Country in Staffordshire, the East End of London, and along the Thames

[5] Kathleen Philip, *Victorian Wantage* (Wantage, 1968), pp. 66–70; BRO D/P 143 1B/2 1B/3, SS Peter & Paul, Wantage, Registers of Services, 1898–1912, 1912–21.

waterside in the diocese of Southwark.[6]

On Berkshire's south-east border the village of Sandhurst had an annual average of nine churchings; in a population of nearly 2,400, its rate of four per thousand turns out to be among the lowest of all these Berkshire parishes. One reason may be that this large population was not an entirely close-knit society, as it included three outlying institutions, The Royal Military College, Wellington School, and Broadmoor Criminal Lunatic Asylum. A few women in the congregation were married to men connected to these bodies ('RMC Servant'; 'Capt. 3rd Hussars'; 'Broadmoor Asylum Attendant'); but the Church of St Michael is seen ministering mostly to the core of an essentially village-sized community, ringed by a dozen large farms among the woods and copses that still dominate the map. From 1881 to 1920 their rector was another rich and powerful figure, the Revd Randal Parsons of Sandhurst Lodge. Like his two predecessors, he was a local benefactor on a large scale, and his influence might have been expected to encourage a higher level of participation by the small inner-village congregation.[7]

Numbering a mere 953 in 1901, and socially dominated by the Barrington family of Beckett House, Shrivenham was destined to become one of the largest villages in the Vale of White Horse. Over time its occupational profile appears increasingly urban, including trades such as railway worker, constable, postman, painter-and-decorator which far outnumber the grooms, gamekeepers and farm labourers normally found on Berkshire's landed estates. Churchings at the church of St Andrew averaged seven a year in a long record of twenty-four years.[8]

But it is in Berkshire's smallest rural communities that churching turns out to have been most popular. When average churchings per thousand per year are counted, eight of the top nine parishes are in villages, their population averaging just 430.

How can their high levels of participation be explained? In five cases: Shellingford, Ardington and Lockinge in the Vale of White Horse, and Radley and Bearwood to the north and east of the county, the nature of their estate connections must have had some effect. The powerful families that dominated their parishes were not only employers but also moral supervisors of their tenants and workers. In Shellingford the lord of the manor in the early twentieth century was Major Harold G. Henderson of Kitemore House (built north of the village in French Gothic style); in Lockinge and Ardington Robert Lloyd Lindsay, Lord Wantage, from his mansion in Lockinge took a personal interest in estate inhabitants

---

[6] BRO D/P 98 1B/3-7, St Mary the Virgin, Reading, Registers of Services 1898–1921; for St Stephen, Reading, see above, note 2, pp. 24–5.

[7] BRO D/P 102 1B/2, St Michael, Sandhurst, Register of Services, 1913–25; P. J. Holmes, *St. Michael and All Angels, Sandhurst: History and Guide* (undated), pp. 15–17.

[8] BRO D/P 112 1B/3, St Andrew, Shrivenham, Register of Services 1907–28; Vivien Moss, *An Illustrated Guide to Shrivenham* (Faringdon, 1995), pp. 7–11.

with the help of his watchful wife, Henrietta. In his autobiography the Revd J. G. Cornish, as well as writing sympathetically of the dire poverty of Lockinge's villagers, emphasised the close eye that Lady Wantage kept on them in the years 1898 to 1902 when he was vicar. Nearly all parishioners in these three Vale villages were farmers, labourers or tradesmen; the Shellingford churching entries varied little between 1898 and 1938: wives of labourers and cowmen, a bootmaker and a shopkeeper, were interspersed with occasional farmers and gardeners, one gentleman, one coachman, one foreman. The social nature of Ardington and Lockinge was much the same, though two upper-class visitors appeared in Lockinge's register among later churchings, Lady Grenfell in September 1933 and Mrs Lane-Fox in November 1939, both visiting the Loyd Lindsays. To add to the landowner's supervision, conformity to village tradition would ensure that women were churched. Of her two churchings in Shellingford as late as 1957 and 1961, one villager, though not the child of farming tenants, referred to the strength of village culture:

> In being young I accepted that that was what happened. I would not have been happy and accepted back unless I had been to give thanks.

This underlines the words of a local vicar about such social codes that even today constrain inhabitants of small villages, as well as recalling a time when girls were still dutiful towards their mothers.[9]

Far less isolated than the parishes of the Vale, St Catherine's, Bear Wood lay close to a crossing on the River Loddon, and not far from the towns of Wokingham and Reading, in the 'model village' of Sindlesham, re-fashioned in the mid-nineteenth century by Sir John Walter. His estate employees were closely supervised: the wife of John Walter II is said to have taken a close interest in all their new-born children, even announcing that she would be their godmother and choose their names at baptism.[10] It is therefore surprising that St Catherine's churching was on average among the lowest in the village list with only four churchings per year from a population of 822.

Close to the Thames in North Berkshire, parishioners of St James, Radley, where churching averaged a middling seven per thousand per year, were also accustomed to show deference to the lords of the manor, the Dockar Drysdale family of Wick Lodge. In the 1930s doffing and curtseying were still expected of the family's employees. Others worked for the tenant farmers in surrounding semi-isolated farmsteads, Peach Croft, Pumney and Goose Acre, or were employed at

[9] BRO D/P 82/ 1B/1, All Saints, Lockinge, Register of Services, 1927–36; M. Havinden. *Estate Villages: a Study of the Berkshire Villages of Ardington and Lockinge* (London, 1966), p. 193; J. G. Cornish, *Reminiscences of a Country Life*, ed. Vaughan Cornish (London, 1936), pp. 16, 28. BRO D/P 109/ 1B/1, St Faith, Shellingford, Register of Services, 1887–1926; interview in Fernham, May, 2002; see below, Chapter Five, pp. 121–2 for the same vicar's perceptive comments on village life.

[10] I am grateful to the vicar of St Catherine's for this information.

St Peter's College, several teachers' wives being among those churched during these recorded years, 1898–1928. Yet more worked in Oxford, nearby, or on the railway, and perhaps escaped the dominating influence of Mrs Drysdale (herself churched in 1910) which is still remembered by present inhabitants.[11]

Not far from Radley, Wootton parish tops the village list in Table I at twenty-one churchings per thousand per year. Yet it was not kept in order by a dominating lord of the manor, indicating that the influence of the local squire should not be over-emphasised. The church of St Peter served a tiny but widely-scattered community of 388, its outlying farms and substantial houses on Boar's Hill and Foxcombe Hill a considerable journey away. Such distances might have been expected to militate against high churching levels; yet its twenty-eight year record has the highest annual rate of twenty-one per thousand of the population. It is not immediately clear why this should have been so. The discipline maintained by Wootton's vicars appears, if it may be judged from their uniquely untidy records, to have been quite lax. No single social tradition can have dominated a parish whose members worked in a variety of locations, including the city of Oxford, and at occupations varying from 'B. A. Oxon', doctor, and gentleman, to labourers, gardeners and small tradesmen. Perhaps an explanation of commitment to churching may lie in the Vestry Minutes for 1913–26 which show that there were several families in positions of influence on the Vestry Committee: Messrs. Winterbourne (engine driver), Edgington, Phipps (cowman), Morgan and Powell, with Mr Hughes (farmer, of Wootton Manor Farm) joining in 1916. A number of their wives appear in the churching list, and may well have provided the influence that encouraged so many women to walk the distance to be churched. In addition, the second decade of the twentieth century saw the incumbency of the Revd W. K. Stude, who wrote in one Oxford diocesan visitation return how much he loved the parish and had enjoyed his time as Wootton's vicar. For all his untidy record-keeping, high churching rates may have been due also to his popularity and leadership.[12]

Far to the south on the Berkshire Downs, West Ilsley with a population of only 276 and average churchings four per thousand per year, appears a tiny parish, though it was by no means a scattered one; Manor Farm and West Ilsley Farm, its two big enterprises, lay actually in the village, while another, Harcourt Farm, was very close by out to the west. The whole settlement is remote, surrounded by bare, rolling downland; Folly Down, Windmill Down, Ilsley Down. The Revd E. A. McConnell, in place at All Saints Church from 1899 to 1917, kept a register nearly

[11] P. Drysdale, R. Ford, P. Groser, M. Orchard, A. Parkes, and K. Williams, *The History of Radley* (Abingdon, 2002), pp. 84, 100; interviews with Radley History and Retirement Groups, June and July, 2002.

[12] BRO, D/P157/1/B/2–3, St Michael, Wootton Preachers' Books, 1903–10, 1910–21; D/P 157 8/2, Vestry Minutes for 1913–21; OCRO Oxf. Dioc. Papers C383, Berkshire Archdeaconry 1924 Visitation, Abingdon Deanery, E1, answers of The Revd W. K. Stude, by then vicar of Besselsleigh.

as chaotic as that at Wootton, but filled with incident and news. Still in use in the vestry, it testifies to the preponderance of carters in its predominantly labouring population, many presumably employed to work the long, windswept roads to Wantage, Newbury and Hungerford.[13]

Still further south, the hamlet of Newtown was even smaller, just a few houses, an inn and St Mary's church, built on the route between Hungerford and the Great West Road. Employment was found at Eddington House nearby, and in several large isolated farms: North Farm, Short's and Newhayward Farms, Little Hidden, Great Hidden and North Hidden. Average churching figures per thousand are impossible to calculate, as Newtown's population is not known: its inhabitants' names are listed in the census as belonging to Hungerford, and they are hard to trace through their addresses as the village's roads have no names, nor are its houses numbered: the register of services has them all living in 'Newtown'.[14]

Berkshire's 1901 Ordnance Survey maps often illustrate the scattered nature of its rural communities, which may have had some bearing on their churching history. This might have been true of East Challow, a small village of 574 souls, which shared its vicar with West Challow, to which it was linked only by a rough, unpaved lane (a subject of bitter complaint by the Revd Henry Sanders, during his forty-four years of service in both parishes). Home to many skilled and unskilled workers on the railway and in the local iron works, East Challow acknowledged the influence of no particular landowner or employer, yet it comes fifth-highest in the churching list at nine per thousand per year. This rate may have been due to its proximity to Wantage, with its strong churching record, or (as in Wootton) to the efforts of a conscientious incumbent, in this case the same Henry Sanders.[15]

For the historian of churching Berkshire's record has proved tremendously valuable. In its parishes the rite was widely observed and often fully recorded. This is in part attributable to its powerful landed families and vigorous clergy, the two often co-operating within the parishes of its villages and country towns.

(b) *Churching in Ten Staffordshire Parishes*

Staffordshire's ten listed churching records introduce a varied range of communities. Map 2 in Plate 5 shows that they come from many parts of the county: the high north where moorland villages lie in mining country, with pottery factories not far off; central flatlands of the rivers Trent and Sow; and the southern powerhouse of Black Country coal, iron and engineering works.[16] The records them-

---

[13] BRO D/P75 1B/2, All Saints, West Ilsley, Register of Services 1902–09; 1B/3, 1909–17.
[14] BRO D/P71 1B/13, St Mary, Newtown, Register of Services 1902–31.
[15] BRO D/P81 B/1B/3, St Nicholas, East Challow, Register of Services 1900–1907; I am indebted to Mary Mann of East Challow for introducing me to Sanders' memoirs.
[16] Map adapted from Cecil R. Humphery-Smith, *The Phillimore Atlas and Index of Parish Registers* (Chichester, 1984), no. 31, Staffordshire.

selves also vary widely in style compared with those in Berkshire. Three were written up in routine registers of services, and two in churching registers; but of the rest, two are in fee books, two in parish magazines, and one in a small, untitled booklet which crowds together marriages, funerals, baptisms and churchings over many years.[17] Details of all are listed in Table II, opposite.

Staffordshire's social variation is sketched into this list of parishes. The top three, lying in its industrial heartlands, the Potteries (Longton) and the Black Country (Wednesbury), contained largely working-class populations. Of the two churches in Longton, the congregation of St James-the-Less near the town centre consisted largely of pottery workers; that of SS Mary & Chad in North Longton of mining families alongside potters. Part of the federation (later the city) of Stoke on Trent, these districts endured intractable poverty through the first half of the twentieth century, and shared some of the highest death-rates in the country. Unforgettable pictures of their urban landscape have been described in the novels of Arnold Bennett.[18] As soon as they could afford it, better-off citizens would move away from the dereliction, pollution and insecurity of the town. Wednesbury, in south-east Staffordshire's Black Country, suffered its own dire problems. Through the twentieth century much of the area fell into decay, with its coalfields on the famous Ten Yard Seam exhausted and flooding, canals redundant and derelict, and in its old terraces the inhabitants still enduring both subsidence and pollution caused by old workings. Medical officers of health in the Wednesbury area had written in 1897 of the high infant death-rate:

> Improper feeding, lack of care, neglect of cleanliness and ventilation, insufficient food, clothing and shelter account probably for the greatest part of our fatalities.[19]

As time passed whole streets had to be demolished as their houses sank into the ground. St Luke's Mission Church itself collapsed and had to be replaced (on a different site) in 1972. That these two notoriously impoverished areas had the county's strongest churching tradition calls for later comparison with several

[17] SRO D5590/1/8, St Edward, Cheddleton, Register of Services 1899–1919; D3959/1/10, St James, Longdon, Register of Services 1898–1952; D1193/5/1, St Luke's Mission church, Wednesbury, Register of Services, Nov. to Dec. 1897; SRO D5014/1, Longton, Ss Mary & Chad, Preacher's Book, 1888–94; D4160/6/41, bound volumes of parish magazines, 1897–1905, 1959–1961; D5676/7/3–5, St James-the-Less, Longton, parish magazines, 1893–1904; D729, St Chad, Lichfield, 1845–83; SRO D834/1/6/1, St Mary, Stafford, 1875-1905; D4242/5, Christ Church, Stone, 1961–84.

[18] Arnold Bennett, *Clayhanger* (London, 1910); *The Old Wives' Tale* (London, 1908); *Anna of the Five Towns* (London, 1906); R. Woods and N. Shelton, *An Atlas of Victorian Mortality* (Liverpool, 1997).

[19] G. J. Barnsby, *Social Conditions in the Black Country 1800–1900* (Wolverhampton, 1980), Ch. 3, p. 76; David Palliser, *The Staffordshire Landscape* (London, 1976), Chapter Five, pp. 195–209, and Chapter Nine, pp. 254–71.

Table II. Staffordshire parishes listed to show total and annual average numbers per thousand of their population churched, in descending order of magnitude.

Parish	Nature	Pop	Dates recorded	Churchings years	total number	Averages per year	per year per 1000
Longton, St James/Less	pottery town	1288	1901–1905	4	1409	352	273
Longton, SS. Mary/Chad	pottery town	918	1888–1894	6	144	24	26
Wednesbury, St Luke	town	1638	1897	0.2	6	36	22
Lichfield, St Chad	city	1848	1879–1883	5	156	31	17
Longdon, St James	village	951	1898–1905	6	114	14	15
Cheddleton, St Edward	village	1938	1899–1904	6	141	24	12
Stafford, St Mary	county town	5921	1900–1902	3	187	62	10
Burton, St Modwen,	town	1982	1914–1920	7	122	17	9
Stone, Christ Church	market town	4413	1880–1883	1	34	34	8
Eccleshall, Holy Trinity	small town	2430	1931–1952	21	59	3	1

parishes of inner London.[20]

Other 'churching parishes' in Staffordshire offer a less dramatic profile. Life in the villages of Cheddleton and Longdon was strenuous and mostly impoverished; not entirely rural, their working men were employed in mining as well as farming. Churching rates were middling at fifteen and twelve per thousand, slightly higher than those in more prosperous parishes. Worshippers at St Modwen, Burton-on-Trent worked in brewing, leather and iron-making industries, and at St Mary, Stafford in the heart of the county, in engineering, leather-working and many lighter trades. St Chad, Lichfield perhaps owed its high participation score of seventeen per thousand per year to the churchgoing society in which it lay, not far from the Cathedral in this quiet, elegant city; while market towns Eccleshall and Stone, miles away on the rivers of central Staffordshire and lowest in churching participation, had social profiles more akin to Wantage or Reigate than to their own industrial neighbours to the north and south.

To develop the impression that social conditions may be part of the explanation for churching's long survival, several further useful parallels may be found between the various regions of Staffordshire and Berkshire, as well as Southwark's Surrey areas which will be seen in Chapter Four. The parishes of mid-Staffordshire, where landowning families oversaw their labourers through the farming year, and which experienced no large-scale movement of population, resemble those of central–western Berkshire's West Ilsley and Shellingford and Surrey's Godstone and Farleigh, in their rural stability; Cheddleton and Longdon share with East Challow the combination of farming and proximity to heavy industry; the bustle and prosperity of Reading and Wantage, Wimbledon and Wandsworth are echoed in Stafford and Stone. In addition, it may have been the working-class culture of St Stephen, Reading and the two churches of Longton, Staffordshire that ensured

[20] See below, pp. 35, 38.

ready participation in the churching rite. More elements of these ideas will be investigated in the analysis of 'Women and the decision to be churched' in Chapter Three, below.

(c) *Churching in Twelve Parishes of Metropolitan London*

Did churching patterns in Metropolitan London differ from those in largely rural Berkshire and rural/industrial Staffordshire? All three studies have been conducted along similar lines; the same sources have been consulted, the same questions asked about who the churched women were, how often they were churched, where they lived and in what circumstances; attempts have also been made to see the connection between churching levels and the nature of parishes. Would the comparatively huge size of Metropolitan London's parish populations, and the distinctly urban character of its communities, have resulted in churching practice unlike that of the other two traditionally rural counties?

A search through catalogues of church registers in the London Metropolitan Archives revealed that there are some records of the churching rite in altogether forty-eight parishes. Eleven, from the seventeenth to early nineteenth centuries, mentioned it briefly in vicar's fee books, or instruments of authorization in which new incumbents were told that it was to be one of their duties. Only from the late nineteenth century did regular and substantial records begin to be kept, of which the twelve listed below have been studied, being the fullest, though of varied length and quality. Their location can be found on Map 3 in Plate 6.[21] Among these it is fortunate that in London no fewer than seven churching registers have been found.[22] Their contents are by no means uniform: at Christ Church, North Brixton and All Souls', Marylebone they give names and addresses of churched women along with the occupations of their husbands and amounts of money offered; at Emmanuel Mission, East Greenwich children as well are entered, along with addresses and occupations, but the offerings have been omitted; at St Peter, Hammersmith and St Paul, Upper Holloway there are only names, addresses and offerings; and at St John the Evangelist, Blackheath and Emmanuel, West Hampstead there is nothing beyond names and addresses.

The remaining five parishes offer only ordinary registers of services containing much less detail. The Lady Margaret Mission, Walworth; St Anne, Shoreditch; and St Chad, Haggerston have entered no names at all, only the word 'churching' and a list of offerings; St Mary, Bromley-by-Bow and St John the Baptist, Hoxton give least detail of all, recording only their huge churching numbers, with nothing

---

[21] The London map is adapted from Hugh Clout (ed.), *The Times London History Atlas* (London & New York, 1991) p. 116; several of the early churching references have been mentioned in Chapter One, pp. 15–16.

[22] For these seven references see footnote 2, above.

Table III. London parishes listed to show total and annual average numbers per thousand of their population churched, in descending order of magnitude.

Parish	Nature	Pop	Dates recorded	Churchings years	Churchings total number	Averages per year	Averages per year per 1000
Shoreditch, St Anne	East End	3845	1910–1915	6	1458	243	63
W. Greenwich, Emmanuel	S. London	2390	1885–1905	20	1800	90	38
Bow, St Mary	East End	14369	1901–1919	18	6372	354	25
Walworth, Lady Margaret	S. London	5290	1913–1922	9	1011	112	21
Hoxton, St John	East End	17425	1927–1930	4	816	204	12
Upper Holloway, St Paul	suburb	6341	1915–1935	20	1428	71	11
Marylebone, All Souls'	West End	11243	1878–1904	26	2541	98	9
Hammersmith, St Peter	suburb	8235	1870–1944	74	5280	71	9
North Brixton	suburb	6797	1907–1971	64	1600	35	5
Blackheath, St John	suburb	5766	1926–1955	29	580	20	3
W. Hampstead, Emmanuel	suburb	9923	1912–1951	39	780	20	2
Haggerston, St Chad	East End	6251	1939–1946	7	72	10	2

about the churched women or their circumstances. Fortunately details from contemporary baptismal registers have been able to provide at least a picture of churchgoing families' residence and occupation during the relevant years.[23]

These selected parishes were extremely varied. Study of late-nineteenth-century maps reveals much social differentiation both within and between them as crowded, unplanned alleys contrast with regular terraces and spacious residences.[24] Four lay south of the Thames: Christ Church, North Brixton; The Lady Margaret, Walworth; St John the Evangelist, Blackheath; and Emmanuel, West Greenwich. The rest are in the city's northern suburbs, and in its East End and West End.

In Table III, it is noticeable that the five highest annual average churching levels are found in the inner-urban area: three from north of the Thames (St Anne, Shoreditch; St Mary, Bow; and St John the Baptist, Hoxton) and two on its southern bank (Emmanuel, West Greenwich; and The Lady Margaret, Walworth). This inner-urban / churching alliance is broken in the case of a sixth: St Chad, Haggerston from the heart of East End London has the lowest average annual rate. This may be because its only surviving churching record belonged to the exceptionally disrupted years of the Second World War. It is also possible that its strong devotion to High Anglican ceremony may have caused some women to seek their churching elsewhere, perhaps at St Anne, Shoreditch, not far away, and less

[23] LMA P 92 /LDM /36, The Lady Margaret Church, Walworth, Register of Baptisms and Churchings, 1913–22; P 91 /ANN/12, St Anne, Shoreditch, Register of Services, 1910–16; P 91 /CHD /5, St Chad, Haggerston, Register of Services, 1939–45; P 88 /MRY2 /61 /1, St Mary, Bromley by Bow, Register of Services, 1901–13; 2 /62, Register of Services, 1913–19; P 91 /109, St John the Baptist, Hoxton, Register of Services, 1927–1930.

[24] Such maps may be found in G. W. Bacon, *The A–Z of Victorian London* (London, 1887).

assertively ceremonial.[25]

To facilitate discussion of the varied social nature of these twelve parishes, five have been designated 'suburban': St John the Evangelist, Blackheath; Christ Church, North Brixton; St Peter, Hammersmith; Emmanuel Mission Church, West Hampstead; and St Paul, Upper Holloway. These suburbs, all originally villages, had grown up in the late nineteenth century as middle-class families moved into them away from the crowding and poverty of the inner city. New railways made it possible to work in central London: by 1900 commuters could reach their offices and workshops from Blackheath on the South-Eastern railway, or by three underground lines as well as the widened Great West Road from the quiet riverside village of Hammersmith. Four railways passed through countrified West Hampstead, offering its clerks and managers quick return journeys to St Pancras and Victoria Stations; and Upper Holloway, once the country home of gentlemen and wealthy merchants, and far enough out of town to have contained farms, and inns for northbound travellers, quickly filled with clerks and engineers as the railway made its impact. As these in their turn moved away, what Charles Booth used to term 'a rough and shifting population' took their place, exchanging the slums around The Angel and King's Cross for Holloway's terraces and tenements, that were soon in danger of becoming themselves dilapidated and overcrowded.

The socialist cleric George Haw wrote in 1906 of the huge blow that all this movement was delivering to parishes close to the capital's centre:

> ... all the strong and prosperous people are running away from the inner belt of London as fast as they can ... The manufacturers, their managers, and all the staff who take salaries as distinct from wages, come in the mornings, and go away in the evenings, and admit no responsibility, social or religious, for the crowded districts where their workplaces lie, and their workpeople live. The chronic poor and the small wage earners are left stranded, a class by themselves.

Roy Porter maintains that this had always been the case:

> In reality London's districts were for ever in flux, turbulent eddies of change, as citizens ceaselessly moved on, to avoid going down in the world.

It was this mobility, the endless leaving and arriving, that was to dominate the Southwark clergy's anxieties in the visitations of 1936 and 1951.[26]

---

[25] See ideas about similar movement towards St James-the-Less, Longton, in Chapter Three on p. 49.

[26] G. Haw is quoted in E. R. Wickham, *Church and People in an Industrial City* (London, 1957), pp. 175–6; Roy Porter, *London: A Social History* (Harmondsworth, 1996), p. 209; on Southwark visitations v. Chapter Four, *passim*.

But it was not so in all cases. In the registers of these suburban parishes only moderate social downgrading is detected, possibly because church attendance was always broadly limited to the same groups: families of the middle and 'respectable' working classes. The churching register of Christ Church, North Brixton, for example, traces little occupational change through more than six decades from 1907 to 1971; husbands' employment remained overwhelmingly Class III: skilled workers and the lower-middle class, living in roads of modest, comfortable houses. Judging by other churching registers and baptismal lists, parish occupations in most of London's other suburbs underwent the same moderate changes over time, with just some levelling of social differences as gentlemen and the higher professions gradually disappeared, to be replaced by clerks and artisans, tradesmen, and always a few more labourers.

Indeed, of all these twelve London parishes, All Souls', Langham Place, Marylebone in London's West End was the only one to appear sharply differentiated. There the occupational lists in both churching and baptismal registers between 1900 and 1904 continued to juxtapose rich parishioners in grand houses and imposing institutions with their poor neighbours in flats and lodging houses; wives of gentlemen, surgeons, army officers and civil servants appear on churching lists alongside others married to porters, milkmen and labourers (see sample in Plate 3). Such a pattern is still to be seen in its baptismal records fifty years later.

Four inner-city parishes in the East End of London offer quite different profiles from those of the suburbs. Three were close neighbours: St John the Baptist, Hoxton; St Chad, Haggerston; and St Anne, Shoreditch. The fourth, St Mary, Bromley-by-Bow, bordered the River Lea in the very east of the diocese. These erstwhile out-of-town villages had been filling since at least 1800 with artisans and labourers in city trades such as food and furniture, printing and shoemaking, and, in Bow, working on the riverside wharves. By the late nineteenth century their clergy, often installed in recently-built churches, were having to confront the squalor, poverty, ill-health and crime that had come to blight many parts of the area. The struggle was to continue through the twentieth century: a letter dated 1981 has come to light among the records of St Anne, Shoreditch in which Canon John Ferley wrote of his time as curate at St John, Hoxton during the very years of its churching record:

> I was in Hoxton in 1930–32 not at St. Anne's but at St. John's ... Hoxton was the chief criminal area in London, there were more ticket of leave men in that area than anywhere else. We hobnobbed with members of race-course gangs and burglars ... John (a fellow-curate) warned me never to interfere if women fought each other in the street, because they would both turn on you.

Yet Ferley also wrote, with some nostalgia, of popular holidays hop-picking in Kent, and of occasionally strong church attendances: of multiple weddings every

Christmas and Easter, and two thousand people crowding into Watch Night services.[27]

Nevertheless, as the old maps show, three of these East End churches were quite handsomely situated in earlier times: St John-the-Baptist on Crondall Street, Hoxton still stands in its own tree-lined churchyard; huge, red-brick St Chad, Haggerston lay on the edge of elegant Nicholl Square (now demolished); and ancient St Mary, Bow was poised at the head of Bow Road, a wide thoroughfare that still has fine houses standing back along its northern side, though the area opposite has been destroyed by bombing and re-developed as an estate of flats. St Anne, Shoreditch lay in far poorer and more crowded surroundings, yet managed, along with twentieth-century Hoxton and Bow, to average over two hundred churchings a year, adding to the perception that churching was most frequent in the least prosperous communities.

This line of thinking is supported by two mission churches in parishes near the south bank of the Thames that were more typical of the inner-city than the suburbs: The Emmanuel Mission Church, West Greenwich, and The Lady Margaret Mission Church, Walworth. Not far from the high parkland of Blackheath, Emmanuel Mission lay on low marshy ground by the River Ravensbourne in one of the poorest parts of the Deptford side of Greenwich. In the 1880s Charles Booth had written of its gardens, alleyways and back-to-backs and the sound of women singing as they washed clothes. He considered drink to be the main social problem. As in Shoreditch, poverty accompanied a churching score of over ninety a year, but here in a population of only 2,390. Not far away, Booth had also visited The Lady Margaret, a High Church university mission set up to minister to the poor of Walworth's crowded markets, later to become part of the commuterland of the southern riverside. He had greatly enjoyed its fine music and spectacular ceremonial. In this relatively small parish population the rate of churching was also amongst the highest.[28]

Records of the Churching Clergy

What is known of the clergy in all these parishes of record? Had they encouraged women in their duty of churching, or merely tolerated requests for the ceremony in order to support habits of churchgoing in the parish? In a century of changing liturgy and practice it seemed important to discover their role in this churching rite, and the ways in which they might have encouraged its continuation, or con-

[27] LMA P 91 /ANN /120, letter from Canon John Ferley, Norwich, Sept. 1981; Maxine Frith, 'Reclaiming Hoxton' (*The Independent*, 14 April, 2004).
[28] Charles Booth, *Life and Labour of the People in London* (London 1902), 3rd Series: *Religious Influence*: on Emmanuel, West Greenwich, Vol. 5, Chapter II, p. 40; and on The Lady Margaret Mission, Walworth, Vol. 4, p. 185. Emmanuel Mission Church was not in East Greenwich (as the LMA catalogue has it), but on Ravensbourne Road some way from Greenwich's west side.

tributed to its demise.

Unfortunately neither the weekly registers of services nor other churching lists reveal much about clerical attitudes. It was not normal practice to write comments on such routine matters as churchings, baptisms or even weddings. Occasionally a funeral might rate a word or two; but in general all that written records can provide are a few clues about the character of the parson and nature of his parish regime. Of the three counties it is again in Berkshire that these records are most numerous and revealing; though some registers are spare and kept to the point, in others a fuller account of weekly services and parish events allows a personality to emerge, displaying commitment and striving, impatience, or remote detatchment.[29]

A few personal memoirs and autobiographies have turned up which tell more. The Reverends Henry Howard of Brightwalton, Henry Sanders of East Challow, S. E. Cottam of Wootton and John Cornish of Lockinge described variously the rewards of successful parish events, frustration about declining attendance, difficulty with intransigent church members, and concern about the suffering of war and of untimely death.[30] Visitations also gave clergy opportunities to reflect on their incumbencies; Berkshire's parsons in Oxford diocese, and South London's incumbents in Southwark diocese were occasionally quite outspoken about reasons for satisfaction or discontent arising from their circumstances. Parish magazines wrote up social events in which vicars were often leading lights. And histories of the local church have been found contributing to the image of former outstanding vicars, as in Radley, Sandhurst, Shrivenham, Sonning and Wantage in Berkshire; Longton in Staffordshire, Walworth and Brixton in London. Sometimes the character of a powerful incumbent lives in the memory of later parishioners: William Mowll of Brixton, Fr Murray of Longton, Randal Parsons at Sandhurst.

Where a successful churching record was achieved by clergy, two elements in their incumbencies could be said to have been important in their relationship with parishioners as they encouraged new mothers to come for churchings: familiarity built on long service; and shared experience of married life, sometimes together with straitened circumstances. These may have helped to overcome the professional and social distance that otherwise lay between them and the major-

[29] For instance D/P157 1B/3, S. E. Cottam's sharp, furious comments at Wootton, 1920–44; D/P102 1B/3, E. O'Malley's increasingly dishevelled pages at Sandhurst, 1938–52.

[30] Henry Sanders of St Nicholas, East Challow, D/P 81 B /1B/3, MF 93804/1, Register of Services, 1900–1907; D/P 81 B/28/5, *Parish Diary 1900*; Edward Hill of St Andrew, Shrivenham, *Diary*, privately-printed, kindly lent by Vivien Moss; Henry Howard of All Saints, Brightwalton (D/P24 1B/172), Register of Services 1879–1900, contains a diary of events; J. G. Cornish, *Reminiscences of Country Life* included an account of the parish of All Saints, Lockinge, 1893–1903; Arthur Jephson, vicar of St John the Evangelist, Walworth 1880–1911, *My Life in London* (London, 1910).

ity of their parishioners.

Long Service

Berkshire clergy in many parishes were remarkable for the extended duration of their incumbencies, as seen in Table IV, below, which names the nine churching parsons whose incumbencies lasted for more than fifteen years, and who must have come to know the parish families very well.

In London and Staffordshire a number of strikingly long incumbencies are also found: William Mowll stayed for seventeen years at Christ Church, Brixton, Arthur Jephson was in place for eleven at St John-the-Evangelist, Walworth. H. B. Freeman served at St Modwen, Burton-upon-Trent for twenty-five years, and Frs Tom Murray and Edward Woodward spent twenty-one and thirty-four years respectively at SS Mary & Chad, Longton. All their records remained tantalizingly silent about churching duties.

Table IV: Duration of incumbency in nine Berkshire parishes

Incumbent	parish	incumbency	duration
Henry Sanders	East Challow	1900–1944	44 years
Edward Hill	Shrivenham	1890–1930	40 years
H. Randall Parsons	Sandhurst	1881–1920	39 years
Alfred Herbert	Shellingford	1870–1909	39 years
George Keble	Lockinge	1904–1937	33 years
W. K. Stude	Wootton	1900–1920	20 years
Edward McConnell	West Ilsley	1899–1919	20 years
Charles Boxall Langland	Radley	1898–1916	18 years
Maurice Ponsonby	Wantage	1903–1919	16 years

Shared Experience

Many clergy were husbands and fathers, which may well have advanced their relationships with the parish mothers. In Berkshire they included Henry Sanders whose wife taught at the Sunday School in East Challow; Alfred Herbert of Shellingford whose wife Elizabeth and their four children (two of them unmarried daughters aged twenty and twenty-six in 1901) perhaps helped Alfred to get to know Shellingford's female parishioners; Fitzwilliam Gillmor of Ardington and his wife Harriet, who was churched after the births of two sons in 1889 and 1901; Edward Alexander McConnell of West Ilsley, who churched his wife, Bertha, in 1901; also Charles Augustus Whittock and his wife Mary at Bearwood; John Cornish at Lockinge and his successor George Keble, each with a wife and daughter, who might all have similarly drawn local wives and mothers closer to the church's activities. Matrimony, of course, was not essential. Bachelor clergy such as Thomas Archer Houblon of Wantage, who lived with his unmarried sister, Maria, and Richard E. T. Bell, remembered as very popular at St Stephen, Reading after 1928, both had full churching records. A number of single High Church clergy in all three counties, running powerful evangelical missions even as they supported education, and supervised pastoral work with the poor and elderly, won in return the loyalty and confidence of their parishioners.

Though it has been suggested that clergy were likely to have been distanced by the relative wealth and comfort of their life in the parsonage,[31] yet there might also have been some fellow-feeling between the parish and the poorer clergy. In visitation replies incumbents in both London and Berkshire claimed to have been hard-pressed financially: small stipends and large expenses (including a number arising from war damage) made it extremely hard to maintain decaying churches and dilapidated, over-sized rectories. Only in a few cases do patrons seem to have contributed to their costs. As congregations declined, and particularly as the participation of the middle classes waned, reducing valuable weekly offerings and other material support, those parsons without their own private funds could not afford to pay for curates, and many complained at the consequent growth in their own workloads. Outside help was urgently needed at Radley where in 1902 the Reverend C. Boxall Langland pointed out: 'the gross value of the tithe is £70 but the net actually received last year was £43. 9. 6d'. Running a parish church was undoubtedly costly, as the Reverend Thomas Houblon itemised in detail for SS Peter & Paul, Wantage, also in 1902:

> ... curates Richard R. Thomas, Edward P. R. d'Alend (£150 each); Michael R. Newbolt (£135) and M. L. Archibald Bates (temporary – the rest are licensed) £140 paid out of the living and chaplaincy then the balance from private income.

In 1918 Houblon's successor, Maurice Ponsonby was paying for three assistant curates and some help from the chaplain of St Mary's Home for Penitents. It was fortunate for these men that they had private means, and that Wantage was a populous and well-supported parish.[32]

Professional Attitudes and Social Distance

Nevertheless it was inevitable that there would be some distance between incumbent and congregation. Differences in class, wealth and education removed clergy socially from their relatively ill-taught, impoverished and (according to the Southwark and Oxford visitations) increasingly indifferent parishioners. Maurice Ponsonby, vicar of Wantage 1903–19, was fourth baron de Mauley; H. Randall Parsons, rector of Sandhurst 1880–1921, was son of the third earl of Rosse, as well as son-in-law to John Mackarness, bishop of Oxford. The 1901 census shows three of

---

[31] David Hempton, *The Religion of the People: Methodism and Popular Religion c1750–1900* (London and New York, 1996), p. 56.
[32] OCRO MSS Oxf. Dioc., replies to visitations, C200, [1902]; C 300 (1906); C372 (1909); C378 (1918); C383 (1924); C389 (1931) and C395 [1936].

Berkshire's churching parsons, the Reverends Gillmor, Whittock and Herbert employing three or even four servants. Many entries in parish records demonstrate a classical education, with dates, phrases and exclamations in Latin and Greek, frequently in tiny, scholarly writing of almost obsessive neatness. Several clergy laid emphasis on their own academic status and that of their distinguished supporters as they recorded their own inductions. Authority as much as familiarity must have governed relations between these parsons and the majority of their parishioners.

At times two further factors might alienate the parish: the drive for strict observance, and divisions over churchmanship. As soon as he arrived in Wootton in 1920 S. E. Cottam began a series of bitter register entries about the slackness of his congregation; and not far off in East Challow Henry Sanders had long been writing of similar problems. Though during a forty-four year incumbency (1900–44) his register did record pleasing moments of full congregations, shared enjoyment of music, and summer outings, his annual summaries of events denounced unrepentant immorality, plotting and defiance as he strove to impose discipline and an unswervingly High Church regime on his parishioners. All, including local women, were to be checked: he wrote in December 1901, reviewing his first year at East Challow:

> My methods differ so radically and profoundly from those of my predecessor (a good and holy man!) that many I fear have not got over the change. As two old maids expressed it – in sermons "he always spoke to us as if we were so good". Yes our methods do differ indeed! ... I've been compelled to "kill" the local branch of the Mother's Union – the members always come to the treats but never to church. A church society cannot be allowed to exist merely for the sake of providing pleasure to unfaithful Catholics! The besetting sin of most of the faithful is Pride & Self Satisfaction. They know everything, and are satisfied with their own goodness. Here it seems to me are the Sins of the Village – 1) Indifference & Carelessness, 2) Pride and Self Satisfaction. May the Holy Spirit enlighten & guide.

During that first year this exacting vicar had refused to church a woman 'on account of her great sin', noting that she had unashamedly departed to be churched elsewhere. He came to be known as 'Black Harry' for his dark, forbidding sermons; and there was soon to be an uncomfortable confrontation with East Challow's members of the evangelical protestant Church Association as they resisted his Anglo-Catholic style.[33] Sweeping severity is also remembered in Longton, Staffordshire. Fr Edward Woodward, incumbent at SS Mary & Chad from 1930 to 1964, a naval man who 'ran a tight ship', was described recently as 'just in charge of absolutely everything ... he was a local lad, came from Stoke, and he just ruled the roost'; his parishioners were said to have 'lived in fear and trembling of him';

---

[33] RO D/P81B/1B/3.

one woman would only agree to be churched if it was the curate who was on duty to take the service.

Both Cottam and Sanders were involved in a struggle that had been going on since the late nineteenth century, between strongly committed High Churchmen with their revived Anglo-Catholic rituals, and Low Church conservatives spearheaded by the Church Association, organisers of the opposition in East Challow. Both groups made strenuous efforts to reach deprived people in crowded towns; such families that would be identified by the Southwark visitation as likely to seek churching. In Staffordshire, SS Mary & Chad, Longton was one of the most strongly Anglo-Catholic parishes, founded as a tin church in 1891 under Fr T. L. Murray to minister to the neglected, impoverished potters of Sandford Hill. Parishioners took sides: inflated churching figures at the nearby town church of St James-the-Less, Longton are thought to reflect a preference among some of these families for its Low Church position.[34]

Such variations of churchmanship can be identified in several of London's churching parishes. Four were to some extent High Church: St Chad, Haggerston; St Anne, Shoreditch; The Lady Margaret, Walworth; and St Mary, Bow. Sometimes parish registers reveal this style in methods of address and choice of sermon texts; in the noting of Black and Red Letter Days, saints' days and festivals; and use of the words 'mass' in various forms (High, Low, Funeral, Commemoration, Memorial, Celebration, etc.). In contrast, the history of Low Church evangelism at Christ Church, North Brixton, starting with its foundation in 1855 by the Revd James McConnel Hussey, soon reaches the famously rousing sermons of his successor, William Rutley Mowll (1891–1917), one of the best known preachers in South London, whose success resulted in an extra pulpit having to be built outside on Vassal Street. Four more of the twelve churching parishes shared this style of churchmanship: St John the Evangelist, Blackheath; Emmanuel, West Hampstead; St John the Baptist, Hoxton; and All Souls, Langham Place (where Mowll was once a curate). There is no evidence that churching rates were affected by these regimes, though they may help to explain the choices made by some women, drawn perhaps to undertake long journeys to be churched in the atmosphere that they preferred.

Glimpses of Staffordshire clergy have proved less easy to obtain for the first half of the twentieth century. The general style of their parish registers was brisk and spare, making no space for illuminating personal comments. Parish booklets, apart from that from SS Mary and Chad, Longton, concentrate more on precious furnishings and monuments (in Stafford and Eccleshall), and glorious windows (in Cheddleton and Burton-upon-Trent) than on the regimes of individual clergy. However, the churching registers of St Mary, Stafford convey something of the

---

[34] R. Cheadle, *A History of SS. Mary and Chad Church, Longton* (Keele, 2000), pp. 49–50; interview in Longton, August, 2004.

painstaking care taken by the record-keeper, as illustrated in the short section from the beginning of 1900 shown in Plate 7.[35]

Many parishes have thrown away their early magazines, abandoning precious collections of social and ecclesiastical information. But those that have survived mention churching services on the cover over many decades. Stored in the Berkshire Record Office are some volumes from Reading's three ancient churches which continued to advertise churchings well into the twentieth century, long after their clergy had ceased to record them in their registers, showing that their willingness to perform the ceremony had certainly not died away. At St Mary the Virgin, early in the century, they were held 'immediately before any service'; after 1918, and again after 1947, 'with at least 24 hours' notice'; and from 1960 until notices ceased in 1962, 'with at least 7 days' notice'; some indication perhaps of reduced demand. The church of St Lawrence offered churchings in its surviving magazines up to 1926; and that of St. Giles until as late as 1970 'by appointment on Saturdays at 6.45 p.m.'. Replying to a query on the 'WHAT DOES THAT MEAN?' page in 1930, the Revd G. R. Oakley explained comfortingly:

> The Churching of Women is the thanksgiving of a mother for the gift of a little child and for bringing her safely through a time of pain and danger.

By such means he and his fellow clergy were perhaps trying to keep interest in the ceremony alive, and maintain its popularity.[36]

A few similar magazine announcements have been found in the London records. Churching appears to have been fitted in frequently: at All Saints, Haggerston 'Churchings – Fifteen minutes before any Service and on Friday, 3.30 p.m.' was on the magazine's front cover from 1913 to 1942; St Matthias, Stoke Newington held 'Churching of Women ... Before or after daily Offices' in 1931; while St Andrew, Newington had 'Churchings after any Service' written on its cover (date uncertain).[37] Staffordshire magazines have not survived so well, apart from those of Longton's SS Mary & Chad and St James-the-Less, both of which used their magazines as registers announcing numbers of churchings and details of baptisms for several years.

Whether they were married or single, High Church or Low, working in town or country, serving for long periods or short, many of these incumbents saw themselves as wrestling with growing ignorance, indifference and declining church attendance in the twentieth century. In his study, *The Anglican Parochial Clergy:*

---

[35] RO D834/1/6/1, St Mary, Stafford, 1875–1905.
[36] BRO D/P98/28A/ 6 (1909), /16 (1918–21, /19 (1930–33), /23 (1947–50), St Mary the Virgin, Reading, 1909–50; BRO D/P97/ 28A/ 9–11, St Lawrence, Reading, 1903–28; BRO D/P96/ 28A/ 17–47, 67, 87, St. Giles, Reading, 1900–20, 1937, 1950, 1960, 1970.
[37] LMA P91 / ALL /93–104, All Saints, Haggerston, P94 /AND /203; St Andrew's, Newington, P94 /MTS / 08; St Mathias, Stoke Newington.

a Celebration, Michael Hinton has actually called the period 1900–50 a time of 'persecution and affliction' in which many clergy became isolated: overlooked and resented by their parishioners, struggling against secularising trends, they were liable to become depressed as their influence waned. He rounds off this account in an 'Afterword' noting that they were still valued when they 'tolerated being made use of', for instance 'by the unchurched when they want a service for a rite of passage'. He offers a telling comment from Nicholas Stacey, Bishop of Woolwich:

> ... the agony of so much of our pastoral work at Woolwich was that the things people did want from us – the name of a safe, cheap abortionist; the loan of £20; a roof over their heads, or a new husband – we were unwilling or unable to provide. But the things that we were able to give they did not appear to greatly want.[38]

Conclusion

Nevertheless, the records of churching in these assorted parishes stand as proof that traditional adherence to this significant aspect of the church's life and ceremonial was being maintained in the three counties in the first half of the twentieth century. They are sufficiently varied in time and scattered in place to suggest that the rite continued widely, and for many years. The following chapter will show more about the churched women and their lives, clothing with detail the dry bones of service registers, fee books and vestry notes.

---

[38] Michel Hinton, *The Anglican Parochial Clergy: a Celebration* (London, 1994), pp. 338–41.

CHAPTER THREE
WOMEN AND THE DECISION TO BE CHURCHED

In this chapter parish records are examined more closely, to see what they can tell us of the lives of women named in the registers, their backgrounds, and their attitudes to being churched after childbirth. For example, what proportion were willing to go along for the ceremony following the painful days of recovery? This is measured by comparing patterns of *churching and baptism* in each of the three counties. Women's decisions will then be looked at more closely in the section *churched women's lives*. This has used records that offer not only numbers of women, but also their names. Names are of huge importance: where they are present, and if a good many years are covered, they reveal *frequency and regularity* of churching: 'repeats' offer a chance to size up such things as individual motivation and commitment, and possibly to glimpse family pressure or even clerical discipline. In Berkshire, named women appearing in the five years 1901–5 were investigated in the 1901 census as well as the churching and baptismal records, so that the size of their families, and ages at giving birth, could also be traced.

Names also open the door to *family networks* present within the parish. Often several women with the same surname are churched; but one major problem instantly arises: once a woman was married she gave up the use of her maiden name, and so her birth relatives cannot easily be detected. This is important, as the influence of mothers and grandmothers was often crucial in making sure that the tradition of churching was followed.[1] Some records also reveal addresses, which introduce the neighbourhood and show whether women living in adjacent roads were churched, which is useful for allowing consideration of possible pressures from neighbours who would see all that went on. Addresses also tell of *proximity to the church* and allow the reality of women's journeys to and from a churching to be envisaged. Women's *social and economic circumstances* emerge when offerings at the churching service are itemised, especially if they are alongside records of husbands' occupations. All this information may be called upon to explain the *intervals of time* that mothers allowed to elapse between birth and churching, and these have been calculated for the Berkshire parishes.

---

[1] This is discussed extensively in Chapter Five.

Patterns of Churching and Baptism

Here churching's popularity is discovered by comparing in each parish the average number per year of mothers choosing to be churched with the number having their babies baptised (some of whom have not wanted churching). Patterns and proportions of women's choices turn out to be remarkably similar in the three counties.

Churching and Baptism in London

For London parishes, women's choices are displayed in Table V. The summary is divided into two groups: (i) West End & Suburban parishes and (ii) East End & Southern parishes. Of these groups, the second contains both the largest and smallest annual churching averages, and has the higher average percentage of new mothers (seventy-two per cent) choosing to be churched. In the first group, the churching average was considerably lower, at fifty-six per cent. The two together average sixty-four per cent. These figures, and the difference between the two groups, appear to confirm that over half of childbearing women were choosing to be churched, and that a markedly higher proportion chose churching in inner urban parishes than in those of the suburbs.

Table V: Women's choices: annual average numbers of churchings and baptisms compared in eleven London parishes

i. West End & Suburban parishes			ii. East End & Southern parishes		
Parish	Averages churchings	per year baptisms	Parish	Averages churchings	per year baptisms
All Souls, L.Place	98	126	St Mary, Bow	354	418
St Peter, Ha'smith	47	69	St Anne, Sh'ditch	243	173
St Paul, Holl'way	71	132	St John, Hoxton	204	496
Ch Ch, N. Brixton	35	60	Emman, W. Gr'ch	90	79
St John, Blackh'th	20	61	St Chad, Hag'ston	10	79
Emman, W. H'stead	20	75			
Totals	291	523		901	1245
Averages	56%	100%		72%	100%

It had been anticipated that baptisms would always outnumber churchings, and so the discovery that in two parishes the annual average rate of baptisms was lower than that of churchings (by twenty-one per cent at St Anne, Shoreditch, and by twelve per cent at Emmanuel, West Greenwich) came as a surprise.[2] One explanation may be that women were coming in from other parts of London to be churched: perhaps to Emmanuel from nearby Blackheath, in which it had a close association with the parish of Holy Trinity (with which its records were to be merged in 1921); and maybe to Shoreditch from its neighbour St Chad, Hagger-

[2] LMA P 91/ANN/12; S/P78 /EMM, note in catalogue.

ston, which had an average of only ten churchings a year, though its population in 1901 had numbered 6,251 (sixty-two per cent higher than that of St Anne). A glance at its service register does confirm the popularity of Shoreditch churchings, which are listed in right-hand columns headed 'Remarks' along with baptisms, banns, weddings and funerals. For example, a typical page, copied on Plate 8 for July 19th to August 9th 1910, has listed seventeen churchings and fourteen baptisms down its right-hand margin:[3]

A detailed comparison of churching and baptism numbers over many years is given in the five graphs of Plate 9. These illustrate in much more detail the relationship between the ceremonies, plotted at three-year intervals in each parish. As the recording of baptisms was obligatory, and therefore undertaken regularly, the baptism lines are virtually unbroken. They show baptisms sometimes in decline, fluctuating markedly during and after both world wars, slowed in the 1930s. Churching lines are less complete, revealing some gaps in the records. They mostly indicate lower numbers than baptisms year by year, though occasionally the two lines converge or even cross.

Though silent about individual women, these interacting lines of churching and baptism allow us to envisage the patterns of choice. Convergence of the two ceremonies was narrowly missed at Emmanuel Mission, West Hampstead when baptisms fell sharply by fifty-two per cent (to fifty-four in 1918 compared with 103 in 1917) while churchings rose equally sharply by fifty-six per cent in 1920 (to fifty-two compared with twenty-nine in 1919). Upper Holloway (1915–35) had several years in which churchings outnumbered baptisms. During this time six mothers whose babies had died were included in the churchings (something also found occasionally in the Berkshire records). Some infant deaths may also explain the apparent meeting of lines at St John the Evangelist, Blackheath, though its sharp fall in baptisms during the Second World War could be explained in many other ways, as it could be by the faltering of the churching record.

In North Brixton the lines are remarkably parallel apart from a fall in the relative position of churchings post-1945. Possibly new immigrant mothers were choosing naming ceremonies, or baptism-only. Baptism numbers had been boosted in 1930 and 1931 by the inclusion of children from homes for unmarried mothers: thirteen from the Anchorage Mission in Jeffreys Road, and three from No. 4, Gosling Way; all the mothers were domestic servants, and none was included in the churching register. Hammersmith churchings rose dramatically to outpace (though not outnumber) baptisms during the early Edwardian period; and the two converged briefly at the end of the First World War. Churchings did not rise along with the big surge of births in the mid-1920s, but the lines remained broadly parallel thereafter.

[3]   LMA P 91/ANN/12, Register of Services 1910–16.

WOMEN AND THE DECISION TO BE CHURCHED

Clearly the churching tradition continued in London through the first half of the twentieth century. Women met the expectation that they should come along to the church, though it cannot be known whether their intention was to give thanks, be 'purified', or simply to do what was expected. Such motives will later be explored in the testimony of women living today as they recall the circumstances of their own churchings.

Churching and Baptism in Staffordshire

It seems that women in Staffordshire displayed about the same level of enthusiasm for churching as their contemporaries in London. The account of participation in five Staffordshire parishes, set out in Table VI, shows an average proportion of churching to baptism of sixty-three per cent, almost exactly the same as that of London, whose parishes averaged sixty-four per cent.[4]

Table VI: Women's choices: annual average numbers of churchings and baptisms in five Staffordshire parishes

Parish	Averages per year	
	churchings	baptisms
Burton, St Modwen	17	35
Cheddleton, St Edward	24	32
Longdon, St James	14	19
Stafford, St Mary	62	100
Stone, Christ Church	34	54
Total	151	240
Average	63%	100%

In fact, Staffordshire's figures would be considerably altered if just one more parish were to be included. At St James-the-Less, Longton, churchings averaged 352 a year, outnumbering baptisms (averaging only 313) by 103%. This unusual case has been omitted from Table VI because it is a-typical, and its inclusion would distort the picture of churching/baptism proportions normally found in the county's parishes. In Plate 10, constructed from the records of St James-the-Less, Longton, which were kept not in registers but in parish magazine entries between 1894 and 1905, it may be seen how often churchings actually outnumbered baptisms: indeed only in 1894, 1897 and 1903 did baptisms reach the churching total. What explanation may there be for this? St James-the-Less may have been chosen for its Low Church tradition; or mothers were choosing to be churched but not to have their babies baptised at all; or women were coming into Longton to be churched, but returning for the babies' baptisms to their home or childhood parishes. Even allowing for unexpected patterns of women's choices, the figures suggest a high and steady rate of churching among childbearing women in this

[4] See above, p. 47.

southern area (known locally as 'neck end') of the Staffordshire Potteries.[5]

Churching and Baptism in Berkshire
It is in Berkshire's records that women's decisions are most fully explained. Only one is a dedicated churching register, but (unlike those in Staffordshire) the ordinary registers of services are full of information, and (unlike those in London) parishes are small enough for thorough searches of baptismal registers to have been undertaken. Table VII, opposite, details women's choices, and shows that annual averages of churchings amount to sixty-four per cent of baptisms, putting Berkshire's figures in line with those of Staffordshire and London.

Summary of Churching and Baptism in the Three Counties
When the question arises about the popularity of churching, this research can provide, at least for the three counties, a confident account. Levels turn out to be remarkably consistent: an average of sixty-four per cent of new mothers in Metropolitan London and Berkshire, and sixty-five per cent in Staffordshire (omitting St James, Longton for reasons already given) were choosing to be churched. This picture agrees broadly with that found in the 1951 Southwark visitation (see Chapter Four), from which it could be reckoned that just over half of childbearing women were still choosing to be churched mid-way through the twentieth century.

Churched Women's Lives
Precious information about churched women in their communities has been disclosed by these parish records. Their varied lists and registers contain details of five useful fields: the regularity with which women went to be churched following the births of each of their children; their kinship networks; where in the parish they lived; the occupations of their husbands; and how much money they offered for their churching. Put together, they allow us to envisage how this ancient rite of passage still fitted in to rural and urban society in the twentieth-century.

Frequency and Regularity of Churchings
Did women choose to be churched regularly after every birth, or only irregularly, following some births but not all? Of the three counties, it is in Berkshire that a pattern has been most thoroughly traced. A selection of record summaries appears in Table VIII, below, to illustrate regular and irregular churchings over one five-year period, 1901–5.

Here, in eight parishes, twenty named women can be seen being churched *regularly* (VIIIa), and twenty-four *irregularly* (VIIIb). Numbers are nearly equal: twenty women considered that churching ought to be undertaken every time a

[5] Interviews with the churchwarden of St James-the-Less and vicar of SS Mary & Chad, both confirmed that an immediate churching would be expected in Longton until late in the twentieth century.

Table VII: Women's choices: annual average numbers of churchings and baptisms in fourteen Berkshire parishes, each over a five-year period.

Parish	Averages per year	
	churchings	baptisms
Ardington, Holy Trinity	5	9
Bear Wood, St Catherine	3	11
East Challow, St Nicholas	4	10
Lockinge, All Saints	4	6
Newtown, St Mary	3	3
Radley, St James	4	9
Reading, St Mary	30	46
Reading, St Stephen	19	27
Sandhurst, St Michael	11	20
Shellingford, St Faith	3	5
Shrivenham, St Andrew	8	10
Wantage, Ss Peter & Paul	65	94
West Ilsley, All Saints	3	7
Wootton, St Peter	12	13
Totals	174	270
Averages	64%	100%

child was born, while twenty-four regarded it as optional. Similar studies were undertaken in two later five-year periods: in one, seven women were found being regularly churched, and nine irregularly; in the second, the proportions were reversed, with sixteen regularly as against six irregularly churched. Clearly churching was a familiar custom, but not something about which women were being put under any overwhelming obligation by either their families or parish incumbents.

Records of frequency and regularity are less easy to collect in the other two counties. Those for London with its (1901) parish populations of between 3,845 and 17,425 and vast baptismal lists have not been trawled nearly as thoroughly as Berkshire's; but in selected years women's names have been noted wherever they appear more than once in churching lists, though always in the knowledge that, as generally only surnames are given, it is never possible to be sure whether they refer to the same woman, or to one of her in-laws. For instance, at St Peter's, Hammersmith some women's surnames occurred three times in samples from decades between 1880 and 1940: on each occasion, tantalizingly, the accompanying addresses had changed. Had they moved house, or married into a family in which their sisters-in-law were bearing children? Similarly Emmanuel Mission, West Hampstead recorded thirteen names being repeated between 1913 and 1933, but often their addresses also differed, and the same enquiry was bound to arise. At St John the Evangelist, Blackheath between 1928 and 1952 the names of twenty-eight women appear as having been churched more than once: twenty-one twice, five three times, and one each four times and five times. But again, changes of address throw the exact meaning of the record into doubt.

Table VIII: Patterns of regular and irregular churching in eight Berkshire parishes, 1901–5

VIIIa *Regular churchings after first and second births, along with baptisms*

Parish	Mother's name	Service I	Service II	Service III
Ardington	Rachel Cross	Ch / B't Apr 1901	Ch / B't Jul 1903	
	Fanny Fuller	Ch / B't Jul 1902	Ch / B't Aug 1903	
	Fanny Collins	Ch / B't Jul 1902	Ch / B't Jul 1904	
Bear Wood	none			
East Challow	Emma Barrett	Ch / B't May 1903	Ch / B't Aug 1905	
	Sarah Shepherd	Ch / B't Oct 1901	Ch / B't Jul 1902	
Newtown	Mrs Middleton	Ch / B't Feb 1903	Ch / B't May 1905	
Radley	Martha Grimes	Ch / B't Jul 1901	Ch / B't Jan 1903	
	Lucy Gibbons	Ch / B't Aug 1901	Ch / B't Jan 1905	
	Martha Stimpson	Ch / B't Dec 1901	Ch / B't Feb 1904	
	Amelia Badnell	Ch / B't Sep 1903	Ch / B't Jan 1905	
Shellingford	Mary Green	Ch / B't Dec 1901	Ch / B't Feb 1905	
	Harriet Pill	Ch / B't Jan 1902	Ch / B't Sep 1903	
West Ilsley	Ellen Maskell	Ch / B't Jul 1905	Ch / B't Sep 1906	
Wootton	May Hughes	Ch / B't Jan 1905	Ch / B't May 1907	
	Rosina Bridges	Ch / B't Sep 1904	Ch / B't Mar 1908	
	Ada Pratley	Ch / B't Jul 1904	Ch / B't Aug 1906	
	Josephine Harris	Ch / B't Jul 1905	Ch / B't Jul 1906	
	Elizabeth Trinder	Ch / B't Jul 1905	Ch / B't Dec 1907	
	Annie Cotmore	Ch / B't May 1906	Ch / B't Apr 1908	
	Laura Bowman	Ch / B't Nov 1906	Ch / B't Feb 1908	

VIIIb *Irregular churchings, not occurring after each birth, along with baptisms*

Parish	Mother's name	Service I	Service II	Service III
Ardington	Belinda Wilkins	B't-only Jun 1903	Ch / Bt Jun 1905	
	Rose Woodley	Ch / B't Jun 1903	B't-only Feb 1904	
	Abigail Anns	Ch / B't Dec 1901	B't-only May 1902	B't-only Feb 1904
	Georgina Anns	Ch / B't Jul 1902	B't-only Nov 1904	
	Annie Taylor	B't-only Jan 1901	Ch / B't Dec 1905	
Bear Wood	Sarah Rixon	B't-only Apr 1901	Ch / B't May 1905	
East Challow	Elizabeth Dennis	Ch / B't Feb 1901	B't-only Apr 1905	
	Edith Crook	B't-only Dec 1902	Ch / B't Feb 1904	
	Sarah Shepherd	Ch / B't Jan 1901	B't-only Jul 1902	
	Emily Lanfear	B't-only Apr 1903	Ch / b't Sep 1905	
	Emily Richards	Ch / B't Feb 1904	B't-only Feb 1905	
Newtown	Mrs Plummer	Ch / B't Jun 1902	B't-only Jun 1906	
Radley	Elizabeth Comley	Ch / B't Mar 1901	B't-only Apr 1903	
	Kate Badwell	B't-only Feb 1902	Ch / B't Jan 1905	
	Susan Taylor	Ch / B't Feb 1902	B't-only Jan 1903	Ch / B't Aug 1904
	Susan Mattingley	Ch / B't Jan 1903	B't-only Apr 1905	
	Katherine Saunders	Ch / B't Feb 1903	B't-only Jan 1905	
Shellingford	Mary Hicks	Ch / B't Mar 1901	B't-only – 1902	
	Annie Carpenter	Ch / B't May 1902	B't-only – 1903	
West Ilsley	Jane Haines	Ch / B't Jul 1902	B't-only Apr 1906	
	Margaret Bailey	Ch / B't Mar 1903	B't-only Jan 1905	
Wootton	Lily Lee	Ch / B't Jan 1904	B't-only – 1905	
	Emily Bullock	Ch / B't Apr 1904	B't-only Jun 1905	
	Gertrude Bargus	B't-only Dec 1903	Ch / B't Feb 1906	

More repeats were found along the river at The Lady Margaret, Walworth (1913–1922), and Emmanuel, West Greenwich (1885–1905), but none in the registers of All Souls, Langham Place (1878–1904), nor, astonishingly, in selected years at St Pauls, Upper Holloway (1870–1947). In one parish, inclusion of women's forenames has shown that a number of regular churchings were clearly taking place. In the years between 1950 and 1971 several occur in the records of Christ Church, North Brixton: Rosina Turner, 1963 and 1967, Sylvia Florence Oris in 1950 and 1960, Lynn Laurence in 1966 and 1968, and Beryl Joyce Hemmings in 1963, 1968 and 1970 (a puzzle remains about the churchings of Susan Grange of 135, Akerman Road, entered in November 1956 and then March 1957). These are the only remaining London parishes with women's names in their churching registers whose churching frequency and regularity can be checked.

Staffordshire reveals still less about churching regularity: only in three parishes, St Edward, Cheddleton, St Mary, Stafford and Holy Trinity, Eccleshall are any estimates possible. Repeats were notably frequent in Cheddleton: of 141 named churchings in 1899–1904 eighteen women went twice, and six either three or four times to the ceremony. Churching here was frequent and regular, apparently a matter of routine. St Mary, Stafford presents a contrast: out of 187 churchings during the thirty-two months from January 1900 to August 1902 only three women, Matalah Allen, Mary Averill and Emily Boult made more than one appearance, though a reading back into the late nineteenth century shows that the wives in the Birtles family had been very frequently churched.[6] At Holy Trinity, Eccleshall lists of fifty-nine churchings over twenty-one years, 1931–1952 reveal that several women were almost certainly churched on more than one occasion, as summarized below:

Table IX: Repeat churchings at Holy Trinity, Eccleshall, 1931–52

Name	1st churching	2nd churching	3rd churching
Mrs Plant	Nov 1931,	Feb 1933	
Mrs Perkins	Oct 1931,	Dec 1933	
Mrs Williams	Mar 1932	Nov 1932	Feb 1933
Mrs Silvester	Oct 1933,	Oct 1939	
Mrs Herriman	Sept 1932,	Apr 1933,	
Mrs Perry	Oct 1933,	Feb 1940	

Unlike St Mary, Stafford, Holy Trinity, Eccleshall did not record Christian names, and so it cannot be known for certain which of these really are repeats. Four may well be (Plant, Perkins, Silvester and Perry); but two others (Williams and Herriman), from the proximity of their two dates, must surely belong to different members of one family.

---

[6] See pp. 54, 64–5 amd Plate 7 for more details from this churching register.

It is tempting to see churching regularity as indicating a well-established custom among a stable parish population in the rural and urban areas of Berkshire and Staffordshire, and also in parts of London's suburbs. Inner urban churches, which have not recorded women's names, do not allow repeat churchings to be traced; but the impression of strong commitment given by the 1951 Southwark visitation replies would suggest that many of those women will also have been churched regularly.

Family Networks, Streets and Neighbourhoods

The hunt for repeated churchings turned up many family networks in which mothers, aunts and grandmothers would have encouraged women to be churched after a new child was born. Often neighbours were also involved and played a vital role. Ellen Ross has described how, in the late nineteenth century, women in urban working-class areas would be expected to take their new-born children to visit each house in the street. It would be assumed that a churching would have preceded these visits.[7]

Staffordshire's records are strong here. The churching register of St Mary, Stafford tells of several women whose families were deeply and continuously involved with children and childbirth, as its columns recorded (among many other details) the number of children already born to the mother. In the Birtles family, Jane and Jemima were churched in 1901, Jessie and Lilian in 1902; we do not know the size of Jane's family, but Lilian and Jessie were each being churched for a tenth child, and Jemima for a ninth. Emily Boult was churched twice during these years, with her fourteenth and fifteenth children, and Amy Boult once in 1902 with her fourth. A few other family names, such as Carless and Clewlow, appear several times, indicating further networks of in-laws. In later decades another form of transmission is found at the local Fernham Maternity Hospital. In a recent telephone interview, one of its retired nurses recalled that in the 1960s the girls who gave birth there 'all knew each other – went to the same dances', and were all churched after childbirth before they left to go home.[8] In Stone, Christ Church's brief lists contain only two families that clearly have more than one branch: the Jacksons of Redford Street and Station Road, and the Brandons of High Street and Aston Lodge; but several families had addresses in the same roads (Newcastle, Victoria and Alexandra Streets, North Street and Old Road) and may have been acquainted with each other, and also with the vicar's wife, Mrs. W. J. Thompson, (named in the baptism but not the churching list) who presumably knew the parish churchgoers.

---

[7] Ellen Ross, 'Survival Networks: Women's Neighbourhood Sharing in London Before World War I', *History Workshop*, 15 (Spring 1983), p. 12.
[8] See extract from St Mary, Stafford register in Plate 7; Interview in Stafford, August, 2004.

WOMEN AND THE DECISION TO BE CHURCHED

Oral testimony has assisted the search for neighbours in Eccleshall. While from the records of Holy Trinity it is possible to find only two related families, Williams and Herriman, there is spoken evidence that a few more on the register would have been familiar to each other: Sillito and Tunnicliffe, Silvester and Plant. They were certainly all known to one parishioner, now in her ninth decade, who ran the Old Post Office for many years. In 2004 she recalled her own churching: 'I remember my aunt going with me after my daughter, Sue, was born – now fifty'. This happened in 1954, missing inclusion in the register by one year.

Written records also deliver several key names at St Edward's, Cheddleton, which boasts a number of women who, sharing the same surname, were almost certainly sisters-in-law or cousins: Kent, Boucher, Blakeman, Bloor, Sherratt, Turner, Lowndes and Wood. Emily Rogers and two other women with the same surname undertook altogether eight churchings. From these families may well have flowed encouragement and example, and perhaps pressure, to fit in with tradition and be churched. This received live confirmation when many of the local Knitting Group, interviewed in 2004, related that it was nearly always the woman's mother who spoke of churching and insisted that it be carried out: a typical statement was, 'my mum wouldn't let me take my children into her house until I'd been churched'.[9]

Where churching records are scarce, names in baptismal registers suggest the existence of groups of relations, and disclose the neighbourhoods in which they lived; baptism indicates that they may have been at least occasional churchgoers. For example, though churching cannot be shown to have taken place in all its families, Longdon's baptismal addresses, seen alongside its 1900 map, reveal a network of kinsfolk and colleagues in which the churching tradition also flourished. Within the register, William and Ellen Gee of Brereton (a baptism in 1900) may well have been related to Thomas and Sarah Gee of Bradley Lakes (a baptism in 1901); and Rowley, a miner of High Street, Longdon to Rowley, also a miner, of Longdon Green, and a third Rowley, again a miner, of Brereton Hill, Armitage. More such family relationships can be detected in Longton from its baptismal record. Two branches of the Imrie family, one headed by a potter, the other by a placer, lived in Gower Street; Byatts lived in Sutherland Terrace and North Road, a miner and a fish dealer; there were the Slates, butcher, joiner and potter; the Locketts, both potters, of Victoria Road and Middlewell Street; and the Burtons, sagger-maker and turner. Many more networks are bound to have existed in this area where it has been said that, early in the twentieth century at least, children did not move away, girls staying with their mothers until they married, boys following their fathers into the farms, mines and potteries.[10]

---

[9] Interviews in Eccleshall and with the group in Cheddleton, August, 2004.
[10] Interviews in Longton, August, 2004.

London's baptismal records also offer evidence of family networks in their populous parishes. In six suburban and West End registers family names quite often turn up more than once: three each at St Peter's, Hammersmith and St John the Evangelist, Blackheath; four each at Christ Church, North Brixton and All Souls, Langham Place. In just two parishes, those of Emmanuel, West Hampstead and St Paul's, Upper Holloway, a total of thirteen names were found being shared by neighbouring families.

Though small by comparison, the parishes of Berkshire have also recorded kinship groups which may have been the influence driving churching practice. To illustrate this, in Table X (opposite), taken from the years 1901–1905, names of women with known churchgoing relatives are cited in italics in three particularly well-recorded parishes: Holy Trinity, Ardington; St Nicholas, East Challow; and St James, Radley. It can be seen that in Ardington, seven women who chose to be churched during the five-year period had their husbands' relatives living in the parish. In the tight neighbourhood of this tiny village (population 433 in 1901) women will have been well-known to each other: Eva Gough was wife of the innkeeper at the Blue Boar, right by the church, and Harriet Gillmor was married to the Rector, Fitzwilliam C. Gillmor. Pressure and support of neighbours and kinsfolk, as well as supervision by squire and parson, can be assumed often to have lain behind these churching rites. Ardington's register also offers information about godparents at baptisms, and the names give evidence of many family friendships and connections: Ellen and Rachel Cross and Rose Coombes belonged to two such families.

The hunt for networks of friends and relations in nearby East Challow uncovered three churching wives belonging to wider families: Anne and Edith Crook and Annie Wiltshire. It is significant that some new mothers in these same families decided not to be churched (Emma Crook, Martha and Elizabeth Wiltshire), indicating that family pressure was not universally felt. A number of women churched in Radley also belonged to well-established local families: Elizabeth Comley and Susan and Elizabeth Mattingley, Katherine Saunders, Annie Denton and Florence Woodley; though again it should be noted that some of their relatives, such as Sarah Comley and Elizabeth Saunders, were among those baptising but not churching. As in East Challow, family custom, though often followed, seems not to have been decisive.

Residence Close to the Parish Church

Living near the church could be expected to have encouraged churchings, and seems to have done so in the case of over ninety per cent of churched women in the three Berkshire parishes shown in Table X: in Ardington's registers, out of twenty-one, only one was extra-parochial, living at West Lockinge, very close to Ardington; at East Challow all of sixteen, and in Radley twelve out of fifteen

Table X: Details of churched women's family circumstances in three parishes, 1901–5

(italics indicates known churchgoing relatives)

Table Xa ARDINGTON

mother's name	age yrs	no ch.	age ch	residence	occupation	service I	service II	service III	offs (s I)
A. Choosing not to be Churched, though Child Baptised, at Ardington (11 Women)									
Ellen Cross	27	5	3–7	Ardington	-	Mar 01 Fred	-		
Mary Phillips				Wimbledn	Corn merchant	Jun 01 Charles			
Ethel Williams				Ardington	Painter	Dec 01 Winif'd			
Elizabeth Strange				Ardington	-	Dec 01 Francis			
Mary Chapman	34	6	1–5	Ardington	Carter	Dec 01 William			
Emily White				Ardington	Carter	May 01 Jane			
Rosetta Cole				Lewes	Trainer	Apr 02 Arthur			
Sarah Wilkins				Ardington	Labourer	Feb 04 Fred		Jul 05 Victor	
Annie Freeman				Ardington	Painter	Feb 05 Ethel			
Louisa Welsh				Ardington	Labourer	Apr 05 Beatrice			
Florence Golding				Theale	Coachman	Dec 05 Arthur			
B. Choosing to be Churched after Some Childbirths, Not Churched after Others (5 Women)									
Belinda Wilkins	32	4	1–8	Ardington	Labourer	B't-only Jun 03	Ch / B't Jun 05		3d
Rose Woodley	38	7	1–13	Ardington	Labourer	B't-only Feb 02	Ch / B't Jun 05		6d
Abigail Anns	28	1	1	Ardington	Labourer	Ch / B't Dec 01	B't-only May 02 B't 04		6d
Georgina Anns	24	2	1–12	Ardington	Labourer	Ch / B't Jul 02	B't-only Nov 04		6d
Annie Taylor	33	2	3–5	Ardington	Carpenter	B't-only Jan 01	Ch'd /B't Dc 05		3d
C. Choosing to be Churched after Their Only Childbirth during These Years (13 Women)									
Alma Moss	-	-	-	-	-	Jan 01			3d
Harriet Taylor	32	3	-	Ardington	Electrician	Jun 01			3d
Harriett Gillmor	34	2	1–2	Ardington	Clergyman	Jul 01			10/-
Eva Gough	36	6		Ardington	Innkeeper	Nov 01			2/-
Rose Coombs	30	2	2–4	Ardington	Machinist	Nov 01			2/6
Mrs Gregory	-	-	-	-	-	Jan 02			6d
Mrs Provis	-	-	-	Lockinge	-	Jan 02			1/-
Esther Williams	35	7	4–17	Ardington	Hse painter	May 02			3d
Mary Church	29	1	3	Ardington	Shepherd	Sept 02			6d
Mrs Werner	-	-	-	-	-	Apr 02			6d
Anne Wickens	-	-	-	Ardington	Painter	Jul 04			6d
Annie Welch	31	3	6-11	Ardington	Labourer	Apr 05			3d
Amy Harris	-	-	-	Ardington	Labourer	May 05			6d
D. Choosing to be Churched a Second Time (Regularly) (3 Women)									
Rachel Cross	27	4	2-6	Ardington	Labourer	Apr 01	Jul 03		6d
Fanny Fuller	22	1	1	Ardington	Labourer	Jul 02	Aug 03		3d
Fanny Collins	31	4	2-7	Ardington	Labourer	Jul 02	Jul 04		3d

Table X: Details of Churched women's family circumstances in three parishes, 1901–5

(italics indicates known churchgoing relatives)

Table Xb EAST CHALLOW

mother's name	age yrs	no ch.	age ch	residence	occupation	service I	service II	service III	offs (s I)
A. Choosing not to be Churched, though Child Baptised, at East Challow (20 Women)									
Marta Wiltshire				E Challow	Labourer	Feb 01 Ernest			
Rose Neale				E Challow	Cabinet mkr	Apr 01 Kate			
Eliz Wiltshire				E Challow	Turner	Apr 01 Alfred			
Kate King				E Challow	Groom	Jun 01 Evelyn	Apr 04 Hilda		
Mary Heynes				E Challow	Carpenter	Jul 01 Sarah	Feb 03 Edith		
Beatrice Dixon				Swindon	Mechanic	Jul 01 Kate			
Carol Wilkins				E Challow	Labourer	Oct 01 Will'm			
Caroline Kent				Sparsholt	Carter	Apr 02 Edith	Sep 05 Fred		
Ellen Lovegrove				W Challow	Iron worker	Sep 02 Cecily	Jul 04 Dennis		
Emma Crook				E Challow	Single woman	Dec 02 Enid			
Annie Booker				E challow	Single woman	Dec 02 Edward			
Eliz Lewis				E Challow	Iron moulder	Mar 03 Eleanor			
Emily Bedford				E Challow	Groom	Jun 03 Meriel	Oct 05 Eric		
Alice Froud				Childrey	Farmer	Sept 03 George			
Annie Cavey				Brompton	Civil servant	Feb 04 George			
Louisa Alder				E Challow	General dealer	Mar 04 Sidney			
Ellen Butler				Charney	Groom	Apr 04 Charles			
Sarah Broad				E Challow	Labourer	Apr 05 Douglas			
Eliza Crane				E Challow	Labourer	Oct 05 Florence			
Annie Brown				E Challow	Blacksmith	Nov 05 Beatrice			
B. Choosing to be Churched after Some Childbirths, Not Churched after Others (4 Women)									
Eliz Dennis	29	-	-	E Challow	Labourer	B't-only Feb 01	Ch / B't Apr 05		6d
Edith Crook	-	-	-	E Challow	Iron worker	B't-only Feb 02	Ch / B't Feb 04		6d
Emily Lanfear	36	9	1-16	E Challow	Labourer	B't-only Apr 03	Ch / B't Sep 05		6d
Emily Richards	-	-	-	E Challow	Stable lad	Ch / B't Feb 04	B't-only Feb 05		3d
C. Choosing to be Churched after Their Only Childbirth during These Years (11 Women)									
Louisa Mason	30	4	-	E Challow	Fitter	Jan 01			6d
Sarah Hawkes	40	6	1-15	E Challow	Butler	Jan 01			6d
Harriet Barnett	30	1	10	-	-	Apr 01			
Cecilia Chainey	-	-	-	E Challow	Fitter	Oct 01			6d
Sarah Wallis	33	2	1-3	E Challow	Farmer	Feb 02			
Annie Fairchild	34	6	-	E Challow	Carter	Sep 02			2d
Ellen Greenaway	24	2	1-4	E Challow	Bricklayer	Aug 02			6d
Anne Crook	52	9	2-22	E Challow	Painter	Jan 04			6d
Annie Wiltshire	33	9	1-17	E Challow	Labourer	- 04			6d
Ellen Bursen	-	-	-	E Challow	Labourer	Jul 04			
Rose Bowman	23	2	1-2	E Challow	Stable lad	Aug 04			6d
D. Choosing to be Churched a Second Time (Regularly) (2 Women)									
Emma Barrett	34	6	1-7	E Challow	Cattleman	May 03	Sep 05		6d
Sarah Shepherd	32	3	4-6	E Challow	Shepherd	Oct 01	Aug 02		6d

Table X: Details of churched women's family circumstances in three parishes, 1901–5

(italics indicates known churchgoing relatives)

Table Xc RADLEY

other's name	age yrs	no ch.	age ch	residence	occupation	service I	service II	service III	offs (s I)
Choosing not to be Churched, though Child Baptised, at Radley (23 Women)									
en Reeves				Radley	Plate layer	Jan 01 William			
ra Chancellor				Oxford	Tailor	Mar 02 Reg'ld			
th Chancellor				Radley	Labourer	May 02 Jessie			
en Drysdale	25	1	1	Radley	Engineer	May 02 Cath'ne			
nie Birkett				Didcot	Porter	May 02 George			
z Abrahanms				Radley	Labourer	Jul 02 Rhyna			
nnah Hearne				Radley	Dom servant	Jan 03 Blanche			
ry Lenwin	44	6	3-19	Radley	Shepherd	Mar 03 May			
rence Wood				Abingdon	Traveller	Jun 03 Irena			
let Elson				London	Manager	10.03 Ambrose			
ah Freeman				Kenningt'n	Gardener	Oct 03 Walter			
ily Gillman				Reading	Porter	Oct 03 Reginald			
cy Tilborne				Radley	Labourer	Feb 04 William			
z Enet				Radley	Gamekeeper	Mar 04 Dorothy			
el Barmby				Radley	Schoolmaster	Jul 04 Rose/Kth			
cy Bennett				Radley	Single woman	Jul 04 Gladys			
z Saunders				Radley	Coachman	Jan 05 Una			
ry Smith				Oxford	Baker	Apt 05 Cecil			
rah Comley				Radley	Labourer	Jun 05 Frank			
el James				M'denhead	Labourer	Jun 05 William			
nie Lay				Abingdon	Butler	Oct 05 John			
Silvester				Radley	Single woman	Oct 05 Robert			
ith Pocock				Radley	Single woman	Oct 05 Ellen			
Choosing to be Churched after Some Childbirths, Not Churched after Others (5 Women)									
te Badnell	21	1	1	Radley	Labourer	B't-only Feb 01			6d
z Comley	46	3	2-18	Radley	Labourer	Ch / B't Mar 01	B't-only Apr 03		6d
san Taylor	29	2	2-4	Radley	Farmer	Ch / B't Feb 02	B't-only Jan 03	Ch/B't Aug 04	1/-
sn Mattingley	32	7	1-7	Radley	Groom	Ch / B't Jan 03	B't-only Apr 05		6d
th Saunders	-	-	-	Wootton	Coachman	Ch / B't Feb 03	B't-only Jan 05		6d
Choosing to be Churched after Their Only Childbirth during These Years (6 Women)									
z Mattingley	-	-	-	Radley	Groom	Mar 01			6d
nie Denton	33	2	1-2	Radley	Blacksmith	Feb 02			1/-
z Bannister	-	-	-	-	-	Aug 04			6d
Woodley	-	-	-	Radley	Labourer	Aug 04			6d
s Bedingfield	-	-	-	-	-	Sept 04			6d
anche Norton	-	-	-	Radley	Solicitor	Sept 04			10/-
Choosing to be Churched a Second Time (Regularly) (4 Women)									
artha Grimes	35	8	1-4	Radley	Shepherd	Jul 01	Jan 03		6d
cy Gibbons	29	1	4	Radley	Shepherd	Jul 01	Jan 03		6d
arth Stimpson	33	1	4	Radley	Labourer	Dec 01	Feb 04		6d
nelia Badnett	-	-	-	Radley	Labourer	Sept 03	Jan 05		6d

women, had homes in the parish. However, proximity to the church, though undoubtedly an enabling factor among mothers still in a state of post-partum recovery, was not by itself a sufficient motivation; fourteen more parish residents in East Challow, the same number in Radley, and eight in Ardington bore children during these years but were not churched. Were the mothers returning to their childhood parishes, or deciding against the churching ceremony altogether?

Problems with establishing proximity of residence in two industrial areas of Staffordshire, and in London's East End, arise from radical changes in the urban landscape. Records of parishes in both the Black Country and the Potteries refer to streets around 1900 which were later to be re-designed, acquire new names, or vanish completely. Subsidence and collapse, clearance of deteriorating properties, construction of new road systems, and commercial and residential development all caused demolition and rebuilding which have confused old landmarks. In the Black Country some of Wednesbury's street names from the registers of 1901 can still be found: Lower High Street and Bridge Street, Foley Street, Union Street and Holyhead Road. These are within walking distance of St Luke's Church. But other roads have collapsed, or been destroyed and built over on this edge of Mesty Croft with its old tube works and coal shafts now smothered in new housing schemes. Certainly an inhabitant has told of buildings (including the old St Luke's Church itself) and indeed whole streets subsiding into the mine workings below.[11]

The towns of the Potteries have also suffered from change and re-building that make their old landmarks hard to find. Longton's crowded courts, alleys and passages, many too small to have been marked on old maps, have now vanished before the march of urban development. Yet many potters' wives will have walked along them to their churchings at St James-the-Less in the town centre. That said, other families are on record coming for baptism (and probably also churching) from the major Normacot, Uttoxeter, Heathcote and Sutherland Roads, and a few down from Anchor Road that runs north up to Sandford Hill. This is where SS Mary & Chad still stands in a landscape that is relatively unchanged, though still threatened by mining subsidence even at the start of the twenty-first century.

Other parish profiles in the county have changed far less, and the majority of churched women's addresses can still be found on the old maps. In the flat landscape of central and eastern Staffordshire, the river vales of the Trent and Sow, walks to church at Burton, Eccleshall and Stafford were straightforward compared with the hills to be climbed at Cheddleton and Longton. On the other hand, many women will have trudged for miles through the parish of Longdon: the old O.S. map etches its scattered outlines which reach far away to the hamlets of Upper Longdon, Longdon Green and Brook End, and outlying Dark Lane, Horseylane and Millbank Farms.

[11] Conversation with an unnamed retired iron-worker, Wednesbury, August, 2004.

WOMEN AND THE DECISION TO BE CHURCHED

Attempts to find residences in London's four East End churching parishes face problems not only of changing urban landscape, but also of women apparently travelling to church events from homes far away. Since the churched women are not given names or addresses in these records, there is no way of establishing where they lived in relation to the churches. Still, addresses from baptismal registers give warning that families were coming in from a wide area to have their children baptised, suggesting that residential proximity should not be assumed in the case of churchings. In the parish of St John the Baptist, Hoxton, children were brought to be baptised from addresses far away from the church: Burrell Street is in St Pancras, and Murray Street in Camden Town; Packington Street lies across the Grand Union Canal as far as Essex Road; Burdett Street down south of the Thames in Walworth; and Oswald Street out beyond the Hackney Downs at Lea Bridge. On the other hand, some of the roads named in the register are close to the parish church: Crondall Road, and Falkirk, Pitfield, Chart, Aske, Cavendish and Buckland Streets. Similarly the baptismal register for nearby St Anne, Shoreditch lists nearby addresses (Hemsworth Street, Luke Street and Mill Row), but then also Smythe Street which is down south in Poplar, and Ufton Road several miles away north of De Beauvoir Town on the Southgate Road.

St Chad, Haggerston follows the pattern of its two neighbouring churches, with families coming from near and far to have their children baptised: from nearby Dunloe Street, Nichols Square, Shap Street, Weymouth Terrace, Geffrye Street and Pearson Road; but also from distant Pollard Street beyond Columbia Market, Goswell Street at the Angel, Whistler Street in Highbury and Groombridge Road in Hackney, beyond London Fields. To a great extent St Mary, Bow's baptismal register affords a similar picture. Roads and streets round the church appear frequently: Ireton and Washington Streets, Devonshire and Egleton Roads; but there are also farther-flung addresses such as Venue Street, well to the south, Hancock and Imperial Roads to the east, and Stratford High Street which lies beyond railway and water-works away to the north.

In the remaining London parishes for which, fortunately, addresses are known, a remarkably high proportion of churched women lived in roads close to the church. Residences in the churching register of St Peter, Hammersmith are almost all remarkably close to Black Lion Lane in which the church stands. Emmanuel, West Hampstead's picture is similar; in its register's final ten entries from 1947 to 1951, five mothers had addresses in Ravenshaw Street and three in Broomsleigh Street; back in 1912 the first ten had also included four residents of Ravenshaw Street and two of Broomsleigh Street, as well as one of Lyncroft Gardens, in which the Mission Church stands. Families attending St John, Blackheath lived, if anything, even closer to the church in roads clearly identifiable on the early maps and still appearing in the records of 1948 and 1955: many came from Shooters Hill, and the Old Dover Road running south of St John, and others from Furzefield and Lizburn Roads and Vanbrugh Park to the north.

Journeys to the 634 churchings in Christ Church, North Brixton between 1907 and 1971 were almost all from adjacent streets: Cowley Street, Gosling Way, Burton Road, Mowll Street, Vassall Road and the northern end of Brixton Road. In Upper Holloway the same roads and streets appear repeatedly in the long run of churching addresses from 1915 to 1935: the main thoroughfares Tollington and Hornsey Roads, flanked by the aspirationally-named Landseer and Alexander, Marlborough, Cornwallis and Denmark Roads. St Paul does not appear to have poached the congregations either of St John to the north or St Luke to the south, but to have effectively reached many of its own local people.

In Marylebone some outsiders might have been expected to patronize All Souls, Langham Place, a church both fashionable and famously evangelical in a largely Anglo-Catholic zone. But Booth had noted that 'the congregation is mainly parochial',[12] and indeed the churching registers from 1876 to 1904 did not contain a very wide range of addresses. The better-off lived nearby, in Portland Place, Cavendish Place and Cavendish Square; the less-prosperous only slightly farther off, in the lodgings of Foley Street, Goodge Street and Alfred Place, close to their work in the hotels of Great and Little Titchfield Street and the shops and restaurants of Charlotte and Bolsover Streets. Henrietta Street was the most distant address, but still lay less than a mile away.

In a town noted in the pages of Charles Booth, and indeed the Southwark visitations, for the high mobility of its population, its people allegedly in frequent movement in and out of suburbs and centres of employment, these records suggest two things: first that the unchanging residential proximity found in several suburbs, over many decades in some parishes, indicate pockets of unexpected population stability; and second, that the far-flung addresses listed in East End baptismal registers might be revealing loyalty to a home parish being maintained by married daughters even after they had moved away. Perhaps this shows that the church's powerful influence as 'the main symbol of community', in the sense outlined, for instance, by Hugh Mcleod in his study of the nineteenth-century church, can still be observed as late as the mid-twentieth-century.[13]

It transpires that throughout all three counties residence was of great significance in the list of factors encouraging and enabling women to be churched. Patterns of close proximity have been found in at least part of all parishes, and must be presumed to have given positive support to churching practice. Conversely, the length and difficulty of some journeys to church will have demanded high levels of motivation and courage: it was not always easy for a woman living far away, often only recently delivered of a child, maybe on foot, unaccompanied, or with only her

---

[12] Charles Booth, *Life and Labour*, Vol. V, pp. 196–9.
[13] Hugh McLeod, *Religion and the Working Class in Nineteenth-Century Britain* (Basingstoke, 1984), Chs. 1 and 6, pp. 9–16, 57–66.

mother for support, to be confident that she could get to the church and then reach home again.

Occupations and Offerings

Up to 1980 the Book of Common Prayer was in use, with its instruction: 'The woman, that cometh to give her thanks, must offer accustomed offerings'. A majority of clergy duly noted these in the margin of their records. As might be expected, amounts varied considerably, generally according to the woman's social and economic status, but sometimes governed by local convention. In London they ranged between nothing and a pound: in Staffordshire and the three Berkshire parishes of Table X from 2*d.* to 10*s.*

Husbands' occupations were noted in rather fewer registers; but where they can be discovered, it is tempting to examine the relationship between occupation and offering. Most is known of both elements in Berkshire where family occupations could be traced in all parishes, and offerings were included in almost every churching list. Elsewhere evidence is patchy; in Metropolitan London, of the twelve churching parishes only three included occupations of husbands in their records, though five listed women's offerings; while in Staffordshire, fees were reported by four registers, but occupations appeared in just one, that of St Mary, Stafford. Fortunately, in all parishes baptismal registers can supply a supporting picture of local employment.

The question may well arise about how far the amounts offered as a churching fee truly reflect class or income; and to this the answer given by Staffordshire records differs in some respects from that found in the other two counties. In a systematic check of one year each from the records of three of its parishes, uniform fees were found being offered by large percentages of women, as follows: at Christ Church, Stone ninety percent, and at Holy Trinity, Eccleshall forty-eight per cent, offered one shilling; while at St Chad, Lichfield eighty-eight per cent offered 6*d*. This suggests expected rates which women felt obliged to give, no matter what their economic status. In Stone, judging from its recorded years from 1869 to 1884, offering the high fee of 1*s.* seems to have been a long tradition, though families had occasionally given 2*s.* or 2*s. 6d.* (Meaford Farm) or 5*s.* (Tennant of Stonefield Brewery), and Mrs Brandon, the draper's wife, twice gave 10*s.* But in the year 1884, out of thirty-one churchings, twenty-eight of Stone's churched women had given 1*s.* irrespective of the level of their husbands' earnings. Their occupations? Of the twenty-one husbands whose work is known from the baptismal record, thirteen were in paid employment, from labourer and servant to coachman, butler and foreman clicker (cutter), and some might well have found it hard to raise 1*s.* for the wife's churching. Only for four (draper, licensed victualler, miller and butcher), assuming that they were running their own businesses, may such a sum have been easier to find.

Tradition also seems to have governed the size of offerings at St Chad, Lichfield, with its routine fee of 6*d*. A current parishioner recalled in 2004 that there was still an accustomed churching fee in the middle years of the twentieth century: 'I remember it had to be silver'.[14]

The opposite appears to have been the case in Eccleshall and Stafford, where women can be seen giving a variety of sums. Eccleshall's fees were to grow over time from 1932 to 1952: by the end of this most uncertain twenty-year economic period churched women's offerings were comparatively high, perhaps reflecting an inflation of the church's expectation, or the way rural incomes held up in the aftermath of the Second World War. In the list of twelve unnamed mothers whose offerings were recorded in 1951 and 1952 all amounts except one (of 6*d*.) were above 1*s*., three were of 2*s*., three of 2*s*. 6*d*., one each of 4*s*. and 4*s*. 6*d*., and one each of 5*s*., 7*s*. and 10*s*. 6*d*.

Similar variety prevailed at St Mary, Stafford, where in the first six months of 1900 mothers gave a wide range of offerings, as may be seen in Table XI, though the majority elected to tender 1*s*., 6*d*. or 3*d*. In general the amount appears not to have reflected husbands' occupations and substance. Although 10*s*. was given once by Mary Averill, married to a parson, and twice by Blanche Brookfield, wife of a Lichfield miller, there was little further differentiation by status: 1*s*. was offered by wives of an ostler, draper, brewer, groom and stoker; 6*d*. by those of a pressman, signalman, platelayer, shoe manufacturer and machinist, and by a single woman from Birmingham; while women married to a soldier, moulder and shoe-finisher found only 3*d*. No offering at all is recorded from three women who were all married to labourers. Impoverishment is not reflected in these offerings: more women gave 1*s*. than any other silver coin, though 6*d*. and 3*d*. were clearly quite normal amounts. No fees were recorded in the remaining parishes in Staffordshire's churching list.

This analysis of Staffordshire's fees and occupations can give only a rough idea of whether churching would have represented a steep, moderate or merely trivial cost to families. Records show examples of both strict uniformity and wide variation in sums offered, but none can reveal whether any women were deterred from being churched by the need to find 3*d*. or 1*s*. from a tight budget.

In London, the most varied offerings came from the West End. At All Souls, Langham Place the record of the 1890s gives perhaps the most persuasive evidence that in the late nineteenth century churching was undertaken by women not of one status in particular but of all classes, no matter whether married to a dining room proprietor or waiter, to a lord, an officer, a salesman or a street cleaner.[15] So it was that several wives of professional men tendered 5*s*., 1*s*. and £1; 6*d*. was the average, and lesser payments ranged down to 1*d*. This variation seems

---

[14] Interviews with the group at St Chad's, Lichfield, August, 2004.
[15] See sample page from this register on Plate 7.

Table XI: Variation of offerings at Stafford St Mary, Jan. 1900–Jun. 1902
(× indicates payment unknown).

Offerings	12s. 6d.	10s.	5s	2s. 6d.	2s.	1s. 6d.	1s.	6d.	5d.	3d.	2d.	1d.	×
Number	1	4	1	5	6	1	34	27	1	22	3	4	80

to reflect attitudes as much as ability to pay: in 1889 the wife of a jeweller of Great Portland Street gave only 4*d*., yet fourteen years later spouses of a carman and a baker were to give 2*s*. and 1*s*. 6*d*., apparently following no tradition or expectation. A range of fees was also found at Christ Church, North Brixton, offered by families largely in skilled manual work, with a scattering of professionals; it varied from 2*d*. and 3*d*. to 1*s*., 2*s*. or 2*s*. 6*d*., continuing largely unchanged throughout sixty-four years, even when in the later decades the register showed the parish's churchgoers to be increasingly artisan.

In two London parishes, their occupational profiles not differing widely in the baptismal records, women gave a uniform 6*d*.. This was at St Peter, Hammersmith in 1920, a skilled area, its families headed by, among others, a signalman, stoker, several engineers and an engine driver, a police constable, painter-and-decorator, printer and fireman; and St Chad, Haggerston in 1942 and 1943, less well-to-do than Hammersmith, its occupations found in an earlier decade to include eighty-nine different trades, from furniture and clothing to food marketing and decorating; none professional or white-collar. St Anne, Shoreditch recorded the lowest sums in this study. In 1910 three churchings together brought in 7*d*., another three, 5*d*., two churchings, 3*d*., one churching, 1*d*.; occasionally there was more, as 6*d*. and even 9*d*. (the maximum) were offered for a single churching. One entry reads '0*d*. unemployed'. Yet many of this parish's occupations taken from the baptismal record for 1913 were skilled and semi-skilled; husbands worked in transport, engineering, furniture and printing. As at St Chad, no white-collar occupations are shown.[16]

The trades and callings specified in the remaining London parishes indicate the economic background of churched women and so hold a compelling interest. Overwhelmingly they are manual, at all levels of skill, reflecting the local trades: wash-house porter and wharf labourers in West Greenwich, French polishers and tailor's pressers in Hoxton, fish porters and cabinet makers in Bow. Leavening of professional men, army officers, accountants, clerks and teachers becomes less and less significant. For instance, the 1930 baptismal register for St Paul, Upper Holloway listed husbands in a range of manual trades: French polisher and piecer's assistant, milkman and fruiterer, Royal Mail driver and railway carriage cleaner. This contrasts with the occupations in its first churching record in 1874, which had included three gentlemen, a solicitor, chemist and manager, five different types of clerk, and an accountant. The practice of churching had carried on unchecked.

[16] See sample page and details from this register in Plate 8.

Offerings in Berkshire were normally low, as illustrated in Table X's three parishes, where larger sums of 10*s.*, 2*s.* 6*d.*, 2*s.* and 1*s.* were tendered by a total of only seven women, while the rest gave 6*d.* or less.[17] This reflects the county's other parishes with their largely artisan and labouring populations, and their leavening of only limited numbers of families enjoying landed wealth or professional status. It therefore comes as a surprise that at St Stephen, Reading, with its low social profile, every single woman paid one shilling, a sum surely hard for many of its families to find from an artisan's wage, even in mid-century.

From an early twentieth-century study, it is possible to estimate the value of the customary sixpence. As Maud Pember Reeves recorded in *Round About a Pound a Week*, the Fabian Women's Group had many occasions to contemplate this sum as they analysed weekly budgets in Lambeth on the eve of the First World War. Sixpence was undoubtedly valuable: enough to buy one person's food for a week; or all the gas; or the wood, lamp-oil, soap and soda that was needed; or seven days' coal supply (though not in the coldest weather). Weekly burial insurance cost a regular sevenpence. Writing on 'Landholdings and Agriculture c.1900' in Berkshire, E. J. T. Collins says that wages were around ten shillings and sixpence a week for male labourers, and reached fifteen to twenty-one shillings for the 'aristocracy' of stockmen, shepherds and carters. Sixpence may only amount to two and a half per cent of a high wage of twenty-one shillings; but it takes almost five per cent out of a low one of ten shillings and sixpence.[18]

Intervals between Birth and Churching

Timing is the final element to be explored in this analysis of women's decisions. There is little evidence that the Biblical intervals of thirty or forty days before purification were observed: some women were churched almost immediately after the child's birth, while others delayed for many months. It is in Berkshire that parish records have been sufficiently limited in size, and at the same time explicit in detail, to make possible an investigation into the extent and variation of such timing. Figures have been collected for nine of its parishes in successive periods of five years, to illustrate how long new mothers waited before churching, and how patterns of delay varied from early in the century to its middle years. The outcome is illustrated in the figures in Plates 11–12, which are concerned with the distribution of delay, and variation in intervals between birth and churching, each covering the first ten weeks following birth. The calculation involved 276 women in three studies: sixty-four in 1901–5, one hundred and thirty-eight in 1915–32, and seventy-four in 1907–40.

---

[17] See above, pp. 57–9.
[18] M. Pember Reeves, *Round About a Pound a Week* (Tiptree, 1979), Chapter VI, *Budgets*, pp. 75–93; E. J. T. Collins, 'Landholdings and Agriculture c. 1900', *Historical Atlas of Berkshire*, p. 110; LMA, DS/VB/001, Visitation Book, A–L, 1907.

The figures reveal how haste and delay varied between the earlier and later studies. They give evidence of a fairly leisurely pattern of churching in the earliest period (1901–5) in which the peak comes in the third to fifth weeks after birth, compared with greater haste in the two later periods (1915–30 and 1907–40) where it begins to quicken in the second week. In the study of parishes 1907–40 there was a steep decline after the third week, in that of 1915–32 a more gradual falling away: both had reached the same low level by the sixth week, then saw a slight surge in the seventh and eighth weeks, and again in the tenth. Plate 11, based on actual numbers of women, gives a vivid impression of how many mothers delayed, and for how long, as the weeks went by.

In Plate 12, to make visual comparison clearer, the number of women churched in the third week after birth has been taken as 100 for each of the three study periods, and the numbers for the other weeks are calculated as a percentage of this figure. For each period the percentage of women churched in each week after childbirth has then been plotted. The 1901–5 line is quite arresting. It shows most delay in the earliest period (women being in not much of a hurry) followed by later activity as they got round to being churched.

Is it possible to explain these timing variations by reference to Berkshire women's circumstances? Table XII sets out what is known about two of those women in each parish, and in particular who left (i) the longest and (ii) the shortest intervals between birth and churching. Finally (iii) the average interval left by all known churched women in the parish is shown.

On the whole these biographical details raise more questions about the variation of churching intervals than they can answer. Did a woman's age, or possibly the demands of her family, some of which may be envisaged in Table XIIa, affect the speed of her churching? It might be assumed that an older woman with a larger family would delay longer before going to give thanks after childbirth than a younger woman looking after fewer children. Certainly in Shellingford 1901–5 Mary Clements, who delayed for fifty-six days, was nine years older, and had many more children (eight compared with one), than her speedier neighbour Jane Ridout, who waited only for two days. However, this was not always the pattern. Ellen Maskell of West Ilsley, 1901–5, thirteen years older and with five more children than Elizabeth Barlow, was churched within one week compared with the other's delay of sixty days; while in Ardington Eva Gough, churched very quickly after just two days, was both older and more encumbered (by six children) than Rachel Cross, nine years younger (and with only four children); yet Rachel waited for fifty-one days.

The more limited material in Table XIIb focuses attention on differences in residence and occupation in the attempt to understand these intervals before churching. Again, no consistent pattern emerges. In Wootton, Ellen Phipps, who delayed for thirteen days in her home on Boar's Hill had a longer journey to St Peter's church than Lizzie Alder, who was based in Wootton itself, yet waited for fifty-six days: perhaps the interval's length was connected in some way with Alder's unmarried status. In Wantage, Edith Weller, delaying only for one day, and Annie Austin, for fifty-five days, were both married to soldiers whose wartime occupations or absences from home apparently affected this domestic event with diametrically opposite results. Annie Austin was scarcely negligent; she had already had her child baptized twenty-three days before her churching, a departure from the normal sequence of events. Gladys Rixon, a labourer's wife in Shellingford, waited forty-five days between birth and churching, far longer than Gertrude Bartlett who was married to a butler, presumably working at Kitemore House, who delayed only for a week. Three years later, Gladys was to have another baby baptized, but this time she was not churched at all, indicating perhaps that she had faced real difficulties. In Sandhurst Annie Cripps waited fifty-six days before her churching in 1913, but this did not establish a pattern: following a second birth three years later she went for churching and baptism within four days. Lily Goswell, also of Sandhurst, waited only thirteen days before her churching; she then postponed the child's baptism for a month, as had Annie Cripps after her first long-delayed churching. Both Annie and Lily were married to labouring men, and lived in the parish.

Clearly, no pattern which might explain how women timed their churchings can be established from the evidence available from census or church registers or even parish maps. But it is possible to speculate about the many possible reasons for delay: weeks might be allowed to pass because of post-puerperal problems; fatigue, or the *lochia* (loss of blood after childbirth), which normally lasts three to four weeks, causing women to be unable or reluctant to undertake walks to the parish church while still in this fragile (and indeed some said 'impure') condition. Women may have been living far from their own mothers, away from any pressure to be churched. Reasons for speedy churching could include a stillbirth, or fear that mother or infant might die; either would bring urgency to arrangements that churching and baptism should be accomplished very quickly. Occasionally women went to be churched even after the deaths of their infants.

In this connection a group of poignant childbirth events can be found in the records of the Preachers' Book belonging to St Peter, Wootton near the start of the twentieth century. They are not neatly arranged, and in places there is some danger of misinterpreting the dates. They tell of four stillbirths, all followed by churchings; intervals of time between these and baptisms were varied. The infant Fred, stillborn son of Alma Vasey (unmarried domestic servant) was baptised on the same day as her churching on 14th February 1904. On the 21st day of the same month came the churching of an unmarried housemaid, Sarah Anne Wake; but her daughter, Constance, had been stillborn, and had already been baptised forty-eight days earlier in January. In 1905 Jane Harris, wife of a gentleman of Foxcombe Hill gave birth to a stillborn son and was churched on the same day, July 18th. Two years later, Fanny Grimes left three days to elapse between her churching and the

Table XII: Intervals between birth and churching related to age, family size, residence and occupation: showing (i) the longest interval; (ii) the shortest interval; and (iii) the average interval in each of six parishes.

Table XIIa: 1901–5

parish	mother's name	children no	age	ages	residence	occupation	interval (days)	average interval (days)
Ardington	Rachel Cross	27	4	2–6	Ardington	coachman	(i) 51	
	Eva Gough	36	6	–	Ardington	innkeeper	(ii) 2	
								(iii) 21
East Challow	Cecilia Chainey	–	–	–	East Challow	fitter	(i) 108	
	Rose Bowman	23	2	1–2	East Challow	stable lad	(ii) 16	
								(iii) 36
Newtown	Harriet Plummer	31	7	1–7	Newtown	hurdle maker	(i) 55	
	Eliz Winkworth	40	5	3–13	Newtown	gardener	(ii) 21	
								(iii) 32
Radley	Florence Goodley-	–	–	–	Radley	labourer	(i) 175	
	Lucy Gibbens	29	1	4	Radley	labourer GWR	(ii) 13	
								(iii) 51
Shellingford	Mary Clements	37	8	1–17	Shellingford	farm carter	(i) 56	
	Jane Ridout	28	1	2	Shellingford	gardener	(ii) 2	
								(iii) 27
West Ilsley	Elizabeth Barlow	25	2	1–2	West Ilsley	gardener & schoolmistress	(i) 60	
	Ellen Maskell	38	7	1–11	West Ilsley	carter	(ii) 7	
								(iii) 22

Table XIIb: 1907–40

parish	mother's name	age	no. of child.	ages of child.	residence	occupation	interval (days)	average interval (days)
Shellingford	Gladys Rixon				Shellingford	labourer	(i) 45	
	Gertrude Bartlett				Shellingford	butler	(ii) 8	
								(iii) 20
Wantage	Annie Austin				Wantage	major	(i) 55	
	Edith Weller				Wantage	soldier	(ii) 1	
								(iii) 23
Wootton	Lizzie Alder				Wootton	spinster	(i) 56	
	Ellen Phipps				Boar's Hill	soldier	(ii) 13	
								(iii) 30
Sandhurst	Annie Cripps				Sandhurst	labourer	(i) 56	
	Lily Goswell				Sandhurst	bricklayer	(ii) 9	
								(iii) 25

baptism of her stillborn child, from 12th to 15th July. One more stillbirth was noted in 1911, when Mrs Griffin was churched and the baby baptised; intervals are unknown.

Conclusion

Such parish lists as these make up the only formal records of women's churching in the three counties during the first half of the twentieth century. Apart from personal letters and diaries they are the last written traces of the ceremony's survival. Judging by their falling numbers, this was a rite of passage going through a time of transition, its observance increasingly seen as optional rather than obligatory. Some women are found hurrying to give thanks soon after every birth; others delaying, or deciding to miss out the service altogether. Perhaps it was unknown to them. Such choices have been measured by comparing churching and baptism lists; families and neighbours have been found, as residential addresses are traced on contemporary maps; and accounts of fees and occupations have hinted at the social and economic conditions of their lives. Sometimes the registers have offered glimpses of the clergy who took the service and wrote the records; an occasional magazine has shown how the whole thing fitted in to the parish programme.

Even so, however deeply her circumstances are probed, dates calculated, or distances measured, real understanding of a woman's decision to be churched remains elusive, and analysis of reasons why some women chose baptism-only for their babies after childbirth while others decided to go along for their own churching as well, has remained mostly speculative. To achieve a measure of certainty, personal testimony is needed. In Chapter Five women will speak of their decisions as they remember how the rite of churching cropped up in their own lives.

CHAPTER FOUR

'TO WHAT EXTENT IS THE CHURCHING OF WOMEN STILL MAINTAINED?' CLERICAL REPLIES TO THE SOUTHWARK VISITATION OF 1951

Here is an immensely valuable record of the churching of women in the twentieth century: a set of 346 visitation replies, sent from all corners of the twenty-five deaneries of the diocese of Southwark. In 1951 every parish priest was faced with Question III.7: *To what extent is the churching of women still maintained?* Nearly all of them replied, revealing their attitudes to the rite, explaining what they saw as its significance, and judging its popularity. At times they discussed quite openly churching's place in the liturgy of the mid-twentieth century. And so from this simple question the visitation elicited the most comprehensive estimate ever drawn up of churching's scale and significance in such a huge area of town, suburb and country. Map 4 (Plate 13) sketches the deaneries. They are shaded to indicate clerical estimates of their churching levels (high, medium or low).

Further exploration of the Southwark archive brought to light a second exciting discovery; a pile of responses to an earlier visitation of 1936, which had opened with the request for estimates of each parish's *social condition ... rich or poor etc.?* About half of the clergy wrote comments which were full of detail; but even those simply limited to 'mostly poor, a few rich', or 'better-off are moving away' helped to establish a social context against which churching levels might be viewed fifteen years later, in 1951.[1]

The Deaneries of Southwark

Southwark was an unwieldy diocese. Created in 1905, it combined the whole of the county of London south of the Thames, formerly in the diocese of Rochester, and the parliamentary divisions of East and Mid-Surrey, once part of the vast diocese of Winchester. There were six archdeaconries: Reigate and Croydon entirely in Surrey; Wandsworth and Lambeth straddling the borders of Surrey and London; and Southwark and Lewisham entirely in South London. Within them lay twenty-five deaneries, each named on the map (Plate 13). An 'historical sketch' in the keeping of the London Metropolitan Archives sums up the task envisaged by its

---

[1] Diocese of Southwark, Bishop's Primary Visitations: LMA, DS/VB/013, 1951; D/S/VB/012, 1936.

first bishop, Edward Stuart Talbot, formerly of Rochester, and his assistant suffragan bishops of Woolwich and Kingston:

> the challenge of building up the church over South London with a population of over two million inhabitants and great social disparities from the prosperous villages of Reigate or Kew and Edwardian suburbs to appallingly overcrowded tenements of inner London.[2]

As late as 1983 the landscape of Surrey was still being described as largely rural, particularly in its most southern deaneries of Caterham, Godstone and Reigate, rather less in Croydon South and Sutton, which had become by then undeniably suburban.[3] Around 1951 in the northern deaneries, Kingston, Richmond & Barnes and Merton, intensive housing developments were still relieved by the preservation of common and parkland, and the tremendous amenity of the River Thames. Neighbouring Wandsworth, Tooting and Battersea lay in the county of London, where suburbs began to merge into a continuous urban landscape. Together with Clapham and Streatham they had retained some part of their open spaces and prosperous areas; but only a short way to the east in Brixton and Lambeth these gave way to narrower streets and more congested housing as they met the poverty of the urban waterside. In contrast the adjacent deanery of Merton, out to the west in Surrey, contained parishes in the relatively prosperous districts of Wimbledon and Morden.

Along the river to the east of Lambeth could be found the rest of the dioceses' poorest deaneries, all in the county of London. Two of the four in the archdeaconry of Southwark (Bermondsey and Southwark) housed crowded streets of railwaymen and printers, costers and waterside workers; while Camberwell was described in 1936 as entirely 'poor', and only in Dulwich, furthest from the river, could as many as fifty per cent of parishes be said to be 'mixed' in their social composition. Three of the deaneries in the archdeaconry of Lewisham (Deptford, Charlton and Plumstead) were on the Thames, Charlton containing the notoriously deprived areas of Greenwich and Woolwich as well as relatively prosperous and spacious Blackheath. Bordering these to the south were the remaining three deaneries: East Lewisham, West Lewisham and Eltham & Mottingham. Each combined poverty in its northern parishes with districts of middle - class settlement to the south.

---

[2] Introductory historical sketch in the LMA Catalogue of Southwark Diocese; http:/www.southwark.anglican.org/history.htm.

[3] N. Pevsner, and B. Cherry, *The Buildings of England: London 2: South* (New Haven and London, 2002); N. Pevsner, and I. Nairn, revised by B. Cherry, *The Buildings of England: Surrey* (New Haven and London, 2002), *passim*.

'TO WHAT EXTENT IS THE CHURCHING OF WOMEN STILL MAINTAINED?'

The Visitations of 1936 and 1951

The 1951 visitation, sixth in Southwark since the foundation of the diocese, was undertaken by its fifth bishop, the Revd Bertram Fitzgerald Simpson. Among the usual batches of questions about staffing, buildings, finances, church services and patterns of attendance, three are of particular interest to this study. The first (Section III: 'Services and Offices') enquired about the nature of the congregation:

> Is the Sunday congregation typical of the whole parish, or mainly of one class? In particular does it contain any industrial or factory workers?

The second, still contained within this Section, was Question 7:

> To what extent is the churching of women still maintained?

Finally, at the end of Section IV: 'Sacraments', clergy were asked about the possibilities of increasing church attendance by home visiting:

> How much time is spent weekly by yourself and your staff in regular visitation of the parishioners? Is house-to-house visiting possible today? If not, have you any definite scheme for visits? What is the best time of day for visiting the homes of your people?

Though it cannot be said that all questions were diligently answered, nor that every reply was illuminating, the returns reveal the character and habits of clergy, as well as giving information about the nature of parishes and, crucially, the extent of churching in 1951. The initial query about class and occupation was simply ignored by many incumbents, or drew only the briefest replies. Accounts of home visiting were given more fully, with target groups and times of day set out, along with complaints about impenetrable blocks of flats, and recollections of repeated frustration when people were always out at work and never at home in the daytime.

Question III:7, however, on churching, was generally answered simply and well, owing perhaps to its being itself so direct. Out of the total of 346 questionnaires sent out, only eight (two per cent) received no reply; the rest elicited more-or-less valuable comments about churching's extent and distribution within the parish, together with numerous clues about its popularity or decline. Thirty-six incumbents connected it directly with requests for baptism, and fourteen with 'superstition'. Some indicated that they valued the ceremony, others suggested that it was no longer appropriate. Altogether a compelling account emerges of mid-century churching activity in this huge and varied diocese that supports and illuminates the parish register evidence from the three counties. At the same time it is nearly as vivid as the oral testimony that has been collected for the second half of the century.

The 1951 replies are complemented by responses to the introductory section of the 1936 visitation articles. For the poorest parts of London these leave a strong impression of the strain under which many clergy worked. Particularly in inner city areas, such as Greenwich, Deptford, Southwark, Walworth, Bermondsey, Rotherhithe and Lambeth, unemployment was seen to be blighting parish life: poverty, ignorance and indifference were often noted. A major problem was geographical mobility; movement of the 'better-off' to homes in the suburbs, leaving newcomers or the remaining poor to fill the crowded tenements, or sometimes themselves be moved out of slum properties into newly-built London County Council housing. At the same time, clergy in the diocese's 'Edwardian suburbs' and 'prosperous villages' such as Richmond and Wimbledon, Caterham and Reigate, wrote of the 'rich' and 'well-to-do' (a favoured epithet), though there were also throughout South-East Surrey numerous 'poor' parishes and 'mixed' settlements of clerks and poorer artisans, chauffeurs, gardeners, and agricultural labourers. Some responses to questions about *difficulties, anxieties, successes* and *problems* were merely perfunctory, but others went into vivid detail about welcome developments, intractable dilemmas, or the struggle simply to hold on to congregations. Thus each parish is revealed in 1936, with its social and economic life, the habits and attitudes of its inhabitants, and something of the personality of its incumbent.

The Visitation Database

In the two visitations of 1936 and 1951 lists of parish replies were organised and numbered in different ways; in 1936 alphabetically, in 1951 in their deaneries. For this study they have been combined to construct a single database in which they are all set out in their deaneries. The full list of these may be seen in Table XIII, along with five keys [a to e] identifying salient facts about each individual parish.

In Table XIII every deanery appears with a Roman reference number (column a) given to it by the visitation administrators (these were pencilled in on the top corner of the 1951 replies). In addition, to help confirm identification, each deanery has been given my own letter of reference (column b). Within every deanery each parish is given its own individual number (column c), a form of reference which is used to identify it with precision, and to enable it, if necessary, to be checked in the archive. The Table also lists the archdeaconry of each deanery (column d), and, finally, in column e, the type of area to which each deanery belonged (*Urban, Suburban* or *Rural*).

Wherever parishes are mentioned in the footnotes of this chapter, the first three forms of reference will be used in order: each will be given its unique combination of deanery number and letter, together with its own parish number within the deanery; eg. St Mary, Battersea: Ia1: St Paul, Clapham: IIIc7.

In addition, names of parishes in the text are followed by an [s/c] score. [s] refers to their social nature, and [c] to their churching level; eg. St Mary, Battersea: [s1/c3]; St Paul, Clapham [s1/c2]. These [s] and [c] scores are based on comments

Table XIII: Deaneries of the Southwark Diocese
These are listed in the order in which they appear in archive of the 1951 visitation.

Deanery	(a) ref. no.	(b) ref. letter	(c) no. of parishes	(d) archdeaconry	(e) area type
Battersea	I	a	1–17	Wandsworth	U
Bermondsey	II	b	1–14	Southwark	U
Clapham	III	c	1–9	Lambeth	S
Brixton	III, IV	c, d	10–17	Lambeth	U
Lambeth	III	d	1–18	Lambeth	U
Southwark	V	e	1–22	Southwark	U
Streatham	VI, XVI	f	1–13	Lambeth	S
Tooting	VI	f	14–21	Wandsworth	S
Wandsworth	VII	g	1–11	Wamdsworth	S
Sutton	VII	h	1–17	Croydon	S
Croydon South	IX	i	1–15	Croydon	S
Godstone	X	j	1–15	Reigate	R
Caterham	IX	j	1–3, 11–15	Reigate	R
Kingston	XI	k	1–16	Wandsworth	S
Reigate	XII	l	1–21	Reigate	R
Richmond and B	XIII	m	1–15	Wandsworth	S
Merton	VI, VIII, XIV	n	1–11	Lambeth	S
Camberwell	XV	o	1–18	Southwark	U
Dulwich	XVI	p	1–13	Southwark	S
Deptford	XVII	q	1–19	Lewisham	U
Charlton	XVII, XIX	q, s	9–19, 1–4	Lewisham	U
West Lewisham	XVII	r	18–27	Lewisham	S
East Lewisham	XVIII	r	1–28	Lewisham	S
Plumstead	XIX	s	5–12	Lewisham	U
Eltham & Mottingham	XIX	s	13–25	Lewisham	S

and descriptions written by clergy in the visitation replies. Phrases commonly used to describe social nature, and the scores accorded to them, included:
 s1 'very poor' to 'moderately poor'.
 s2 'mixed'; 'middle class with artisans, clerks etc'; 'not rich', and 'not poor'.
 s3 'rich', 'well-to-do', 'comfortable'.
whilst among those telling of churching frequency were the following:
 c0 'not at all'
 c1 'negligible', 'occasional', 'very little' [estimate, below 33%].
 c2 'mixed', 'considerably', 'quite regular' [estimate, between 33% and 65%].
 c3 'frequently', 'almost all', 'very strong', [estimate, between 66% and 99%].
 c4 'universal', 'fully', 'all women' [estimate, nearing 100%].
 Table XIV shows how scores have been given for comments by clergy in the parishes of two very different deaneries, Lambeth and Caterham:

Table XIV: Summary of social conditions and churching levels in two Southwark deaneries based on the 1936 and 1951 visitation records

Lambeth Deanery	1936 Visitation Social Condition (S)	1951 Visitation Level of Churching (C)	Scores S	C
1d. Lambeth, St Mary	Poor, changes, slum clearance etc	'about 40 per year'	1	2
2d. Lambeth, St Andrew	Poor, People gambling, indifferent	'not a great many'	1	1
3d. Lambeth, Emmanuel	Poor. 'Fear of loss of people owing to proposed demolition'	*no reply*	1	–
4d. Lambeth, St Mary Less	Poor.	'almost 100%'	1	4
5d. Lambeth, St Philip	Poor; 'moving populations'	'about 100 each year'	1	3
7d. Lambeth, Holy Trinity	Very poor.	'frequent'	1	3
8d. Lambeth, St Anne	Poor, lack of home life, floating population. Visits impossible.	'only occasionally'	1	4
9d. Lambeth, St Stephen	Poor.	'completely'	1	4
10d. Lambeth, All Saints	Poor, people move to outer suburbs.	'about 1 in 4. Good deal of superstition.'	1	2
11d. Kennington, St Mark	Very poor.	'very common'	1	3
12d. Kennington, St John	Poor.	'all women churched before baptism.'	1	4
16d. Kenn. Cr., St Anselm	Mainly poor artisan.	'the number down this year to 50 from 80'	1	3
17d. Kenn. Hill, St Peter	no reply	'a superstition about it very general'	–	2
18d. W'loo Rd., St John	Poor. Shifting population	'whenever required.'	1	2
		total of code points	13	34
		no. of parishes giving useful information	13	13
		parish average	1	3

Caterham Deanery	1936 Visitation Social Condition (S)	1951 Visitation Level of Churching (C)	Scores S	C
1i. Caterham, St Mary	Few rich, many moderate, 4,800 poor.	'some 20 a year'	3	1
2i. Caterham, St John	Well-to-do, moving away; many poor.	'more than half'	3	2
3i. Whyteleafe, St Luke	A few well-to-do; a few really poor.	'not much, 4 or 5'	3	1
11i. Farleigh, St Mary	All very poor except one family.	'still the custom'	1	3
14i. Warl'ham, All Saints	Mixed, increasingly poor.	'they come to Warlingham'	2	1
14ai. Chesham, St leonard	Mixed, increasingly poor.	'they come to Warlingham'	2	1
15i. Woldingham, Ss Paul	Rich	'very little'	3	1
		total of code points	17	10
		no. of parishes giving useful information	7	7
		parish average	2	2

'TO WHAT EXTENT IS THE CHURCHING OF WOMEN STILL MAINTAINED?'

Three Caveats

This attempt to impose numerical codes on the written phrases of the visitation returns raises three important problems: (1) how did clergy understand the questions? (2) what did they imply in their responses? (3) how should association of the 1936 and 1951 data be handled?

Caveat 1. Clergy interpreted Question III:7 in different ways in 1951. On churching's popularity, some referred only to its observation among women who were regular churchgoers, or had taken their children for baptism, while others wrote as if they thought that they should reply for 'all mothers'. Quite often clergy counted women who were churched in hospital as part of their parish total, as in St Michael, Woolwich [s1/c3]: 'Very generally in parish and hospital', while others discounted them, as in St John the Baptist, Eltham [s3/c2]: 'Not in great numbers, hospitals do more'.[4] Such variations make it impossible to be certain just how extensive churching really was among the mothers of each parish.

Caveat 2. Interpretation of phrases used in the replies of both visitations is not always straightforward, since they reflect the cultural assumptions of past decades. In 1936 clergy of relatively good education were asked to make judgements about the 'social condition, rich or poor etc' of their parishes. How were they to define notions of wealth and poverty? It is hard to know how those parishioners in Southwark and Camberwell, whom they called 'poor, many very poor', or 'poor type, many casual workers', were comparable with the 'poor', or 'not really poor: working class' written about in Kingston and Reigate, whose inhabitants were generally 'suitable people', 'the best', 'upper middle-class', 'the well-to-do'. This word 'poor' has to be seen as a relative description, by no means an absolute. Judgments of religious non-participation were probably also affected by the norms of the area: non-churchgoers were described tolerantly as 'retired and passive Christians' in well-off St Margaret, Putney [s2/c2], but sternly criticised for 'ignorance, apathy, little apparent belief' in St Luke, Camberwell [s1/c2].[5] Interpreting the replies to Question III:7 in 1951 meets the difficulty of imprecision not only in social verdicts but also in accounts of churching frequency such as 'quite a lot', 'only slightly', 'still demanded', or 'fairly often'. It follows that even the most careful attempts to group replies according to the levels of frequency [c] that they indicate are bound to achieve only approximate accuracy.

Caveat 3. The social code [s] is based on the information given by clergy in the 1936 visitation, while the churching code [c] comes from that given in the 1951 replies. Continuity of attitude has normally been assumed: in both years the clergy were ordained men of broadly the same outlook and expectation, and attached to the same churches and congregations. Yet it must be acknowledged that it can only be guaranteed in thirty-seven of these 346 parishes, those in which the same

[4] St Michael, Woolwich, XIXs2; St John the Baptist, Eltham, XIXs13.
[5] St Margaret, Putney, XIIIm14; St Luke, Camberwell, XVo6.

incumbent was in place for both years.

Before moving to further analysis of the Southwark returns, and because many clerical comments on 'social conditions' were impressionistic rather than informative, it is worth looking at the contributions made by *The New Survey of London Life and Labour* of 1930–35, a massive attempt to bring up to date the findings of Charles Booth; and *The Report on the 1951 Census*, to see if they concur with the 1936 visitation replies.

The New Survey, Volumes III and VI, gives detailed estimates of Inner London's affluence and poverty in the 1930s.[6] In these Arthur Bowley's 'House Sample Analysis' looked at overcrowding, and the Survey team's 'Borough Summaries' itemised death rates, employment patterns, and proportions of the population living in various grades of poverty. In Volume III, 'The South-Eastern Survey' ranged over Bermondsey, Deptford, Greenwich, Lewisham and Woolwich; while South and North Lambeth, Southwark, Battersea, Camberwell and Wandsworth were investigated in 'The South-Western Survey' in Volume VI. Emulating Charles Booth, a series of maps was produced showing the levels of poverty in each area by use of a code of colours. These contributed to the classification of each borough. Table XV gives a tabulation of the 'London Street Survey Classification' findings. It is tantalising that the 1936 team failed to share Charles Booth's interest in the social implications of religious belief and affiliation (found in his seven-volume religious survey), and included no word about London's churches; indeed it mentioned religion only once in its own nine volumes, to observe that 'the weakening of religious sanctions' was, together with 'decline in parental authority', one of the 'contrary influences' militating against any decrease of crime in Greater London.[7]

The second source used to test clergy opinion of changing social conditions is the 1951 Census Report, in which population figures can be found for the ten boroughs in South London and sixteen in Eastern Surrey that make up the diocese of Southwark. One of its tables was particularly helpful, giving changes in population in the diocese between 1921 and 1951. A transcription is seen in Table XVI.[8]

Here the contrast can be seen between urban and suburban/rural settlement from 1921 to 1951: populations fell in all but two of London's boroughs, and rose in all but two of Surrey's. Many clergy commented in 1936 on the constant movement of their parishioners, complaining that longstanding church members were leaving to live elsewhere, and being replaced by newcomers who showed little interest in churchgoing. Nearly all in the Metropolitan area bore witness to a high degree of poverty and overcrowding. Other census tables compared the occupational skills found in different districts using the measurement Social Class I to V.

[6] Llewellyn-Smith, Sir H., *The New Survey of London Life and Labour,* 9 vols (London, 1930–5), pp. 1030–35.
[7] *New Survey*, Vol. XIII, p. 396.
[8] *Report on the 1951 Census* (HMSO, 1953).

Table XV: 1930–35 London street survey classification
(South London boroughs)

Constructed from the figures given for each borough in the *New Survey of London Life and Labour* of 1930–5.
Key given by the authors to explain their use of colours on street maps to illustrate poverty and affluence:

Black	'the lowest class of degraded or semi-criminal population'
Blue	'those who are living below the poverty line'
Purple	'the mass of unskilled workers who are above the poverty line'
Pink	'skilled workers'
Red	'the middle class and wealthy'

SOUTH-EASTERN AREA

	Bermondsey		Deptford		Greenwich	
	Total	%	Total	%	Total	%
Blue / Purple with blue stripe	28,100	25.2	17,800	16.9	12,400	13.1
Purple	52,100	46.8	25,800	24.4	27,600	29.2
Pink with red stripe / red	1,190	2.0	7,600	7.2	7,100	7.5
Red	—	—	9,900	9.4	9,500	10.0

	Lewisham		Woolwich	
	Total	%	Total	%
Blue / Purple with blue stripe	1,300	0.6	5,400	4.0
Purple	14,900	7.2	46,100	33.6
Pink	113,100	54.7	57,700	42.1
Pink with red stripe	19,900	9.6	8,700	6.3
Red	57,700	27.9	19,200	14.0

SOUTH-WESTERN AREA

	S. Lambeth		N. Lambeth		Battersea	
	Total	%	Total	%	Total	%
Blue / Purple with blue stripe	2,200	1.4	10,700	8.2	12,900	8.2
Purple	15,200	10.0	59,600	46.0	56,800	36.3
Pink	86,600	56.7	47,500	36.6	61,600	39.3
Pink with red stripe / red	19,400	12.7	11,900	9.2	9,600	6.1
Red	29,300	19.2	—	—	15,800	10.1

	Southwark		Camberwell		Wandsworth	
	Total	%	Total	%	Total	%
Blue / Purple with blue stripe	14,300	8.6	16,200	6.6	11,300	3.4
Purple	70.400	42.2	57,600	23.4	32,700	9.9
Pink	76,600	45.6	129,600	37.9	141,700	42.9
Pink with red stripe	5,900	3.6	18,200	7.4	36.700	11.1
Red	00	00	24,100	9.8	108,000	32.7

Table XVI: Census 1951 report: changes in population in the Diocese of Southwark, 1921–1951

Boroughs	pop. 1921	pop 1931	pop 1951	% change '31–51
(a) London				
Battersea	167,739	159,552	117,140	–26.2
Bermondsey	119,452	111,542	60,640	–45.6
Camberwell	267,198	251,294	179,777	–28.5
Deptford	112,534	106,891	75,495	–29.4
Greenwich	100,450	100,891	89,846	–11.0
Lambeth	302,868	296,147	230,240	–22.3
Lewisham	174,194	219,953	227,576	+3.5
Southwark	184,404	171,695	97,221	–56.1
Wandsworth	328,307	353,110	330,493	–6.4
Woolwich	140,389	146,881	147,891	+0.7
(b) Surrey				
Croydon	191,468	233,108	249,870	+16.8
Barnes	34,299	42,440	40,567	–4.4
Beddington & Wallington	16,451	26,328	32,757	+24.4
Carshalton	13,873	28,586	62,721	+119.4
Caterham & Warlington	17,108	21,774	31,293	+43.7
Coulsdon & Purley	23,115	39,795	63,773	+60.3
Kingston on Thames	39,514	39,835	40,172	+0.9
Maldon & Coombe	14,495	23,350	45,566	+95.1
Merton & Morden	17,532	41,227	74,730	+81.3
Mitcham	35,122	58,872	67,269	+18.3
Reigate	31,733	34,547	42,248	+22.3
Richmond	37,105	39,276	41,944	+6.3
Surbiton	20,149	30,178	60,875	+101.7
Sutton & Cheam	29,733	48,363	80,673	+66.8
Wimbledon	61,405	59,515	58,141	–2.3
Godstone	23,196	24,928	31,851	+27.8

They illustrate the contrast between boroughs in the inner city (Bermondsey, Deptford, Southwark) and those in Surrey's outer suburbs (Wimbledon, Richmond). In the 1936 visitation clergy generally agreed about the huge number of men in Social Class III (using phrases such as 'very poor to moderately poor') in metropolitan parishes. In Surrey their alignment with the census was more varied. For instance, they agreed about Coulsdon & Purley being largely 'professional and artisan' (at St Andrew, Coulsdon [s3/c2]) and 'rich; small village people' (at nearby St Mark, Woodcote [s3/c1]); and two parishes at Mitcham being 'poor, artisans' and 'poor': but considered that at St James, Purley ([s1/c3]) the parishioners were 'mainly poor', with no mention of even middle class people, let alone the professionals who had been found in the census.[9]

[9] St Andrew, Coulsdon, IXi5; St Mark, Woodcote, IXi10; St James, Purley, IXi9; Christ Church, Mitcham, VI, VIII & XIVn4; St Barnabas, Mitcham, VI, VIII, & XIVn5.

'TO WHAT EXTENT IS THE CHURCHING OF WOMEN STILL MAINTAINED?'

Each of these sources will be called upon to help explore the varied backgrounds of Southwark's nine urban, twelve suburban and three rural deaneries, as their record of churching in the middle of the twentieth century is reviewed.

Nine Urban Deaneries: Social Conditions

Bermondsey and Deptford, Southwark and Camberwell, Lambeth, Brixton and Battersea, Charlton and Plumstead: these nine deaneries lay within those parts of London designated by planners in 1945 as the 'Inner Ring'.[10] Their relative poverty was constantly referred to in the 1936 visitation, and illustrated in the *New Survey* street maps with much blue and purple colouring (below and just above the poverty line) though some pink ('skilled workers') was also in evidence. On Map 4 seven of them are heavily shaded to denote high average churching frequency, suggesting that there is some association between this and the nature of parish life.

Inner South London might not appear promising churching territory. Levels of church attendance were low: clergy deplored repeatedly the departure of those who had worked their way out of poverty and into better housing taking 'the better sort' of families away from the parish and out of sight. In both 1936 and 1951 they wrote repeatedly of the 'apathy' and 'indifference' that undermined church attendance, for, as a number of historians have observed, the working classes normally went to church only for special events: in her study of popular religion in Southwark, Sarah Williams quotes the Revd W. Thompson of St Saviour's, Southwark [s1/c3] telling Charles Booth in 1902:

> The poor think it proper to have their children baptised, marriages solemnised and burial services read in church but anything more is generally conspicuous by its absence.[11]

(But St Saviour's mothers 'generally' went to be churched in 1951.)

Conditions in the deaneries of the Southwark archdeaconry were notorious. Alan Bartlett says in his study of Bermondsey's clergy: 'the inner ring of riverside parishes were generally perceived to be in a bad way': and he quotes Bishop Cyril Foster Garbett's observation:

> Most of the churches on the riverside had minute congregations: the people did not even know where their parish church was. I very soon discovered that, when I came to take a confirmation, it was useless to ask the way to St. – 's: I had to find out beforehand from the incumbent the name of the nearest public house.[12]

---

[10] Stephen Inwood, *A History of London 1914–1997* (London, 2000), pp. 814–15.
[11] S. C. Williams, *Religious Belief and Popular Culture in Southwark c. 1880–1939* (Oxford, 1999), pp. 87–8; C. Booth, *Life and Labour* (London, 1902), 'Religious Influences', IV, p. 20; St Saviour, Southwark, Ve10.
[12] Bartlett, 'The Churches in Bermondsey', p. 329.

Bermondsey's clergy gave the most frequent accounts of unrelieved poverty in the 1936 visitation, repeating the words: 'poor', 'poor & very poor', 'extremely poor', 'many very poor', 'very poor – casual dock labourers'; the Revd Thrift, incumbent at Holy Trinity, Rotherhithe [s1/c4] since 1921, explained that it was linked to 'much unemployment ... only about two of my men could demand a week's notice from employment.'[13] (Unemployment was running at thirty-three per cent of Bermondsey's insured population in 1933). Where there was work, it was mainly on the waterside; even in 1951 the census showed that 319 per thousand were in Class V occupations, the highest proportion in the diocese. As Alan Bartlett showed, the cost was spelled out in the *New Survey*:

> one man who worked as assistant to the relieving officer being sickened by the filth, the bugs, the semi-starvation of the poor and the old, and indeed the mental illness caused by prolonged unemployment.[14]

Predictably, no streets in this borough were coloured 'Red' ('middle class and wealthy'), but 25% were 'Blue / Purple with Blue Stripe', close to the poverty line. Programmes of slum clearance in the 1930s, as they started to bring improvements to the dilapidated tenements and cottage houses, also forced the families who needed to stay and work in the area to crowd into the remnants of older 'ill-lit and insanitary' properties. Meanwhile the better-off were leaving: the Revd G. R. Ballein, vicar since 1928 of the second largest parish of St James [s1/c3], wrote in his *History of St James* (1936) of the loss of the lower middle class 'who had formed the backbone of most of our local congregations'.[15]

Not unlike Bermondsey, the borough of Southwark was rated second in the list of Social Class V boroughs, with 277 per thousand in unskilled occupations in 1951; and though it had been given higher ratings than Bermondsey in the *New Survey* street classification, it still had the third highest proportion of 'Blue / Purple with Blue Stripe' streets in the South London area. In this study all its parishes, as in Bermondsey, have been coded s1. The clergy described in a variety of ways their undoubted poverty: 'extremely poor', 'growing poorer each year', 'very many unemployed', 'poor type, many casual workers', in 1936. By 1951 this was confirmed, though its detail was bound to have altered: the census showed that Southwark's population had fallen by fifty-six per cent during the twenty years since 1931, due to the damage and aftermath of war, and earlier clearance and resettlement programmes of the London County Council. Almost as poor, with 226 per thousand in 1951's Social Class V category, was the borough of Deptford, and though its *New Survey* street profile looked less impoverished than that of Bermondsey, largely because its poor northern half (with almost seventeen per

---

[13] The Revd Thrift in 1936, Holy Trinity, Rotherhithe, IIb13.
[14] Bartlett, 'The Churches in Bermondsey', p. 40.
[15] Bartlett, 'The Churches in Bermondsey', p. 328.

cent 'Blue / Purple with Blue Stripe' streets) was balanced by the 'pronounced middle class elements' of the more prosperous south, even so five of its parishes were notoriously derelict and low-lying, and described by clergy as 'poor', 'poor, very', with their inhabitants, as in Bermondsey, 'indifferent', and 'moving away'. In Camberwell, the spaces of its greens and markets long invaded by new housing, and a borough twice as poor as Southwark in the percentage of 'Blue / Purple with Blue Stripe' streets, all but one of the eighteen parishes were described in 1936 as 'poor' or 'very poor'; the only exception being St Giles, Camberwell [s2/c2]: 'artisan with a small proportion of the clerk type'.[16] Indeed, away from the docks, the proportion of its men in unskilled occupations (175 per thousand) was lower than those recorded in its two riverside neighbours.

Impressions of poverty remain dark to the west in Lambeth deanery, where all twelve incumbents in 1936 described their parishes as 'poor', and gave some additional details: the impact of slum clearance and demolition; people 'gambling', 'unkempt', and 'indifferent' (St Andrew's [s1/c1]). The Revd Matthews, who had been at Holy Trinity [s1/c3] since 1932, wrote in 1936 of the damaged circumstances of his parish:

> Constant emigration of the 'best' people with corresponding immigration of inferior type ... Their places are filled by slum dwellers whose houses are being pulled down, who come and go before we can get to know them ... We feel that we are losing ground, though the church is still in a very much less depressed state than it was in 1923–5 ... How to arouse the careless is the big problem.[17]

The deanery is only in the northern part of Lambeth Borough, which may be seen in the *New Survey* with half of its streets coloured 'Purple' ('unskilled, above the poverty line'); a striking contrast with South Lambeth, whose colouring was over fifty per cent 'Pink' ('skilled workers'), and just over nineteen per cent 'Red' ('middle class and wealthy').

More prosperous Brixton, Clapham, Merton and Streatham also lie well south of the river. Of these only Brixton, with its strong similarity to Lambeth and Camberwell, may be counted as an inner city deanery. Seven of its nine parishes were described in 1936 as 'poor', 'mainly working-class', 'poor but not slum'. Once a middle-class area, its residential houses were being replaced by flats and terraces for clerks and artisans during the inter-war period. The Revd Walker of Christ Church, North Brixton [s1/c3] wrote in 1936 of his 'poor, continually changing and unresponsive congregation'.[18]

[16] St Giles, Camberwell, XVo1.
[17] St Andrew, Lambeth, IVd2; Holy Trinity, Lambeth, IVd7.
[18] Christ Church, Brixton, IVd15. It is worth noting, though, that its 1951 churching level was high.

The gloom lifts somewhat when the survey reaches Charlton deanery, which lay in the three London boroughs of Greenwich, Woolwich and Lewisham (in which relatively prosperous Blackheath is included). All three had high scores of skilled workers in the *New Survey* scheme of classification, and indeed three of its seventeen parishes were described as 'mixed' [s2]. Nevertheless, a further thirteen were recorded as 'very poor' to 'moderately poor' [s1], mainly those in Greenwich and Woolwich which were both suffering the disruption of unemployment and major slum clearance between the wars.

Nine Urban Deaneries: Levels of Churching

In these Thameside urban deaneries levels of churching were remarkably high in 1951. Thrift, still at Holy Trinity, Rotherhithe [s1/c4], was able to testify that the rite was 'practically universal amongst all nominal church women', and many from neighbouring parishes echoed his confident tone: 'universally', 'largely maintained', 'very strongly' (at St James), 'all come' (at St Luke), 'still demanded', 'the majority', 'still the common practice', '90%'. Of Bermondsey deanery's twelve parishes, all rated as s1 ('very poor' to 'moderately poor'), three scored the highest churching rate [c4], six a score of over 66% [c3] and two a score of 33%–65% [c2], leaving only one, St Augustine, with a negligible rate [c1]. In Deptford deanery the churching record was also strong with all but two of its nine parishes returning answers to Question III:7 that scored [c3]: the ceremony was 'frequent', 'usual' and 'very popular'; 'Never a week without a churching' was entered by the Revd Hutt, vicar of St Luke [s1/c3] since 1930; mothers had kept coming to the ceremony despite the 'increase in drunkenness' and 'growth of indifference' that he had noted in 1936.[19] Altogether the rite appears to have been important to this poor riverside area with seven parishes having a rate of over 66%, [c4 and c3], and only two scoring a mixed [c2]; in three parishes the local maternity hospital supported the ceremony, and in another, Ss Paul & Mark [s1/c3] churching was said by the incumbent to be a 'very popular superstition'.

Southwark deanery's churching levels were not quite as high as those of Bermondsey. In 1951, out of nineteen parishes two were rated very high [c4] both in the borough of Southwark itself; eight were rated at over two-thirds [c3] three of them in Walworth; six scored between one and two thirds [c2], and three, reporting only 'occasional' churchings were given a [c1]. In Camberwell rates were undramatic but steady, with half the parishes scoring [c2] and the other half [c3]. Two incumbents in [c3] parishes connected churching with superstition: Emmanuel, Camberwell [s1/c3] and St Chrysostom, Peckham [s1/c3] whose vicar, the Revd Potter, had been presiding over a high-church regime since 1923. Two more, one a parish with a mixed churching rate [c2], mentioned the large pro-

---

[19] Deptford: St Luke XVIIq3, Ss.Paul & Mark, XVIIq4.

portion of mothers who were churched in hospital before leaving for home.[20] The ceremony was regularly observed in Lambeth deanery in 1951, and with churching levels evenly distributed. Three out of thirteen parishes have been given the highest score of [c 4], four of [c3], three of [c2], and three of [c1]. Clergy in two parishes, St Peter, Kennington Hill [s-/c2] and All Saints, Lambeth [s1/c1] noted that 'superstition', of which there was 'a good deal', was 'very general' concerning the churching ceremony. It is hard to know the churching level at St Peter: the vicar's comment was simply: 'A superstition about it very general', giving no idea of its frequency; in this case a mixed rate [c2] has been awarded.[21] In neighbouring Brixton the churching record was spectacularly high. Six out of eight parishes returning comments in 1951 were rated [c3] with 'very good indeed', 'frequently', 'most mothers come', 'very considerably', and 'every Sunday'. Two added that it was 'largely due to superstition', and 'most seem to regard it in a superstitious way'. In Charlton, the last in this account of Inner London deaneries, there was quite an even distribution of churching, similar to that in Camberwell and Lambeth: scores of [c2] went to four parishes, [c1] to five, and [c3] to the remaining six (all described as 'poor'). Hospital churchings were reported as common in three parishes.

Two further deaneries on the outer edge of the 'urban' group, Battersea to the west and Plumstead out to the east, remain to be considered. Each was made up of a poorer northern river border, and more prosperous area in the south. Battersea's clergy reported little enthusiasm for religion: the Revd Carroll of St Bartholomew's [s1/c1] wrote:

> People who used to come to church have moved to Cheam, Morden, etc.
> The new families that arrive seldom if ever have any desire to attend church.

while at St Luke [s2/c2] '120 churchgoing families have left the District in 6 years'.[22] Others, echoing those in nearby Brixton, wrote regretfully of the area's social decline as old family homes were divided into hostels and flats of 'artisans and casual labourer types', 'tradesmen and small dealers'.

Over in Plumstead there was more than mere indifference to trouble the church: among the Arsenal workers were found 'atheistic, communistic and materialistic influences' at St Mark, Plumstead Common [s2/c2], and 'quarrels among the faithful' together with 'general godless socialism' among the parishioners of The Ascension [s1/c2]. 'Materialism' was also deplored at St Nicholas [s1/c4] and 'few signs of conversion' had been achieved at St John the Baptist [s1/c2] with its

[20] Emmanuel, Camberwell, XVo4; St Chrysostom, Peckham, XVo15; Camden, Camberwell, XVo11; St Andrew, Peckham, XVo14.
[21] All Saints, Lambeth, IVd10; St Peter, Kennington Hill, IVd17.
[22] St Bartholomew, Battersea, Ia9a; St Luke, Battersea, Ia11.

strong Labour Club.[23] Here in Plumstead the 'better off' were also moving out and the poor arriving: 'Arsenal workers', 'working class' and 'industrial workers' alongside the 'clerks and typists'. Yet in both areas over ten per cent of the streets were coloured 'Red' ('middle class and wealthy') in the *New Survey* maps, and proportions of Class V workers were relatively low in 1951 (177 per thousand and 149 per thousand respectively), whereas they reached 23 per thousand and 38 per thousand in Class I. On the churching map both these deaneries have medium shading, for churching was only moderately frequent; it took place more regularly in Battersea which scored [c3] in eight of its fifteen parishes, less so in Plumstead with nearly all scoring [c2] apart from one [c1] and a remarkable [c4] at St Nicholas Church [s1/c4] with 'almost 100%'.

Comments in these nine urban deaneries point to a common clerical opinion that local mothers adhered quite strongly to the churching ceremony, and that its frequency was higher in the poorest parishes with their unemployment and wretched housing than in those that were better-off. Though religious indifference was often prevalent, women still thought it important to attend the service in almost every urban parish replying to Question III:7.

Churching in Twelve Suburban Deaneries: Inner Suburbs

The four deaneries here designated 'inner suburbs' are Dulwich and its three eastern neighbours, East Lewisham, West Lewisham and Eltham & Mottingham. Still included in the system of London boroughs, they lay outside the inner city, bordering on the county of Kent. On Map 4 Dulwich has a 'low frequency' shading, the other three 'moderate frequency', none having had any clusters of 'high frequency' parishes. During three decades up to 1951 social traditions, often including church membership and rites of passage such as the churching of women, had been lost in many suburbs as residents moved in and out, transforming the shape and custom of their communities, and often separating different generations of their families, crucially, mothers from daughters.

Were these deaneries different from those of the inner city? Certainly all four lie well away from the Thames waterside with its crowded dwellings and press of casual workers. Yet the *New Survey* made it clear that the three in Lewisham, in their northern 'older and lower-lying parts', contained elements of the poverty of their neighbours, Greenwich and Woolwich, just as conditions in North Dulwich were similar to those of Camberwell and Brixton. It was in their southern parts, the areas to which the better-off were heading, that the social profile became far more middle-class. This is the dual nature of all suburban deaneries: crowded city streets, giving way to broad avenues, parks and open spaces. Even so the word 'poor' appeared somewhere in almost every 1936 'social condition' comment,

---

[23] St Mark, Plumstead Common, XIXs11; Ascension, Plumstead, XIXs12; St Nicholas, Plumstead, XIXs8; St John the Baptist, Plumstead, XIXs7.

since low-earning artisans and industrial workers were among the number of those starting to arrive, moving south away from the river, drawn to flats or housing in new estates. Despite so much transition, the practice of churching was retained in the three most eastern of these deaneries 'to a surprising extent in a town parish', according to the Revd Anderson of St Luke, Eltham Park [s2/c2] and '100% a year' at St Edward the Confessor, Mottingham [s2/c4].[24]

Dulwich alone stands out, more stable and prosperous than its South London neighbours, and manifesting the least enthusiasm of the four when it came to the churching of women. Only three of its sixteen parishes scored [c3], while five were rated [c2] and seven [c1]. Four vicars noted its infrequency without comment: 'could be more frequent', 'rare', 'very little', 'only very occasionally', hinting at little surprise or regret for its evident decline. A fifth, the Revd Morris, vicar of St Matthew, Denmark Park [s1/c0] replied simply 'Not at St Matthew' in the 1951 visitation: he joins St Alban's, Cheam [s-/c0] as conspicuous in the whole survey for apparently doing no churching at all. The curtness of his phrase might seem to suggest impatience at the very question, perhaps understandable given his parish's allegedly slow and difficult recovery from massive material damage sustained during the Blitz.[25]

In East Lewisham, with nine [s2] and seven [s1] parishes, churching was quite strong. It held seven [c3] parishes in which such phrases as 'most women', 'most mothers', 'about 75% of baptisms', 'pretty generally', and 'those bringing babies for baptism come first to be churched' were used. At St Cyprian, Brockley Rise [s1/c2] the Revd Hurst, in place since 1922, wrote:

> Women who seldom if ever come to church come to be "churched"! How
> far this is due to superstition rather than to thanksgiving I cannot say.[26]

From some clergy replies it is hard to judge just how much churching was going on: 'held every Wednesday at 10.0 am', or 'fairly widely' are not revealing. In West Lewisham's eleven parishes clergy answers on churching levels divided evenly between high, medium and low, varying from enthusiasm: 'in nearly every case', 'almost universally', and 'prevalent, very popular here', to curtness: 'infrequent, 1 in 12', 'very little', and 'rarely'. Eltham & Mottingham's churching was said to move similarly from 'rarely' [c1], to 'regularly but not very frequently' [c2] and 'very largely', 'to a surprising extent' [c3]. Only at the church of St Edward the Confessor [s-/c4] did every mother allegedly go in for a churching.[27]

Running a parish was not easy in any suburban deanery. In these four, clergy comments constantly deplore high levels of indifference to church membership, and allege local competition from other denominations: militant protestants in

[24] St Luke, Eltham Park, XIXs17; St Edward the Confessor, Mottingham, XIXs25.
[25] St Matthew, Denmark Park, XVIp2, but cf St Barnabas, Dulwich on p. 93.
[26] St Cyprian, Brockley Rise, XVIIIr14.
[27] St Edward the Confessor, Mottingham, XIXs25.

Dulwich, Roman Catholics in Lewisham. They found it almost impossible to bring newcomers into church life and establish familiarity with them as parishioners. Ceremonies such as churching might have been expected consequently to have fallen away. Yet for all its uneven distribution, it was still found in every parish save one.

Churching in Twelve Suburban Deaneries: Outer Suburbs

Deaneries in the nine outer suburbs of South-West London fall into two categories on the churching map: five are shaded for medium churching frequency, found not far out of town in Wandsworth, Tooting, Streatham, Clapham and Merton; the rest show lower frequency, along the Thames in Kingston and Richmond & Barnes, and well out into Surrey in Croydon South and Sutton. These different churching levels appear to reflect two now familiar aspects of the suburban church: apathy among its parishioners, whether rich or poor; and instability of church membership as they kept moving away to different areas.

These Southwark incumbents gave quite broad estimates of parish income levels, tending to describe their parishioners as 'mixed', with few 'poor' and even fewer 'rich' among them. Two of these deaneries, Wandsworth and Tooting, are covered by the *New Survey* street map. This confirms their undoubted prosperity, with a huge number of 'Red' ('middle class' and 'wealthy') streets, well over twice the number of 'Purple with Blue Stripe' and 'Purple' (below and just above the poverty line) combined; and in the 1951 census, its proportion of Social Class I males in employment was, at forty-eight per thousand, the highest in South London. For other glimpses of parochial life we can learn much from the clergy's written testimony.

The commonest lament about these mixed and varied parishioners was that they were apathetic and indifferent: newcomers failed to get in touch, attend the church, or even send their children to Sunday School; the poor showed no interest; the rich had other things to do, with their 'love of pleasure' in prosperous St Andrew, Streatham [s2/c1]; or else, rather than seeking the consolations of religion, 'displayed a belief that a well-mannered life needs no more' in the quiet roads around Holy Trinity, Roehampton [s3/c1].[28] Though they were free from both rural remoteness and the worst of urban overcrowding, suburban parish clergy were frustrated by such apathy, whether they were wishing to visit families, church new mothers, or build up Sunday attendances. In addition, parish membership was not stable, and, as in inner London, clergy were dismayed and infuriated by its constant shifts: in 1936 the vicar of St Mary, Mortlake [s2/c1] wrote of 'a floating population', while the incumbent of St Mary, Long Ditton [s2/c2] observed: 'Change from old village to London suburb. Old helpers moving out'.[29]

[28] St Andrew, Streatham, VIf12; Holy Trinity, Roehampton, XIIIm15.
[29] St Mary, Mortlake, XIIm12; St Mary, Long Ditton, XIk15.

'TO WHAT EXTENT IS THE CHURCHING OF WOMEN STILL MAINTAINED?'

Not surprisingly, churching levels in the suburban parishes showed less uniformity than those in inner London. All but two of these nine deaneries had at least one high level [c3] parish: two each in Croydon and Sutton, Kingston and Richmond & Barnes; three each in Clapham, Streatham and Tooting (with one [c4] in each of the latter); four each in Wandsworth and Merton (with two [c4]s). At the same time, no deanery had fewer than two low level [c1] scores. It appears that, while on occasion rich parishes churched frequently and poor ones infrequently, more usually it was the other way round. On the whole 'about half' of mothers went in for churching 'sometimes' in these mixed and middling suburban parishes.

Churching in Three Rural Deaneries

It might be imagined that inhabitants of Godstone, Caterham and Reigate, the three deaneries out in the countryside of Surrey, far from the disturbance of city pressure or suburban population change, would support a traditional ceremony such as the churching of women. These were extremely small communities. Populations of under 1,000 are found in twelve parishes in 1936 (three of them under 500 strong), and in nine still in 1951, with a further six remaining below 2,000. Far from taking in immigrants with their unfamiliar ways, many were losing people during these twenty years; St Mary's, Farleigh [s1/c3] fell from 100 to 80, St James, Titsey [s2/c3], from 163 to 119, and Ss Peter & Paul, Nutfield [s2/c2] from 1,093 to 953. Would women in these parishes not have felt obliged to follow the traditional churching rite when living so under their neighbours' eye? Not so: for it turns out that these predominantly rural parishes are all shaded 'low frequency' on the churching map. A number did apparently contain conservative, church-going folk, as in Reigate's main church of St Mary [s2/c1] where the congregation, a mixture of 'moderately wealthy and poor' was reported in 1936 to have 'many earnest Christian workers' even though they were found lacking in 'aggressive witness'. But it appears that this was not always the case: the vicar of St Margaret, Chipstead [s3/c1] a parish of 'landowners, businessmen, gardeners, chauffeurs, and labouring villagers (really poor)', regretted that 'large numbers come only to the great festivals'. Well-attended or not, both these churches had a low churching record ('very little' and 'not good') in 1951.[30]

It was in these parishes that the churching rite's decline was mentioned most. Several clergy recorded particularly low rates. The Revd W. Palmer-Godwin, in place since 1926 at St Luke's, Reigate [s2/c1], thought that it was 'nothing like a few years ago'. In Godstone deanery the scattered nature of the parish of St Nicholas, Godstone [s2/c1] seems to have discouraged the wives of agricultural workers from coming to be churched; it was 'suggested to all but often postponed'. The vicar of Holy Trinity, Redhill [s2/c] observed that there was 'much less

[30] St Mary, Reigate, XII l 151; St Margaret, Chipstead, XII l 6.

here than in, say, Bermondsey'. Churching was not being maintained at all in the tiny parish of St James, Titsey [s2/c0] which consisted in 1936 of 163 'poor agricultural workers and the Squire and his agent': the Revd S. T. Ayers simply wrote 'No babies for years'. Surely numbers were bound to decline.[31]

Yet there is evidence of support in some of Surrey's country parishes. Each deanery had at least one claiming above 66% churching [c3], and Godstone had one of 100% (c4). In St Philip, Reigate [s-/c1] the vicar wrote rather unexpectedly: 'this has recently been introduced'; close by in the parish of St Bartholomew, Leigh [s2/c3], described in 1936 as 'ten rich families, the remainder farmers and labourers', churching was being maintained in 1951 as 'the usual custom'. The vicar of St Michael, Betchworth [s3/c3], also a place of 'several large houses and a few farms, gardeners and chauffeurs etc.' wrote that 'most mothers still come' to be churched. Perhaps in explanation, he described the religious conservatism of his tiny parish of 900 souls:

> So many good church people in a village like this live in the religious and intellectual atmosphere of 60 years ago. The whole of the modern critical outlook on the Bible is not known. Sometimes I recommend modern books to them, but I find that hardly any read them.

The most enthusiastic response in the whole of Reigate archdeaconry came from St John, Outwood [s3/c4], a parish of 707 conducting only four baptisms in 1936; in what Pevsner calls this 'simple weald hamlet' churching was maintained 'fully, and recommended by many mothers'.[32]

It is hard to be certain how social class may have influenced churching rates in rural Surrey. At Christ Church, Nutfield [s3/c3] in Reigate deanery, where people had been described simply as 'rich' in 1936, churching in 1951 occurred 'in nearly every case', yet in nearby St Peter, [s2/c2] it was noted, perhaps rather dismissively, that 'working-class women are usually churched'. Nevertheless from the mixed parishes in the small deanery of Caterham come two illustrations of churching's connection with social class V: in another 'rich' parish, that of Ss Paul & Agatha, Woldingham [s3/c1], 'the better-off people come less than the poor to be churched'; while among the eighty souls in St Mary, Farleigh [s1/c3] it was 'still the custom' in a congregation described as 'all very poor except one family'.[33]

---

[31] Holy Trinity, Redhill, XII l 20; St Luke, Reigate, XII l 16; St Nicholas, Godstone, Xj4; St James, Titsey, Xj14.

[32] St Philip, Reigate, XII l 17; St Bartholomew, Leigh, XII l 10; St Michael, Betchworth, XII l 1; St John, Outwood, Xj2.

[33] Christ Church, Nutfield, XII l 14; St Peter, Nutfield, XII l 13; Ss Paul & Agatha, Woldingham, IXi15; St Mary, Farleigh, IXi11.

'TO WHAT EXTENT IS THE CHURCHING OF WOMEN STILL MAINTAINED?'

The Role of Southwark's Clergy

This survey of the churching of women in the diocese of Southwark in the mid-twentieth century demonstrates that the ceremony had by no means disappeared, but was performed, with varying degrees of frequency, in practically all parishes. Militating against its continuance was the geographical mobility of Southwark's population, in which people lost the habit of church attendance, families were scattered, and mothers no longer lived close to their daughters. In the background is the growth of a secularised culture bringing about the 'apathy and indifference' upon which these incumbents commented so frequently. To what extent, though, may the clergy themselves have contributed to churching's survival or decline?

Whether in the 1930s, a decade of unemployment, slum clearance and massive re-housing, or the early 1950s, still close to the end of devastating war, a positive outlook must often have been hard for parish clergy to sustain. As they respond to visitation questions, writing about poverty and ignorance, indifference and worldliness, occasionally also loyal and uplifting service, some display confidence and optimism, but many more a patient resignation shot through with weariness.

Attitudes to the visitations varied. Some clergy gave replies so brief as to appear impatient of the whole enterprise. The Revd Flack at St Michael, Stockwell [s1/c0] offered only the curtest of comments: 'poor' in 1936; 'not possible', 'doubtful', and 'up to a point' in 1951. Maybe this was because, in an impoverished Brixton deanery, Flack had ministered to 10,000 souls with no help from curate or woman worker since 1931. Other incumbents, on the contrary, were eager to communicate, cramming the visitation papers with figures and explanations, sometimes clipping on additional sheets of argument and suggestion. This was, after all, for the bishop's attention; and the opening words of the 1951 visitation questionnaire may have seemed encouraging:

> N.B. – the main emphasis in this visitation is on the local unit of church life in the parish and the urgent importance to our nation in present circumstances of its faith, witness and vitality. For this purpose statistics have been reduced to a minimum and some of the questions are of a searching and private nature to which a frank reply is requested in the assurance that such information will be regarded as strictly confidential and not for administrative use.

Thus reassured, some clergy felt able to be quite outspoken in their impatience with overwork, inadequate means, and the apparently unshakeable indifference of their parishioners. In the visitation of 1936, when invited to write about 'difficulty and anxiety', 'happiness and hope' in their work, they had been still more candid, complaining about newcomers, flat-dwellers and women who went out to work and were never at home in the afternoons. The Revd Hutt has already been noted writing of his undisciplined flock at St Luke's, Deptford [s1/c3]. Thomas

Reakes at St Peter, Walworth [s1/c3] complained of 'materialism, poverty, jealousy, lack of sense of responsibility'; he had written earlier, in a 1929 visitation, of the problems of bringing up his children in Walworth, adding: '7 years is the outside limit for men in these inner parishes'. At the same time some Southwark clergy wanted to applaud faithful and supportive parish members, especially commending the young who had not left, though few took the robustly evangelical approach of the Revd K. Hurst of St Cyprian, Brockley [s1/c2], in place since 1922, who in 1936 answered Question 23 on whether he went in for home visiting:

> Literally no. But paying definite visits & chatting to the people in the streets does get one known in the parish after a quarter of a century! It is a joy to learn that anybody in trouble, difficulty or need seems to imagine that the vicar is the solution![34]

How did the Southwark incumbents regard the churching ceremony itself? In 1951 a few already disliked the service. Actually critical in 1936, Hutt of Deptford [s1/c3] had suggested: 'The Churching service is unsuitable and needs revision. Especially choice of Psalm. Could *Magnificat* be said by those being churched?' The Revd G. Hudson at Holy Cross, Raynes Park [s-/c2] echoed this desire for change: 'Little used apart from its regular use by church folk. We would welcome a service of thanksgiving in place of the present office'. At St John the Evangelist, Caterham [s3/c2] the Revd Longton had already 'slightly altered' the service 'as it is an act of thanksgiving'. Possibly they wished to cut out intimations of purification that they felt had become unacceptable. These reactions apart, readiness was the prevailing attitude. Churching was noted throughout as a normal part of parochial routine, 'habitual with the majority of mothers' (Ss Andrew & Michael, Greenwich [c1/c3]). This was the case in at least one parish in each of the twenty-five Southwark deaneries, and churchings were fitted in 'whenever required' 'by appointment', 'Tuesday evenings', 'Wednesdays at 4.0pm', 'Saturdays at noon'. A certain number of clergy in both town and country areas emphasised their success, some connecting churching with baptism, a few inviting both parents to attend.[35]

In nine out-of-town deaneries clergy seem to have been making some effort, as they claimed that churching had been 'suggested', 'taught' and 'urged', 'instructed', 'explained' and 'encouraged', often after baptism. And here and there throughout the visitation epithets such as 'strong', 'habitual', 'prevalent'; 'very popular', and 'it flourishes' claim continuing success for this childbirth rite.

Even so, thirty-three clergy (nearly ten per cent of those responding) noted the ceremony's decline in brief phrases: 'nothing like a few years ago', 'it is largely diminishing', 'the number has dropped this year', 'often neglected by the present

[34] St Peter's, Walworth, Ve21; D/S/VB/010, Visitation, 1929; for the St Cyprian, Brockley Rise reference v. note 25.
[35] D/S/VB/012, Visitation, 1936, St Luke, Deptford XVI lq3; Holy Cross, Raynes Park, Vin3; St John the Evangelist, Caterham, IXi2; Ss Andrew & Michael, Greenwich, XVIIaq12.

generation', 'rarely asked for', 'losing ground', 'declining very fast', 'much rarer than formerly'. Remarks of this nature were distributed throughout the visitation replies, again occurring in at least one parish in every deanery. No regrets were expressed, and only a few suburban and rural clergy offered any explanation: the Revd Jenkins, vicar of Croydon deanery's St Mary, Sanderstead [s2/c1] since 1935, thought that it was to do with the area, saying that churching there was now 'very seldom, as compared with the "inner circle" parishes'; the Revd S. Isaacson of St Paul, Plumstead [s-/c2] wrote of the different thanksgivings offered by the maternity hospital in Woolwich.[36]

In words such as 'many', 'most', 'usually' and 'often', the part played by maternity hospitals in delivering churching services as well as babies was emphasized by twenty-eight clergy (eight per cent of those responding). Some welcomed their contribution; the Revd T. A. Young, vicar of St Michael & All Angels, Woolwich [s1/c3] was himself chaplain at Woolwich Maternity Hospital. From St Barnabas, Dulwich [s2/c3] the Revd Brown wrote of '500 a year at the hospital', adding that 'cards sent home to parishes notifying this' were welcomed. For clergy, as well as mothers, hospital confinements that reduced the pain and danger of childbirth must have been a bonus; and many struggling with large parishes, particularly those still offering frequent services, were probably relieved to have churching taken off their hands. This may have been suggested by the Revd Crockford when he wrote from St George, Westcombe Park [s1/c3]: 'when not churched in hospital, I have the service in church.' Only the Revd Ross at St John the Evangelist, Malden [s2/c2] was less pleased: 'We church about 50% of all mothers, but then the others are churched (regrettably) in hospital'. One is left to speculate about this regret: whether it was about the loss of immediate contact with a new baby who might eventually become a churchgoing member of the parish; the non-payment of an offering which could amount to as much as 1*s*. or 1/6*d*. in this area; or another blow to the church's perceived pastoral significance.[37]

Of the mothers who were churched it is difficult to catch from this 1951 visitation more than a fleeting glimpse. Incumbents often described how the women themselves 'ask, 'desire', 'request' or 'demand' the ceremony, and they were aware that this might be from a variety of motives. Two, at St Mary, Beddington [s3/c2] and St John, Outwood [s3/c4] mentioned the influence of grandmothers; and at St Saviour, Battersea [s1/c3] the Revd Sergeant wrote 'Nearly all (Midwives see they do)', these presumably in domiciliary as well as hospital work.[38] To some women being churched clearly mattered: at nearby St Peter, Battersea [s1/c3] it was 'considered more important than baptism'. But others were apparently reluc-

[36] St Mary, Sanderstead, IXai12; St Paul, Plumstead, XIXs10.
[37] St Michael & All Angels, Woolwich, XIXs2; St Barnabas, Dulwich, XVIp3; St George, Westcombe Park, XVIIq13; St John the Evangelist, Malden, XIk16.
[38] St Mary, Beddington, VIIh1; St John, Outwood, Vj2; St Saviour, Battersea Park, Ia14.

tant to fit it in: the vicar of Christ Church, South Nutfield [s3/c3] wrote: 'In nearly every case I find the suggestion welcomed, but with some I have failed'; while the mothers belonging to St Mary, Welling [s-/c2] were suspected of resorting to deceit in order to avoid the ceremony: The hapless incumbent wrote:

> All women who bring their babies for baptism are encouraged to be "churched". I think many say they have been churched but have not.[39]

Where it was offered, testimony was divided over whether it was churchgoing women who were most likely to be churched, as at St Swithun, Woodcote [s-/c2], and at both St Andrew [s3/c2] and St Saviour [s-/c2], Limpsfield; or 'women who rarely come to church', as at St Cyprian, Brockley Rise [s1/c2]. The Revd Thamford, vicar of the parish of St Andrew, Earlsfield [s1/c3] clearly ran a popular churching service:

> I find people from other parishes come to be churched. I suppose the time suits them, 10.0 am daily.

There were remarkably few comments about the class to which churched women belonged, apart from 'particularly with the poorer class' at St John the Evangelist, Kingston [s2/c2], 'mostly the poorest' at St Silas, Nunhead [s1/c2], and 'the women belonging to the older families in the parish still desire to be churched' at St Peter's, Petersham [s3/c2]; it is not entirely clear to which class these families might belong in this 'rich, middle class and prosperous working-class' parish.[40]

Thirteen clergy made the interesting observations that churching was in some way involved with women's 'superstitious' beliefs. Two among them made clear exactly what this meant. The Revd C. Rowe of Emmanuel, West Dulwich [s2/c3] wrote in answer to Question 7: 'considerable, largely owing to superstition about not crossing other women's doorsteps, but some more genuine'; while at The Ascension, Blackheath [s2/c3] the Revd J. F. Wedmore judged that the 'purpose of being churched is almost universally regarded as rendering them fit to go shopping etc'. For the rest, 'superstition' is a possible motive for churching: 'still regularly used, often perhaps from semi-superstitious motives'; 'by most people, I presume largely on account of superstition'; 'as a superstition, very prevalent'. Only in the parish of St Barnabas, Coulsdon [s-/c3] was it firmly (but perhaps revealingly) ruled out: 'most women, but no superstition in the practice'.[41]

[39] St Peter, Battersea, Ia7; Christ Church, South Nutfield, XII l 14; St Mary, Welling, XVI-IIs21.
[40] St Swithun, Woodcote, IXai10; St Andrew, Limpsfield, Xj8; St Saviour, Limpsfield, Xbj8; for St Cyprian, Brockley Rise, v. note 30; St Andrew, Earlsfield, VIIg6; St John the Evangelist, Kingston, XIk3; St Silas, Nunhead, XVo13; St Peter, Petersham, XIIIm2.
[41] Emmanuel, West Dulwich, XVIp8; The Ascension, Blackheath, VXIIIr13; St Barnabas, Coulsdon, IXai4.

'TO WHAT EXTENT IS THE CHURCHING OF WOMEN STILL MAINTAINED?'

Sarah Williams has discussed this question of superstition in relation to churching in her book *Religious Belief and Popular Culture in Southwark, c.1880–1939*. In some cases she found women in the deanery who believed that in being churched they were performing a rite that would ensure good luck, having been told to do so by their (superstitious) mothers. They were also doing their duty to God, and asserting their membership of the local church. Williams tells how one mother 'specifically associated the ritual with the avoidance of bad luck'; while another related in a vivid passage how she accompanied her friend who had been sent on a foggy November night to find a place to be churched before she might be allowed to enter her own mother's house. Jeffrey Cox found in Lambeth during the same period little 'evidence of the semi-pagan magic and superstition which historians have discovered among English villagers in the early nineteenth century'; by this time it had subsided into 'luck', as with the determination to be churched:

> In these matters as in everything else associated with popular religion, evidence is scanty and motives were almost certainly mixed. Respectability may have played as large a role as 'luck' along with the notion that God as well as one's neighbour was in some way pleased with the performance of sacrificial rites of passage.

Cox thought of the clergy as 'reluctant' over churching; they disapproved of 'the mother's confident expectation that the ceremony would prevent a future miscarriage'. Alan Bartlett in his work on Bermondsey, while discussing the area's struggle to recover after the devastation of the Second World War, noted only the continuing popularity of weddings and 'surge of popularity of rites of passage, eg. "Thanksgivings" and funerals', despite the loss of the old community and as yet imperfect development of any replacement. The area found itself in 'a world of uncertainty and isolation'. It is noticeable that the parishes dealt with by these three historians had high churching levels, confirming the rite's long endurance through this period of significant transition and difficulty.[42]

By 'superstition' clergy almost certainly meant belief in 'good luck' that would give the new mother protection from various forms of ill-fortune that might befall her. Looking into the meaning and significance of the term, and its connection with religion, four young sociologists held a series of interviews in the 1960s in the borough of Islington. Their conclusions, based on an admittedly small sample, may throw some light on answers given to the 1951 visitation. They concluded that it was women rather than men who were superstitious; women in the working class rather than the middle class; and women who were not churchgoers rather than regular attenders. Though 'about a quarter of our religious respon-

[42] Williams, *Religious Belief and Popular Culture*, pp. 89–97; Cox, *The English Churches*, pp. 97–9; Bartlett, 'Churches in Bermondsey', pp. 380–1.

dents were found in the very superstitious group', they were likely to be non-attenders, since 'going to church reduced the proportions of superstitiousness among people who prayed', as 'the church exercises a genuinely counter-superstitious influence among its adherents'. Finally the authors hazarded the notion that superstitiousness is liable to increase in times of anxiety such as war, uncertainty or depression, and that 'one would expect people who are least able to control their situation to be most superstitious', this being the lot of women dealing with the insecurities of working class life:

> The women need the security most because they have to feed and rear the children yet there is little they can do to obtain it except rely on their husbands.[43]

This idea could lead to an understanding of the grandmother whose daughter has married, gone to live in her own home, and given birth to her own child: insisting on a churching is one way in which she may be able to maintain, or regain, some of the control that she has lost over her daughter, and to bring her back, however briefly, into the culture of the community in which she grew up, a life where her mother was in charge. It will be seen in Chapter Five that such ideas fit in well with the oral testimony of mothers and grandmothers.

Table XVII, below, summarizes all references to superstition in the 1951 visitation. It is noticeable that eleven (85%) of the parishes in this list, have a social code of [s1] ('very poor' to 'moderately poor'), and nine (69%) one of [c3] that records 'frequent' churching. This might seem to confirm a general conclusion that superstition is a largely working-class phenomenon. In these records at least, it can generally be associated with a high level of churching.

The Significance of the Southwark Visitations and of the Year 1951

Here in the middle of the twentieth century is a unique set of statements about the churching of women made by Southwark's incumbents, dealing with the extent of the practice and revealing their attitudes towards its continuance. Among the 1951 visitation replies, neat, scribbled, occasionally typed, can be found the wide variety of churching regimes, and some ideas about their meaning. Answers to the 1936 visitation provide an account of social context. Inner London's parishes are discovered in the distress of unemployment and poverty, while its outer suburbs are seen to have been destabilised by the arrival of settlers, working people of all classes who have moved in to new homes and occupations. The remoter rural areas of the diocese are still composed largely of labourers and artisans living alongside their wealthy employers. In the 1951 returns it is possible to

---

[43] Nicholas Abercrombie, John Baker, Sebastian Brett and Jane Foster, 'Superstition and Religion: the God of the Gaps', in David Martin and Michael Hill (eds), *A Sociological Yearbook of Religion in Britain,* 3 (SCM Press, 1970), pp. 121–3.

Table XVII: Distribution of superstition references in the 1951 Visitation returns

Parish	code	deanery	comment
Suburban Deaneries			
Wimbledon, All Saints	s1/c3	Merton	'as a superstition, very prevalent'
E. Dulwich, St Clement	s1/c1	Dulwich	'still a lingering superstition'
W. Dulwich, Emmanuel	s2/c3	Dulwich	'considerable, owing largely to superstition about not crossing other women's doorsteps, but some more genuine'
Blackheath, Ascension	s2/c3	E. Lewisham	'purpose ... rendering them fit to go shopping etc.'
Brockley, St Cyprian	s1/c2	E. Lewisham	'how this is far due to superstition ... I cannot say'
Urban Deaneries			
Deptford, Ss Paul & Mark	s1/c3	Deptford	'very popular superstition'
Southwark, St Stephen	s1/c3	Southwark	'it flourishes to a superstitious degree'
Camberwell, Emmanuel	s1/c3	Camberwell	'by most I imagine largely on account of superstition'
Peckham, St Chrysostom	s1/c3	Camberwell	'often perhaps from semi-superstitious motives'
Camberwell, St James	s1/c3	Brixton	'most seem to regard it in a superstitious way'
Stockwell Grn, St Andrew	s1/c3	Brixton	'many churchings but largely due to superstition'
Lambeth, All Saints	s1/c2	Lambeth	'about 1 in 4 ... a good deal of superstition'
Kennington Hill, St Peter	s–/c2	Lambeth	'a superstition about it very general'
Other References to Superstition			
Coulsdon, St Barnabas	s–/c3	Croydon South	'no superstition in the practice'
Plumstead, St Nicholas	s1/c4	Plumstead	'Sacrement of Baptism is largely regarded as superstitious'

catch up with thirty-seven clergy who had been in place since at least 1936 (in the earliest case since 1919) struggling to re-establish the life of their parishes after the physical devastation of war and dispersal of old communities.

The two visitations illuminate some challenges which faced religion in the mid-twentieth-century. Both took place at a time when the Church of England was still striving, with mixed success, to achieve its evangelical targets and maintain its national significance. This can be illustrated for the years between 1918 and 1951 in the diocese of Southwark's history. Alan Bartlett has analysed how the church in the inner urban area of Bermondsey lost authority and power between the wars. Short of funds, its clergy had to cut back on their social projects; lacking manpower they could no longer attend all the meetings or support the old organisations in parishes and settlements. Deterred by the middle-class leadership of church social organisations, their working-class parishioners were choosing to join the new London County Council committees with their egalitarian atmosphere, driven by municipal socialism rather than overt Christianity. Bartlett also illustrates how, at the same time, the lives of women were changing in Bermondsey. Young girls were becoming liberated from long-established traditions of matriarchal supervision:

> ... this closely confined culture, of which the Church was an integral part, was slow to break down, not least because of the continued grip of poverty, but it was to dissolve in the face of freer social mores, wider leisure opportunities, smaller families and increased prosperity.[44]

These were two important challenges: the growth of a confident, secular socialist ideology, which was already flowering in the 1950s in national and local politics; and changes in the lives of women, for long the main participants in parish life, now leading more independent lives, with less time or inclination to keep in touch with the world of their upbringing.

By 1951 the Anglican church was approaching not so much a frontier as marcher country. There was no great clash of arms between the old participating communities and the new individualism which was to contribute to their decline; but the battle to reclaim the indifferent was being lost. Bishops of Southwark had been checking the situation in visitations since 1911. One of the most distinguished among their number, Bishop Cyril Foster Garbett (1919–32) was to write from York in 1953, of 'a general retreat in Christianity' which went back at least to the beginning of the century. He saw it largely in institutional terms: a loss of ordinands since the War; a 'falling off of late by the upper class, in suburbs and villages':

> with the passing of power from the old aristocracy, from the manor and the squire, the church has lost channels through which it might influence the nation. With the diminution of the powers of the House of Lords the political influence of the bishops who at one time crowded the episcopal benches has been greatly reduced.

Garbett reckoned that 'the Christian ethic is no longer regarded as universally binding', and wrote of men questioning 'the truth of ancient tradition', as they developed 'acquisitiveness and materialism, mass amusements and the fear of silence'. Looking back on his earlier days in Portsea he wished that clergy could deal with parochial indifference as he had, through relentless visiting:

> When I was first ordained I was taught to visit four hours on five days of the week. My fellow curates did the same; and when after ten years I became vicar of the same parish I expected the tradition of visiting to continue.

He and his successors in the diocese of Southwark had tried to instil this into their parish clergy, with the mixed results recorded in the 1936 and 1951 visitations. In 1953, now an archbishop, he seemed to concede that it was 'no longer possible' for the old structures of influence to prevail either at national or parochial level.[45]

Southwark's visitations of 1936 and 1951 were peppered with clerical reaction to these problems; nevertheless, the returns on churching in 1951 showed that the church was retaining something of its power, and at least this parish ritual was still taking place 'to a surprising extent'.[46] Quite apart from the testimony

[44] Bartlett, 'Churches in Bermondsey', pp. 323–5.
[45] Cyril Garbett, *The Church of England Today* (London, 1953), pp. 29–68.
[46] St Luke, Eltham Park, XIXs17.

of the visitation, analysis of the three Southwark parishes that have left detailed churching records for as late as this shows that, in two at least, numbers were holding up well: at St John the Evangelist, Blackheath [s2/c1] there were nineteen churchings in 1931, and seventeen in 1951; while Christ Church, Brixton [s1/c3] held sixteen in 1931 and eighteen in 1950. Between the same years at St Mary Magdalen, Mortlake [s2/c2] they had dropped from seventy-two to only nineteen. In 1971 the latter two parishes recorded only a couple of churchings each; by then the Blackheath register was no longer being kept.

In his recent study *The Death of Christian Britain* Callum Brown also sees the 1950s as the ultimate period of the ecclesiastical 'world we have lost': still a time of sustained church attendance, based on surviving belief, where churches maintained moral authority and were even enjoying a recent surge of support:

> Christian Britain survived into the 1950s with a medley of well-observed rites, some of which were stronger than they had been in 1800 or 1850.

Time and again he claims that these were still years of conservatism and maternal authority; that most women had not been liberated from former constraints by the experiences of war; even 'the discourse of modernisation was in fact riddled with traditionalism'. Well-chosen literary discourses serve to illustrate his theme: home and family remained central; magazines stayed with cookery, motherhood and gardening; fiction with catching a husband. He is adamant that secularization had not yet entered its final phase; popular religion remained strong; there was as yet 'no great haemorrhage'; not until the end of the decade, from 1958, did all indices begin a decline, which entered 'free fall' from 1963, 'levelled off' in the 1970s and 1980s, then became 'catastrophic' in the 1990s.[47] In their depiction of the early- to mid-twentieth century parish these visitation replies could have supplied evidence for both Garbett and Brown in support of their different judgments. Some Southwark clergy tell of devastating loss to parish stability and attendance between 1930 and 1951, but others point to remarkable vitality through these years of hardship, change, and mighty shock.

But by the 1960s and 1970s an enquiry such as that in 1951's Question 7 could almost have been dismissed as an anachronism. Already liturgical debates and experiments were preparing to make changes, among them altering the form and meaning of the churching service. Six Southwark clergy were openly dissatisfied and had recommended in the 1951 visitation that the rite should be changed, and the element that offered thanks to God given more emphasis. The Revd Sixton at St Mary Magdalen, Bermondsey [s1/c4] wrote, 'We use a form of Thanksgiving for the Birth of a Child compiled by the Bp. of Sheffield'; and the Revd Huston at Emmanuel, Sidlow Bridge, Reigate [s2/c1] said that he used a Thanksgiving,

[47] Callum Brown, *The Death of Christian Britain: Understanding Secularization 1900–2000* (London and New York, 2001), pp. 1–15, 168–9, 172–3, 188–9.

though 'this has not the Bishop's permission'. 'Use P.B. but add a short extempore prayer', was in the reply of the Revd Wiglan at St Mark, Camberwell [s1/c3], while the Revd Longton at St John the Evangelist, Caterham [s3/c2] ran a service 'slightly altered, husband too, as it is an act of Thanksgiving'; the Revds Egan at St Saviour [s2/c1] and Hudson at Holy Cross, [s-/c2], both at Raynes Park, agreed that something new was needed.[48] When it appeared in the Alternative Service Prayer Book of 1980, the new service was indeed an unambiguous 'Thanksgiving'.

---

[48] St Mary Magdalen, Bermondsey IIb7: Emmanuel, Sidlow Bridge, Reigate XII l 121; St Mark, Camberwell XVo7; St John the Evangelist, Caterham IXi2; St Saviour VIn3 and Holy Cross VI an3, both of Raynes Park.

CHAPTER FIVE

CHURCHING DISCOVERED THROUGH PERSONAL TESTIMONY

Here the churching rite is brought to life by personal testimony. In interviews, letters, conversations and questionnaire replies, women and clergy told what they could remember about the ceremony and offered their (sometimes outspoken) comments about its meaning and long survival.[1] The questionnaire and a summary of replies obtained in the first stage of research are found in the two following tables; the replies formed the focus of later enquiry and discussion, all of which confirmed that the rite of churching had been part of parish routine and family life in all parts of the country and through almost the whole of the twentieth century.[2]

Location, Distribution, Timing

Questionnaire answers identified churching in forty-six places (counties, towns, suburbs and villages) with a 5:3 predominance of rural over urban areas. Clergy, often recalling their curacies and first incumbencies, wrote of many different locations: of churching among 'the fishing community' near Caistor-on-Sea and also Cleethorpes; 'workhouse visits' at Cannock, Staffordshire; gipsy women at Evesham and Llandaff, and 'fairground people' visiting Bloomsbury.[3]

Churching dates cropped up in every decade from 1910 onwards, the numbers rising (along with the reach of memory) from two in the 1910s to a peak of thirteen in the 1940s and then falling back (as instances declined) to one each in the 1970s and 1980s.

On differentiation the words of one cleric summed up the feelings of most, that 'the lower the socio-economic group, the more churchings' took place. Another offered the verdict that churching 'has largely died out among better-educated people but continues in rural communities and close-knit working class urban areas'. It was said to be common in Hull, 'still a close-knit largely working-

---

[1] A list of contributors may be found in *Personal testimony*, pp. 137–8.
[2] See the Preface, p. 1.
[3] Taken from an interview in Benson, Oxfordshire, in December, 1997, describing churching in Caistor-on-Sea, 1940s; letters about churching in Cleethorpes, 1959; Cannock, 1961; Stafford, 1955; Essex, 1942–7; Broad Clyst, Devon, 1977; Evesham, 'quite recently'; Llandaff, 1958; Bloomsbury, undated; and Lincoln, 1948.

Table XVIII: The Churching Questionnaire

1. Location, Distribution, Timing
Location: are there any areas where you know that Churching has been widely practised?
Are there any areas where you know that it was practised, but not widely?
Are there any areas where, as far as you know, it has not occurred at all?

Distribution: does there seem to have been any differentiation –
– between rural and urban areas?
– between classes or occupational groups?

Timing: can you give any particular date(s) when you know that Churching occurred?
– when it was widespread? Or occasional? Or not going on at all?

2. The Ceremony
In any churchings that you know about
– did the mothers attend alone?   – with the new baby?
                                 – with the father?
                                 – with any of the wider family?
                                 – with friends?
– did they wear anything special?   – cover their heads?
– did they pay a fee to the clergyman?
– or sit in a special place in church?

3. Transmission of Information about Churching
As far as you know, how did women learn about the ceremony?
– from their mothers?   – both parents?
– any of the wider family?   – neighbours?
– the midwife?   – the clergy?

4. Understanding and Interpretation
What did women understand the ceremony to be about?
– purely personal thanksgiving to God for a safe delivery?
– something to please mother / the family / the community?
– duty / obedience to the church?
– something to do with purification which had to be seen to after childbirth?
Feelings about the Ceremony:
– pleased / proud?
– indifferent? It was just routine?
Do you know of anyone who, when requested, refused to undertake the ceremony at all?
Do you know on what grounds they might have objected to it?

5. Sanctions and the Climate of Opinion
– Can you give any examples of any understanding (or warning) that new mothers would not be allowed out, or into other people's homes, until they had been churched?
– or that unchurched mothers might bring bad luck?
– or that their children would not thrive?

Table XIX: Summary of Questionnaire Responses

1. Location, Distribution, Timing

– 46 places were mentioned (counties, towns, villages). No comment on rural/urban concentration.

– 4 mention 'working class'; others 'lower class' - *'uneducated', 'the lower the socio-economic group, the more churchings'; 'more prevalent with non-churchgoing families'* ; 2 refer to 'middle classes'.

– many churching dates, sometimes several on one sheet:

decade:	1910s	1920s	1930s	1940s	1950s	1960s	1970s	1980s
no. of churchings	2	7	9	13	11	10	1	1

2. The Ceremony
– 23 attended churchings alone: 8 with their mothers or mothers-in-law: 4 with husbands.
– 11 took the baby along.
– 12 paid fees or gave donations; in two cases it was demanded, otherwise optional.
– 10 covered their heads and/or wore their best clothes.
– 13 went to a special place (Lady Chapel, altar rails, by the font, in a side chapel, at the back of the church, in the front pew).

3. Transmission of Information about Churching
– 34 that it came mostly from their own mothers or mothers-in-law.
– 11 that it came from clergy.
– 4 that it came from a friend, grandmothers, wider family, or midwife.
– 11 that it was 'just known about' *('I was brought up knowing that')*.

4. Understanding and Interpretation
– 23 that it was a 'purely personal' thanksgiving to God.
– 8 that it was something to please the family.
– 7 that it was done from duty or obedience *('we were young, but would never agree now')*
– 11 were concerned / warned about cleansing / purification.

Feelings about the Ceremony:
– 28 had pleased / proud feelings about the ceremony.
– 11 were indifferent or felt that it was 'just routine'.
– 2 knew of refusals on account of shyness and self-consciousness, or denominational hostility *('My Mum was scornful, being a Methodist')*.

5. Sanctions and the Climate of Opinion
– 12 were not allowed out until they had been churched.
– 8 were warned that there would be back luck, or that the child would not thrive, if not churched.

class place, and more traditional than many other English towns', and in Stretford, Lincolnshire where it 'involved working-class girls who were doing what their mothers told them'.⁴ On the other hand, in an accompanying letter, an undeniably middle-class event was recalled in Leicester, in 1951, where one incumbent's mother was churched when he himself was twelve:

> ... and so were those of my prep-school chums ... in four cases known to me (and including my own mother's Churching), the officiating priest was invited back to the family house to bless the infant and partake in a simple meal which was attended by close family members (viz grand-fathers and god-fathers).⁵

Clergy were the only respondents who could indicate the frequency of churching. In the late 1950s, 'rarely was there a week when no-one came for this' from the fishing families of Cleethorpes, or Caistor-on-Sea. From the 1950s to 1980s it was 'common' in South London, 'routine' in South and East Yorkshire, 'often found' in Stockport, Congleton and Spalding, 'continuing' in Hull and Broad Clyst, Devon. Most had tried to fit it into a routine, carrying it out 'by appointment', 'fifteen minutes before baptisms', 'on Wednesdays', 'at 11.0 am. on Fridays', '10.0 am. every Wednesday and Friday', 'most Monday afternoons'; but some faced women arriving with 'urgent' requests 'at any time'.

The Ceremony

Women had much to say about their experience of the churching ceremony. A majority of twenty-three respondents had attended alone, eight with mothers or mothers-in-law, four with husbands. About one-third of them had paid fees, worn appropriate clothes, covered their heads, and sat or knelt in a special place in the church. This might be a pew right at the front, at the back, next to the font, or in the Lady Chapel. Nearly all letters confirmed the private and unceremonious nature of the churching rite in mid-century.

Transmission of Information about Churching

Who saw to it that new mothers continued to be churched? A majority of both women and clergy respondents were quite certain that they would have been directed by someone in the family, most probably mother, mother-in-law or grandmother. To eleven others it was the clergy who told these women of the importance of the churching rite. A further eleven reckoned that it was 'just known about'.

Understanding and Interpretation

Questionnaire replies contained a wide range of interpretations. In many, these were quite straightforward: women had been to their churchings in a spirit of

---

[4] Letters from Hull and Stretford.
[5] Letter from Leicester, October, 2000, about churchings around 1951.

thanksgiving, pleased, proud and grateful about their successful childbirth. Family background was clearly of great importance, the urging of grandmothers obviating the need for any particular enquiry about the ceremony's meaning by the new mother. To eleven, it was 'just routine'. Memories of opposition broke into a few replies: from eight women who could see little point in churching apart from pleasing the family; and from eleven who had reacted critically to any idea of purification. Two women, writing jointly, added their regrets: 'We were young, but would never agree now'. Only two outright refusals were remembered, one arising from the new mother's shyness and self-consciousness, the other discouraged by her Methodist grandmother.

Sanctions and the Climate of Opinion

Here, over a dozen replies became truly revealing, as women, having been through their memories of the whole question of churching in the first four questions, were moved to frankness by the fifth. Their reactions had ranged from bafflement to outrage as they told of being confined at home and forbidden to see friends and family members until after they were churched, and of the warnings of bad luck to themselves, their own mothers, or the baby.

Altogether this initial response to the subject was of immense value. As well as facts about places and numbers, women offered recollected feeling and opinion; memories of their relief that childbirth was over, some questioning about the urgency with which churching had to be accomplished, and their own combination of amusement, indignation and scepticism about those threats of ill-luck if it should be delayed. Clergy wrote of the ambivalent meaning of the service, and expressed surprise that it had continued for so long. Most were relieved that it has been superseded by a more general type of thanksgiving, though some had been glad to offer the church's comfort to women in this time of heightened anxiety and stress. Insights were offered into what it is in society that has prolonged its use: survival of close-knit communities, unbreakable tradition, matriarchal power.

On the whole, these lines of recollection and interpretation were to be confirmed rather than altered by later testimony as the study moved on to look at evidence from personal correspondence and conversations, both continuing to contact those who had already replied, and finding a host of others who lived in the 'churching parishes' of Southwark and the three counties. All were invited to say how they had come to know about the churching rite, what the experience had been like (whether for mother or priest), and how they understood its meaning and significance. Again and again, the same topics emerged: insistence of mothers, obedience of daughters, power of tradition and superstitious fear of ill-luck, willingness of clergy to undertake a ritual that parishioners asked for. Occasionally daughters are defiant, and incumbents uneasy as they confront the notion of female purification.

Further Testimony, from Women

Among women in the three counties mention of churching was to generate vivid recollections and many comments. In Staffordshire such oral contributions were particularly rich, and especially welcome, given the scarcity of its written records. They came from nine women gathered in Cheddleton in a monthly knitting group and luncheon club; gatherings of roughly the same number who stayed on to talk in the church after mid-week services in Stone and Lichfield; six who were present in Burton-upon-Trent at the opening of a new church café and drop-in centre one Saturday morning; and three or four at meetings arranged in Norton-in-the-Moor (near Cheddleton) and in Wednesbury. In Longton, Eccleshall and Stafford individual women were visited or telephoned. All contacts were organised with the help of the local incumbents: they were with known churchgoing women, who were of an age to remember when churching was normal practice.

For members of the Cheddleton knitting group the understanding was simply that churching 'was the thing that you did': 'when you'd had a child you came to church to be churched; it was a thing that my mother told me'. All had thought the ceremony to be primarily a thanksgiving for a safe delivery; but they also had memories of sanctions (largely being kept inside at home) which were to do with 'being unclean'. One their number, who came from Eccleshall, had not been allowed in to Christmas dinner in the 1960s; another, from Cheddleton, remembered being shut out of her own mother's house as she arrived to visit with her new twins on her way home from hospital. They nodded as a fellow tricoteuse, this time from Stafford, recalled her confusion and disbelief when she was told 'that you were unclean until you'd been to church'.

Pressure would come from church and family combined. A conversation with a member of the congregation in St Chad, Litchfield about the churchings of two of her friends revealed elements of genuine thanksgiving, some sort of superstition, and obedience to vicar, mother and mother-in-law:

> She had her baby in the '60s, and it was insisted upon by the church [author asked 'here?'] no, St Mary's; [it was] insisted upon that they should go into the church; taught by the church that they should. But she went in with the vicar Mr Creswell; the difference being that the lady who – the other lady I spoke to you (about) – was not a churchgoer but was well into this procedure. She had to call in to the church. I said, 'will you go in with anybody?' and she said, it might be the person who was driving them, transporting them; there wouldn't have been a priest there at that time. And I said, 'should you go in and just say a prayer?'; and I said, 'what was your prayer about?', and she said it was just a prayer saying thank you for a safe delivery. And she said 'Ooh', she said, 'yes, if I hadn't done that my mother wouldn't have allowed me in the house; I could go to my own house but not to anybody else's.' I said, 'was this a sort of superstition?' And she said, 'oh no'. And I said, 'what would have happened if you'd gone to your mother-in-law's house and you hadn't been churched?' And she said, 'Oh she would have

had bad luck'. So it is a superstition, isn't it?

Similarly, a recently-churched Cheddleton mother described herself as very close to her own mother, aunt and sisters, and attached to the church since she was a child. Her maternal grandmother and grandfather, a sidesman, were 'great churchgoers', as was her uncle who rang the bells. Maternal and family direction were all-important to her.[6]

In London, women's testimony was harder to find. This was partly because of recent parish history. Several vicars wrote that they knew no parishioners who had attended their churches for longer than around fifteen years. St Paul, Upper Holloway had been destroyed in 1940 and never rebuilt; its old parishioners would have to be sought in neighbouring St Saviour, Stroud Green, whose vicar thought that he would not recognise them. In All Souls, Langham Place; St Mary, Bow; and St John the Baptist, Hoxton, no individual women were found who could help with this research. Lucille Barber, parishioner and historian of Christ Church, North Brixton, could suggest no people who would remember even the recent past from which they might provide testimony on churching. Because of profound changes in the community and crises in the running of the church early in the 1970s, there is 'no-one left from the old days'.[7] However, social gatherings were found at St John the Evangelist Fellowship Group, Blackheath, and a luncheon club at St Chad, Haggerston; two sisters were consulted at St Anne, Shoreditch; and individuals were interviewed at St Peter, Hammersmith; Emmanuel, West Hampstead; and St John the Evangelist, Walworth.

On the whole, London women described their churching experience quite freely, but with perhaps more detachment and less relish than in Staffordshire. This may be because at the time few had been living in their original home parish, and so most had been far from pressure and encouragement of mothers and close family. Many had suffered disruption of community and family life in the Second World War. Hospital sisters and chaplains emerged as family substitutes, directing several women in the Haggerston group to churchings in the 1940s to 1960s. None had been churched in Haggerston itself. Four were matter-of-fact about the whole subject, and one perhaps confused it with baptism:

> – Yes that's the first thing that happens, you've got to be churched first, then you can take the baby out, yes.

> – When I had my son, my first one [1954], in Barts: when you come out the sister makes the appointments for the churching and you go down to the chapel. ... and if you haven't been churched when you come home, you go

[6] Comments from Groups in Cheddleton, Lichfield and Burton-upon-Trent; interviews in Eccleshall, Stafford and Lichfield, August 2004.

[7] Lucille Barber, *Chronicles of Christ Church, North Brixton, 1855–2002*, Vol. 3 (London, 2002); written testimony of ex-vicar of Christ Church, North Brixton; see Chapter Six, below, p. 135.

and be churched at home.

– Yes in the mothers' home. The Salvation Army: it did the churching before you came out.

– No, I didn't have children. But I know my mother was churched in Shepherd's Bush. I never forgave her – she couldn't think of a second name, so she called me after the hospital; it was Charlotte.[8]

Several older members of the Fellowship Group in Blackheath talked of being churched; but all had been living somewhere else, and none retained more than a general, vague memory, though they became animated as they agreed that 'it had to be done'.[9] Two elderly women, of Hammersmith and West Hampstead, remembered their churchings in the 1950s, and another, of Shoreditch, her three in the 1940s. The Hammersmith testimony recalled the guidance of a much-loved mother who could always count on her daughter's obedience:

> *Author – tell me more about your mother. Did she tell you, you must be churched?*
> – Oh yes; my mother wouldn't let me go out. You come home when you've had the baby and before you go anywhere you have to be churched. My mother made the arrangements and you just go and pray for thanks – but they don't now. We all had to be churched. We had to cover our heads. Just by myself.

As in Staffordshire, there was little recollection of resistance in London. In Walworth a younger woman, still living in the street where she had grown up, with her own mother still close by, said that after the births of each of her four children in the 1970s she had welcomed the churching ceremony in the church of St John the Evangelist round the corner. She had regarded it just as a thanksgiving. Later on it was her friend, a woman minister, who said to her with some horror, 'how *could* you?', and explained about the idea of purification. The mother was intrigued, but not inclined to reject or denounce the ceremony.[10]

Testimony in Berkshire largely echoed that of the two other counties. It was gathered from meetings of Mothers' Unions, historical societies, a retirement group, and individuals in Reading, Caversham, Sonning, Wantage, Radley, Windsor, and Shellingford. An example of obedience came up in Sonning where a woman recalled how, in 1952, her mother-in-law, shocked that she was outside in the garden soon after giving birth, insisted that she had no choice but to go at once to be churched. There were also instances of compliance in Fernham and Shellingford, where maternal expectations had been made clear: one mother was churched after the birth of her son in 1980 in the nearby parish where she had

---

[8] Luncheon Group in Haggerston, February, 2004.
[9] Fellowship Group in Blackheath, February, 2004.
[10] Interviews in Hampstead, Hammersmith and Walworth; conversation in Shoreditch; January–May, 2004.

grown up and her own mother still lived:

> My mother wouldn't let me go out anywhere until I was churched and she said: right, you're not going anywhere else until you've been churched; and I had to make an appointment with the vicar.

No insistence, merely the pleasure of continuing family and parish custom, was behind three generations of churchings in Earley, Reading:

> We'd always been to church, it was a thanksgiving for bringing new life and that everything went OK. That's what I thought about it. And the same thing with my daughter; she said 'I'd like to be churched, Mum, like you were' ... I think it's family. Talking to people at church, too, I think it's family.[11]

Two more accounts of filial acquiescence came from Oxfordshire and Lancashire. One was given by a woman in her eighties who had been taken to be churched by her mother in 1928 in Garsington:

> You're not supposed to go out till you've been churched. I don't know why not. You thank God for it. My mother wouldn't have let you go outside till you'd been churched. You know'd you'd got to do that afore you 'ad a baby. Yes I was churched there. I come up to me mother, and we went up to the church. Nobody else: a special do, see. They don't do it now, my duck. We left the baby down with my sister. Yes, the vicar, Mum and me. Yes, kneels there and says your prayers and what the vicar says to you and that. I remember it as plain as yesterday. Don't have no more of that nowadays.

The second testimony came from the daughter of a Lancashire Catholic family who had travelled twice from her new home in Yorkshire to be churched in her old home parish in 1969 and 1970:

> My mother definitely was churched, and she thought it was absolutely *de rigeur* you couldn't – she came from a very devout Irish Catholic family; myself and my brother; and all her sisters, she came from a big family; and that was absolutely *de rigeur* because I still – she said 'you've got to go and be churched before the christening'. I said, 'what do you mean?' 'You've got to go to the church and be blessed before you can go out'.[12]

But there was also resistance. Not all women meekly obeyed their mothers, partly it seems because of the way in which the idea of churching was presented to them. Two elderly members of a Reading church reacted sharply against the very mention of churching, and still felt angered and affronted by the notion of purification. One offered her conclusions:

> I've been reading about, in Genesis, the idea that women were unclean, and that after childbirth they were unclean; and my mother very definitely felt

[11] Conversations with groups in Caversham and Radley, and with individuals in Reading, Sonning, Wantage, Windsor and Shellingford during 2003 and 2004.
[12] Interviews in Reading, August, 2004 and Oxfordshire, December, 2000.

that churching was a way of going because you were regarded as unclean and you were going to be purified. She never emphasised the giving side of it, only the purification side of it. I didn't feel that it was right at all because I don't think of myself as soiled by having a child. I do think that going to church and saying thank you for your baby and for your own health is lovely, but the old-fashioned view of it: well! She may have been wrong but that old-fashioned view I felt strongly was not right.'

The other added:

> That reflection [sic] of you of the fact that you're dirty and have got to be purified after having a child, how do these sort of people who believe in that expect the human race to continue?

Three further expressions of hostility were heard in oral testimony from Berkshire women. One had also been instantly offended by the whole idea of churching, which she had flatly rejected in the late 1930s; a member of the Radley Historical Society declared in July 2003 that she never wanted to go again to this 'dark, gloomy service'; and a Reading mother remembered her reaction with some feeling, even after thirty years:

> I was annoyed and upset at the first service and I thought, 'I'm not going to do that again'. I was cross and I've never forgotten it; well I was cross because I felt I'd done something wrong. Rather than have a baby and be happy about it, it felt as if it was something wrong, to me.
>
> – You'd expect to have a joyful, happy occasion with a new baby; but it wasn't. There was something about it. And reading this now I'm wondering if the clergyman who was there said something extra.
> *Author– What might he have said?*
> – I don't know. I just have that impression, that I wasn't really very happy doing it.[13]

Six women sent letters that also recorded objections to churching. One wrote from Norfolk that her mother, churched five times between 1909 and 1923, had:

> disliked the service intensely because there was 'no joy whatsoever' in it; it was just 'a matter of hygiene'.

Several others expressed a critical view of clerical demeanour during the service. The first wrote of a churching experienced in Nottingham, probably in the 1950s:

> The 'older' vicar didn't appear till 5 or 6 young Mums were kneeling at the altar. He then walked down the row holding out an offertory bag (I don't know whether they had money to put in or not). Then without any greeting he gabbled through the service, turned his back on them & walked out. Some of them had been kneeling a quarter hour and one fainted.

[13] Interviews in Radley and Reading, July and April, 2003.

CHURCHING DISCOVERED THROUGH PERSONAL TESTIMONY

A second told of a nursing colleague who had begun to move towards atheism, so shocked was she by an order from her vicar to repent and repeat the words 'I am unclean'. From Lancashire, two women 'recalled being churched with absolute horror'. They wrote their comment on the churching questionnaire:

> Both of us felt anger at being made to go through an archaic ceremony. We were young, but would never agree now. We both thought we had to have forgiveness for any sexual pleasure we received in procreation.[14]

In contrast to this hostility and indignation, some women in their oral testimony had entirely positive reactions to the churching rite with its notions of purification. They understood its purpose as re-establishing equilibrium after a nerve-racking experience. Talking on the telephone from Stafford, a mother churched in 1960, '62 and '70, explained how she understood and valued its meaning: Her mother and mother-in-law had said that you were unclean until you had been to church. She indeed felt that giving birth to her children had taken her through the pains of Hell: she was grappling on her own to bring these children into the world; maybe she doubted God. Then it was over, and she found that God had been with her. In the churching ceremony she got over the feeling of isolation. Also it was a purification of the body after the ten days' lying-in. Spiritual and bodily purification went hand-in-hand.[15]

Another, also from Staffordshire, followed similar ideas. She thought that the idea of purifying after childbirth might be connected in particular with the pain, difficulty and danger that women in childbirth endured. Women's faith might have been shaken while they were in this vulnerable state. That was why they needed this service of blessing. Her first child had been born in 1952, and had lived only for a short time:

> Oh yes, you weren't to visit anyone. Oh no, you weren't to visit anyone.
> *Author – do you know why?*
> – because you'd been in that much pain and sort of in touch with the devil.
> *Author – is that what they said?*
> – well, more or less.
> *Author – so what would happen if you went out?*
> – well, you brought bad luck to the people that you went…
> *Author – and did you believe that?*
> – no. I believe that it was really a blessing after having pulled through the time. I prefer to believe that really, it was a blessing. I mean my first baby was *spina bifida* really, you know what that is? Having lost one you were only thankful that they're alright.[16]

---

[14] 1997 letters about churching: in Poplar and Clapton, 1909–23; in Nottingham; in Milford-on-Sea, 1952; in Lancashire.
[15] Telephone interview with a mother in Stafford, August, 2004.
[16] Interviews in Burton-upon-Trent, August, 2004.

Was this superstition? Certainly both women captured the notion that during this rite of passage a mother, in her pain and isolation, might have been vulnerable to the danger of dark forces.

Recollection of huge relief after childbirth lay behind the appreciation of churching expressed in two further testimonies, from Norton-in-the-Moor, near Cheddleton:

> – I thought of it as a blessing; when I had my son I'd had a really bad time, so really I couldn't wait, I wanted to do it. I didn't regard it as a superstition, though I remember hearing people say, 'Ooh you've got to go along.' This was 1956. I was very moved by the service, because of the bad time. I'd been in bed most of the pregnancy, resting. ... I did hear about superstition, but it didn't affect me in any way.
>
> – it was just a thanksgiving, that I've had the baby after having a bad time. That's why I cried all the way through.[17]

Recalling their emotional state following the trial of childbirth led other women in their letters to support the churching rite. One had endured a stillbirth; another 'a long and traumatic birth (34 hours and a Caesarian and three weeks overdue)' leading to 'an overwhelming need to have our baby blessed'.

Straightforward belief in the importance of churching did not often arise in women's letters and conversations; but one account came from Wales concerning a mother known to have been churched in 1932. In her case, strong commitment to the church's ruling had led to her determination to be churched:

> She was very religious, not well-educated, with a blind faith in the church's teaching. She said that she would have felt very unclean and unable to go to normal church services if unchurched.

Enduring faith also lay behind the words of a woman of Barnsley, South Yorkshire, churched seven times between 1939 and 1960. She wrote:

> I have always been a big believer in churching of women ...Perhaps I am old-fashioned, but I do believe we are all in God's hands at the birth.[18]

These attitudes are still to be found even in the twenty-first century. Three women, all churched since the year 2000, were prepared to talk about their experiences. To one the rite was quite familiar: her own mother had been churched in 1960, and several of her contemporaries had been churched in the 1990s. They saw it as a purification, and were 'quite evangelistic' about it. Approaching childbirth she had found 'quite scaring; one needed faith just to get on with it'. She had untroubled births in 2000 and 2002, but was acutely aware of the danger of the process; suffering some depression after her second child was born, she could

---

[17] Group in Norton-in-the-Moor, August, 2004.
[18] 1997 letters on churching: in Whitehaven, 1951; in Redhill, 1989; in Wales, 1930s; in Barnsley, 1939-60.

accept and understand the rite's references to protection from harm.[19]

The old churching service had not been used by the second of these mothers, but she had clearly enjoyed those of its ceremonial features that had been retained in her Thanksgiving:

> – Now the service we had was not the long and very ... it's a very emotional service, the Prayer-Book service, there's a lot of going to deep waters and that sort of thing, and we didn't have that, we didn't have those readings.
> *Author – you had a different psalm?*
> – yes, and it was something that Fr Michael had already established with the other family, so he just did that. We didn't really discuss it hugely in advance, just said we'd like that service for coming back on a particular Sunday, would that work? And it was a very good way of getting ... of showing ourselves to the community there, but also for me feeling that I was glad to be back.
> *Author – were you on your own when you were churched?*
> – no, it was during the main Sunday morning service. What they do is, they have a procession from the vestry up one of the main aisles and then they sort of turn at the head of the church and go down the nave. So when they came to the top, Fr Michael stopped and I – I think he was wearing a stole or something, and I held on to the end of his stole, or part of his vestment, and I was carrying [the baby], and was taken up to the steps, and then there were prayers said over both of us. And then I went back to my pew and they continued as normal; but it was just a way to – it was probably over in five minutes; but it was built into the main Sunday morning service.

Asked why, unlike many women, she did not mind references to sin and danger, she said:

> – well that was very much what I appreciated, because I felt that we had gone through a crisis and been carried through it and come out the other side...

Her husband was articulate, even eloquent, about the meaning of the service: for him it was definitely a thanksgiving:

> – I am sorry, because I think it's probably misunderstood. I think it's just seen as part of a medieval past; a rather arcane and possibly misogynistic sort of thing to do. And in the medieval world I don't think it was that at all. I think it's one of the only times in the church calendar when women came centre stage and women seem to have been celebrated after childbirth in this way.

He said that his wife had not had a particularly easy birth:

> – and we had a lot to give thanks for. So it wasn't in any way a feast of purification after childbirth but a sort of sacramental thanksgiving really.[20]

---

[19] Telephone interview, July, 2003.
[20] Interview in Oxford, July 2003; cf. Fr. Michael's understanding of the love of ceremony, p. 119; and Becky Lee's account of it in medieval churchings, Chapter One, pp. 9–10; testimony about the third very recent churching is included in the next chapter.

RITE OUT OF TIME

One remarkable oral encounter with a group of four women at St Luke, Wednesbury, contained a number of these key ideas about the significance of churching. Just occasionally all spoke at the same time, confirming and adding to one another's stories. Their contribution is here given in full:

– I know that my Gran wouldn't let anyone in her house until they were churched, but I haven't been churched. *[she has no children]*
Author – how did you know that about your Gran; would she have told you?
– Oh yes, I knew that me auntie, mum's twin sister, came to see her; she had twins, and Gran wouldn't let her in the house because she hadn't been churched. I remember, she had to sit outside.
Author – she must have felt terrible, having to walk away.
– I think it was accepted, though you realised that you couldn't go visiting anybody, you couldn't go into anyone's house, or shops, until you'd been. I mean it was accepted; people knew this, you see.
Author – they knew it because they were told it when they had their child, or they just grew up knowing it?
– well you grew up with the idea of it didn't you?
– there was something, you couldn't touch raw meat.
– bacon, flour; I cooked my own breakfast, they said 'off with you'. It wasn't clean.
– I don't remember that part. Not to touch flour, meat, do the cooking, go into a shop.
– go through a door.
– when you'd had a child you were probably in bed for seven days weren't you? And then when you were well enough to get up the first thing you did was to be churched.
Author – and you went with your mothers? Sisters? Or by yourselves?
– just by myself, with the baby.
– with my sister.
– with my mother.
Author – did you get churched after each of your babies?
All – yes, at St Luke's.
Author – and you've always lived here?
– I came to Wednesbury when I married; I lived at Rushall, the other side of Walsall.
– I've lived in Wednesbury all my life.
Author – the friends round the corner would know if you'd been churched; would they care?
– would you say a bit of superstition?
– yes, I think it was a superstition.
– like the same it's for baptisms for a lot of people, that was a bit of superstition.
Author – so what do you think people think will happen to a baby if it isn't baptised?
– won't thrive.
Author – and what about if a mother isn't churched? Is it the same?

CHURCHING DISCOVERED THROUGH PERSONAL TESTIMONY

– in those days it was took for granted you'd be churched.
Author – but if you'd said 'no, I won't be churched'. Or resisted or defied your mother?
– I suppose we'd have been looked bad on, wouldn't we? Probably be shunned, like in the Bible when they shunned people, you know, for not doing ...
– they'd talk about it, they'd talk about it.
– but it was something you wanted to do anyway; no objections to it at all.
– I lived at the Moor, and I had to walk a long way to St Boris, a long way right up the hill.
– I have known one person come to this church with the baby for a thanksgiving in twenty-five years.
– I just wondered if it happened now.
– I haven't had children, but if I had I would have been churched.
Author – who did you get churched for?
– first and foremost for yourself and your sister. Not because you were religious, just one of those things you'd got to do. Because your parents wouldn't loose you into anyone else's house, you know, or go on the bus or anything, or into anywhere.
– a lot of it is, people have their babies in hospital, don't they.
– you can tell them to have the baby christened, but they'll please themselves.
– really it was our age-group wasn't it? My daughter would certainly never think about having been churched.
Author – could I ask you in what year you had your first babies?
– '44, '55, '59. The very age-group you mention.
– I think it is a superstition. I haven't come across not preparing food.
– yes; raw meat. Women would be barren, or miscarry. It's superstition, superstition.
Author – any other superstition?
– the 13th; not walking under ladders; salt over the left shoulder; not cross knives.
– my daughter-in-law wouldn't tell any of her children's names till after they were born; 'because people will change me mind'; so we never knew the names.
– they were aware of the devil – more so than we are today, aren't we? They were frightened of the devil; and the sermons that were preached – I mean I can remember sermons when I was a kid and it was all fire and brimstone.
– yes, it frightened you to death.
– more so than today, the sermons. Did you think that, Lil?
Author – do you know why they thought you were unclean?
– was it something to do with the blood?
Author – there's obviously an 'unclean' element in having a baby – a lot of blood around...
– when a woman's having a period she's always unclean isn't she?
– they do say something rude about men.*

---

*   Perhaps this was 'All men are liars', Psalm 116: v. 11 from the 1661/1928 service (optional in 1928).

– when you've been churched, you feel a cloud has lifted – you've completed your …
– and it's lovely once you have been churched to be able to carry on with your life normally; take the baby out, show the baby off.[21]

Considerable embarrassment was evident at times in these testimonies and conversations. Some women were reluctant to recall experiences of real physical mess and uncleanness in past times when modern plumbing and adequate routines of hygiene were not available to them. The notion that sex is connected with shame and uncleanness will have been drummed into many women who are now reaching old age, and they were not at ease in discussing whether or not the churching service might have had a point with its offer of 'purification'. Several had felt inhibited about these matters since early in their lives, saying that they had at no time been given information about menstruation, sexual intercourse or childbirth. Such subjects were taboo even between mothers and daughters; perhaps neither had possessed the vocabulary needed to discuss them.

Other women expressed surprisingly little indignation at the suggestion that they had been considered in need of 'cleansing'. They treated the whole subject of uncleanness and bad luck as a straightforward matter, as is described by a vicar's wife writing of life in Dagenham in the 1950s:

> I always answered the front door – a tired, pale young Mum accompanied by her Mum – not the baby – it was unlucky to bring the baby out before Mum had been churched. The girl's Mum would say 'She's come to be done' & expect to be walked into church at once and 'done'. I had to say that churchings were at 11 am. on Fridays when there would be 5 to 10 women each week. Mum would be very angry saying, 'Well I can't look after her any more – she's got to get out to shops & so has the baby'. To do with the not-understood idea of being unclean from child-birth. The neighbours wouldn't allow her to 'infect' the area with bad luck until she'd been churched.

A woman at St Chad's, Litchfield was similarly matter-of-fact as she told how she had been swept into being churched by her mother:

> *Author – you were churched – was it in this church?*
> – no it was in [thinks] Newcastle-on-Tyne. But I was born in Leeds in West Yorkshire, and my mother was a Roman Catholic, but we were all christened Church of England because my dad was Church of England. But her mother was Irish, so she had all the Irish superstitions; and so we weren't allowed to go into anybody's house until we'd been churched because she considered, you know, that we weren't clean. It was just something that you had to do; so I've got two sons and one's 45 and one's 47, and more or less as soon as I came out of hospital it was a case of making an appointment and off to church.
> *Author – were there a lot of you from the hospital?*

---

[21] Group interview in Wednesbury, August 2004.

CHURCHING DISCOVERED THROUGH PERSONAL TESTIMONY

– no, it was a case of once I got home I made an appointment with my own sort of vicar
Author – did she say why you 'weren't clean'?
– no. There were six of us, and I was the fifth out of six; so by the time it got to my turn it was just the thing; it was just, everybody, it was just the thing that we'd all done.[22]

As already noted in Haggerston and Southwark, women were often churched before returning home from their maternity hospitals. Interviews conducted in the three counties between 2001 and 2004 often included the influential roles of chaplains and ward sisters who saw to it that this was done, as the new mothers, often in groups, were churched in chapel before they left for home. This has been described by Helen Gribble and Sheila Allen, archivists of St Bartholomew's Hospital in London:

> The services were held twice a week, when new mothers would go across to the church in a group ... churching continued certainly into the 1960s and most probably until the midwifery unit was moved to the Mothers' Hospital; not sure of the date, 1980?[23]

Such initiative was not always welcomed, as one woman remembered from her experience in Lancashire in the 1960s. She had borne her first child in hospital, where she reflected that she must have been 'a bit mental' in agreeing to be churched, as she 'wasn't very religious'. The chaplain had come to her bedside and performed what he called 'a cleansing ceremony' after the 'unclean business' of giving birth; there was apparently no question of its being a thanksgiving. Another new mother said that, not having expected to be churched, she had been dismayed by the severity of a Bristol chaplain in a joyless and impersonal hospital service which made her feel that she had 'done something wrong'. But others said that they enjoyed the hospital ceremony as it signified a successful conclusion to the anxious process of labour, birth and recovery.

Further Testimony, from Members of the Clergy

Few clergy apparently took the initiative in churching women: mothers told their daughters what to do and, together with aunts, sisters and grandmothers, made sure that unwritten social codes were handed down:

> When you had women in their twenties, mothers in their forties, grandmothers in their sixties; those were the two generations that controlled family life.[24]

Only twice have incumbents been found making the first approach themselves: in Lambourn, Berkshire whose vicar (now retired) admitted to having played an

[22] Letters, conversations and interviews between 1997 and 2004.
[23] Letter, March 2004.
[24] Interview in Oxford, April 2002.

encouraging role; and in Goosnaugh, Lancashire, where in 1942 'the vicar came round and suggested it'.

Churching created endless work in a large parish. Two interviewees tell of daily demand in the Black Country in the 1980s. Twenty years earlier, another had tried to avoid unexpected requests in nearby Stoke and Fenton but had still faced problems with numbers:

> We were available to do churchings after Evensong and at times published, and whoever was on duty for that week would stay behind for any who came. On one very memorable occasion four all arrived at once, and I had them lined up along the communion rail and I was just beginning when a fifth one came in – it was almost mass-production.[25]

When clerical time was scarce 'churching' would be left to take place without the presence of curate or vicar. Routines in the 1960s were described in Lancashire and Staffordshire parishes: young mothers returning from confinements in the local maternity hospitals would call at the curate's house, collect the church key and a churching card, drop into the church, and read over the service for themselves. A vicar's wife (herself now ordained) when asked, 'Didn't your husband go into the church with them, to perform the churching?', replied that no, he was far too busy.[26]

Oral testimony introduced several examples of clergy who were not just reluctant but actually unwilling to perform churchings. Three, vicars of St Modwen, Burton-upon-Trent, St Mary, Cheapside (formerly of St Anne, Shoreditch) and St Mary, Bow said in 2004 that they would not be prepared to do churchings, even if a request were made. Women also spoke of such cases. An elderly member of the Cheddleton Knitting Group remembered:

> My next-door neighbour asked me to go to the church with her. I said, yes I would. She rang the vicar and he said: 'you can come by all means and I'll have a talk with you and give thanks, but I don't church women'.

A second woman, in Norton-in-the-Moor, recalled her experience in the late 1950s:

> I wasn't actually churched, but I had a blessing ... my mother said to me: 'you can't go out until you've been churched'; so I went to the Reverend Pollitt and I asked him, and he said: 'It's a pagan thing. Don't do that, but happily come along with your husband and have a blessing and a thanksgiving service'.

A friend agreed: 'I remember with Michael Pollitt talking about it and he didn't like it at all'.[27] Another incumbent, in 1940s Walworth, remembered trying to insist that

---

[25] Interviews in Longton, Oxford and Stafford, all in 2004.
[26] Interview in Oxford, April, 2002; telephone interview with a former hospital chaplain, June, 2002.
[27] Interviews in Lambourn, May, 2004; Reading, June 2002; Staffordshire, August, 2004.

churching should be only 'by appointment, after a personal talk'.[28] There were others who detailed their dislike of 'superstitious' sanctions that were applied to still-unchurched mothers: being forbidden to cross the thresholds of their own houses or the houses of others 'because unclean', and told not to handle food: facing disapproval in family, street, church and community. Dismay is still etched onto one vicar's account of a woman's exclusion and confinement to the hen-house over Christmas in Yorkshire fifty years ago, all part of 'a folk religion, powerful in people's lives'. He had discovered during a long career in Yorkshire that demand was greater for 'cleansing' than for 'thanksgiving'.[29] Another wrote, 'curiously there were far more mothers *not* from a committed church position who wished to be churched than the faithful', suggesting that folk or pagan tradition actually contributed more to churching's popularity than did Christian liturgy. In Oxfordshire this was echoed during a long interview with a minister in the Vale of White Horse:

> You were up against a folk-religion ... paganism is getting worse; it's everywhere, indicating a huge spiritual void. People will believe almost anything that fills that void.[30]

Nevertheless there were other clergy who appreciated that, even late in the twentieth century, some people hankered after ceremony and ritual such as might be found in churching's thanksgiving and purification. One Oxford vicar commented on people's lingering hunger for ceremonial. He referred to a man whose wife he had recently churched:

> [he] was of an old Jericho family, very devout, traditional Anglo-Catholic, became Orthodox a couple of years ago ... Feels that the Church of England has neglected its great traditions and is drifting in a liberal tradition. Now he can have as many ceremonies as he could possibly want ... I used the 1662 service with Catholic ceremonies. I met her at the church porch and wearing a stole. She held the end of my stole and a lighted candle coming into the church. We went into the Lady Chapel and held the service there. It's what I had done when I was first ordained, on the couple of occasions when I first did it.[31]

A century earlier, Charles Booth had noted how much ritual was loved in London, commenting with detached amusement on its 'imitations of Rome', 'church millinery' and 'men in coloured garments sprawling before the altar'.[32]

For some parishes, particularly those following an Anglo-Catholic tradition, a question of the church's proper attitude to women arose when ministers talked

---

[28] Interview in Benson, Oxon, December, 1997; letters about churching in Dulwich, Peckham, and Clapham, 1948–60; Don Valley, South Yorkshire, 1950s; Hessel, South Yorkshire, 1958–62; Spalding, 1960–1, Leicester, 1969–75, Guildford, 1975–93.
[29] Letters about churching in Spalding, Llandaff and South Yorkshire.
[30] Letter from Norfolk; interview in Oxford, May 2002.
[31] Interview in Oxford, April, 2002.
[32] From Owen Chadwick, *The Victorian Church*, Part II, pp. 312–13.

of churching's survival. Indeed, for some the notion of women's purification was still a controversial matter. One of them, working in South London, began by describing his own mother's views:

> – When my sister-in-law had her children my mother was appalled that she didn't go to church to be churched.
> *Author – what would she have said?*
> – she would have said that after giving birth (we were born in hospital) when she came home from hospital, the first thing she did – the first time she left the house to go anywhere – she went to church to be churched; she said that you had to do that; that was what you had to do. It was about giving thanks that she had survived the childbirth, for purification, and making an offering to the church. And the old offering was one penny.

He went on to explain his understanding that these ideas of his mother's are echoed in the Anglo-Catholic fear of menstrual impurity. It has to be added that his own churchmanship did not allow women to enter the Sanctuary, and he personally did not believe that women should be ordained. This perhaps coloured his own supportive attitude to churching. He continued:

> It's the uncleanness: and giving birth, it's the uncleanness; and of course, it's harking back, so that the child is the product of original sin.

The survival of churching he attributed partly to the church's teaching:

> It's still going on with the shame factor, and the purity and impurity factor in it: it's sort of keeping women in their place, I suppose.

He quoted the words of an 'old girl' recently expressing this association of sex with shame at a social gathering in the immediate neighbourhood:

> 'You never did it till you were married ... and isn't it awful because, when you had a baby, everyone knew what you'd been doing?'

He ended by endorsing the ceremony, in his own way:

> Oh, I wouldn't refuse ... if anybody asked me to do it, I'd do it, of course; because it seems to me ... but then I hark back to the folklore bit; because I've heard it resonating down the generations, I think it must be important.[33]

The incumbent of one of Staffordshire's strongly Anglo-Catholic parishes recalled his first vicar's belief in the importance of purification, in terms which seemed to echo this London woman's sentiment:

> He was a bachelor, Rector of St John's, Longton, and I can remember his sermon clearly. He quoted the psalm, *In sin did my mother conceive me*, and I remember him making the point very clearly that even if you only indulge in sexual intercourse for the purpose of producing a child, there is still an

---

[33] Interview in Walworth, January, 2004.

CHURCHING DISCOVERED THROUGH PERSONAL TESTIMONY

element of sin, because no matter how long it takes to do the deed, there's a time when you're enjoying it.[34]

A third minister to tackle this subject was equally outspoken, though he personally had no sympathy with the churching rite. His parish was in London's East End:

> – I've probably done about two churchings, and I've been a priest now about 33 years.
> *Author – So you wouldn't have been urging women to have it done?*
> – No; I don't approve of it. I mean they've written a service now of thanks; most women would want to do that, I mean you've come out of it safely. I'm a father and a grandfather, so I know all about that, and the dangers which are still inherent in it. But it gets mixed up with all this rubbish about impurity, and I suspect – since you wrote me the letter, actually, I've thought quite deeply about it; areas like this were very Anglo-Catholic and in general Catholics hate women; I was brought up as a Roman Catholic and ...
> *Author – Would you say perhaps that they fear women?*
> – I think they hate them actually.
> *Author – Do you really?*
> – Yes I do. It goes all the way back to Thomas Aquinas who thought that women's sexual organs were the gate to hell; I mean he actually said that, I've read it in Latin and in English (I used to teach Classics once) and they dislike women intensely ... a lot of this came out during these discussions about women priests; you can catch the echoes if you've got any historical sense at all – this sort of Catholicism thing which was: women are unclean.[35]

As a further explanation of churching's endurance, several vicars in the three counties emphasised the entrenched conservatism of communities in which churching was still valued. One, while still incumbent of at least four small country parishes in the Vale of White Horse, shared his thoughts at some length about the unchanging outlook of villagers in remotest Berkshire and their failure to articulate or develop their ideas, or question their own traditions:

> How do people think? Well they don't, really ... When you bury people who have reached eighty-five or ninety you can ask their children (by now aged sixty or seventy): 'Tell me about your mother, or your father'. And they can't. They have no categories. All they can say is: 'She was a good woman; always dressed us kids OK; she was a kind neighbour'. They can talk with feeling about how they fulfilled their role. But it's not thinking – it has only a limited application.

In his opinion, being churched was part of the battle of village life:

> Villages: they are idealised. Actually the trouble is you can't get away from them; the family is always there, as are old friends and rivals; *enemies*. To

---

[34] Interview in Longton, Staffs., August 2004.
[35] Interview in Bow, February, 2004.

survive, the requirement is to minimise the chance of being marginalised or cut off. There is a drive to conform, certainly in externals; to *accommodate* to this small feudal community. There are various rituals, concerned for instance with harvest, stock, drinking, church. Church is the area for accommodating religion, the squire, God. You accommodate to this, do the right thing; go along, pay dues, put on your best frock. You just do it. A *gemeinschaft* approach. Or you can have a *gesellschaft* approach, which is more urban.

Another expressed similar ideas about the nature of villages in his North Staffordshire parish, where close familiarity put pressure on young women to conform:

> The whole of this area, the whole Staffordshire Moorlands area, is immensely conservative with a small *c*. People don't move very far from here. Ladies whom you'll meet at the old people's 'thing' [knitting group] are all known and 80% of them were born in or around Cheddleton, and went to school and were married here and lived here.[36]

Clergy who actually expressed appreciation of the churching rite were few in number. One, writing from Spalding in Lincolnshire, was annoyed that it appears to have been under attack:

> The view that it was superstitious, or demeaning to women, which began to be promoted a long time ago, seems generally to have been victorious, which I regret.

In a different way a parson in Wales testified to its value. He said that he had taken only two services in forty years between 1958 and 1998, one for a 'gypsy woman' asking for immediate attention, the other for a mother who had been through a terrible childbirth experience:

> Her pregnancy had been fraught with problems and her doctors had urged her to have a termination because they judged it a danger to her life to bring the child to birth. She decided against the advice and spent many weeks in hospital and nearly died before the child was born ... She was accompanied by her whole family, all rejoicing in the situation, and glad that the church had provided a special service for her.[37]

Thus oral and written testimony demonstrates a range of clerical interpretations and attitudes. To most older clergy, ordained by the middle of the century, churching had been a part of parish routine, best seen as a service of thanksgiving for new mothers, to be performed without delving into its superstitious nuances; and they were aware of the power of grandmothers to have their way: if thwarted they really might make life hard for their daughters. For some, aware of the dis-

---

[36] Interviews in Berkshire, June 2002, and Cheddleton, August 2004.
[37] 1997 letters from Spalding and Llandaff.

ruption caused by current liturgical innovation and knowing how many women churchgoers still cherished old traditions of worship, it was good policy to keep the churching rite alive. But for younger generations entering the ministry in later decades the old ritual and its associated ideas almost certainly became hard or even impossible to accept. This generational division was made clear at a Chapter meeting at St Peter's, Hammersmith in 2004. Most of the incumbents present were young and had scarcely, if ever, heard of the churching service. They listened to an account of it given by the oldest of their number with ill-concealed disbelief:

> *Tom (an elderly vicar, close to retirement) on churching in Warrington*: Women came to churching before having their children baptised; and they came on a weekday, and they asked for churching; sometimes it would be two or three mothers on the Wednesday morning after midweek communion; and the folklore behind it was, as you probably know, that if they weren't churched mother-in-law would become pregnant.
> *Author – was it at your suggestion or theirs?*
> Tom – no, theirs. It was a fairly strong local tradition.
> *Author – was it a high church?*
> Tom – no – sort of very intermediate Catholic.
> *Author – what did you feel about it?*
> Tom – well I'd never heard of it before I arrived in the parish; but it seemed to be a good pastoral opportunity. Apart from what mother-in-law may or may not have been saying, it was a good pastoral opportunity on the way towards baptism; and also when I moved to Matlock in Derbyshire as well ... it was still not infrequent for people to come for churching; but they wouldn't come that soon; generally two or four weeks, not in the first week.[38]

Conclusion: the Value of Oral and Written Testimony

All those offering personal testimony have lent a dramatic quality to this whole study. They have confirmed that churchings have been located in all parts of the country, both rural and urban, and in every decade of the twentieth century. There is broad agreement about details of the ceremony, such as location in the church, who was present, and the wearing of hats. In the matter of transmission, accounts ring with powerful matriarchy, as the rite's survival is attributed overwhelmingly to the new mother's mother, occasionally to sisters and mothers-in-law, almost never to clergy. Husbands are never mentioned. All social classes were involved.

Where understanding and interpretation of the churching rite are concerned, explanations have inevitably varied. In women's testimony, motivation has varied from genuine thanksgiving and obedience to mothers, to dismay at the prospect of social exclusion and possible ill-luck. Some spoke of the welcome feeling brought by the churching ceremony as it marked closure to the whole long business of pregnancy, parturition and *lochia*; and expressed appreciation that it

---

[38] Chapter Meeting at St Peter's, Hammersmith, March 2004.

had acknowledged in public that this birth had been a time of travail and apprehension, courage and achievement. Today's young will never know, the Cheddleton Group emphasised, the prolonged pain and real danger of death that mother and baby used to face at each and every birth. Others rejected the ceremony as quite unacceptable, and already out of date even by the middle of the twentieth century.

Clergy have explained their willingness to church women. Though a few refused, seeing the ceremony as 'pagan', or demeaning to the mother, many were prepared to accede to requests for the ancient rite, offering as it did thanks to God, and comfort to women in their vulnerable post-partum days. At the very least it placated their families. There were always hopes of a later baptism. Churching also seemed to suit the High Anglican style of churchmanship with its problems about female purity. But almost all expressed relief at the arrival in 1980 of the ASB service of Thanksgiving, which managed to avoid such controversies. One vicar wrote in August 1997:

> My hope is that 'thanksgiving' will completely replace all the old conceptions, especially the superstitious notions, as I imagine is already happening.[39]

The final topic in the questionnaire, *Sanctions and the Climate of Opinion*, raised speculative talk of modern society's links with ancient tradition. Confirmation was given of the forces behind churching. In towns and villages (especially those of Staffordshire) there was still awareness that people would notice, and that unchurched women would 'be shunned'. Folk tales linger of ill-luck attending such a woman after childbirth, and though nearly all speakers in the early twenty-first century dismissed them as ridiculous, the word 'superstition' persisted in a few testimonies.

Above all, whether for or against, those who have offered these testimonies combine to paint a picture of unmatched value, which is vivid, reliable and detailed, recalling their churching experiences fluently and with humour, many still intrigued about the true nature and value of the rite.

---

[39] Letter from Stretford, August 1997.

CHAPTER SIX

OUT OF TIME: THE DECLINE OF CHURCHING IN THE TWENTIETH CENTURY

Difficult to define, its meaning hard to explain and often guarded behind pursed lips, what has become of the rite of churching at the end of the twentieth century? Clergy and their parishioners, women and their families and neighbours appear to have all but lost track of its very existence. Churchgoers now pursue a different version of thanksgiving to celebrate a mother's achievement after the birth of her child. The historian must ask: how has this ancient ritual been abandoned after so long? When did it begin to disappear, and for what reason? This chapter will look for answers as it reviews the evidence of churching's decline found in the visitation returns from Southwark, parish registers from the three counties, and personal testimony from around the country.

Problems with the Measurement of Decline

Any attempt to measure the rate of churching's decline has to acknowledge that the written record is incomplete, as parish clergy tended to give up, some quite early in the century, the practice of registering any account of names, dates or offerings. Staffordshire incumbents, both current and retired, are quite unapologetic about their lack of records, pointing out that they were not obliged to register churchings, which anyway were so numerous that there was no time to write them all down.[1] Churches in London and Berkshire also suffered from problems of high workload: the administrative support that might be given by curates was becoming scarce quite early in the century in both city and country parishes, as new ordinands failed to come forward, deterred by the cost of training, and prospects of social isolation and poor pay. Things were made worse by the Tithe Act of 1936 which caused some livings to lose income; their inability even to support a parson led to amalgamations and further overwork for those who remained.[2] In the Southwark visitation returns for 1936 and 1951 vicars protested that they needed more assistance as they struggled with enormous livings, whose populations sometimes numbered over 20,000; while Berkshire returns in earlier decades told of many rural clergy attempting to run far-flung parishes often on

---
[1] Testimony from clergy who had served in Longton, Tipton and Wednesbury.
[2] Roger Lloyd, *The Church of England 1900–1965* (London, 1966), pp. 356–8.

allegedly pitiful incomes.³ It is no surprise that recording duties were kept to a minimum.

Another explanation for the lack of records is that vicars simply decided to abandon the burden of registration. In 1921 this was apparently the case in two well-supported Berkshire parishes, Ss Peter & Paul, Wantage and St Mary, Reading, and at Staffordshire's St James-the-Less, Longton. The incumbent at All Saints, Lockinge probably ended his records in 1950 because numbers had fallen by then to only one or two a year, and anyway he had completed the last page of the service register. It must have been lack of demand that also caused the lists to close at St John the Evangelist, Blackheath in 1956 and Christ Church, North Brixton in 1971.⁴

Levels of Decline in Southwark Diocese and the Three Counties

Nevertheless, some form of measurement can be attempted. For the diocese of Southwark numerical values have been given to verbal comments in the 1951 visitation replies, and a pattern of these describing decline is drawn up in Table XX, below. Area rates are clearly differentiated, inner-urban Southwark contrasting noticeably with more countrified Reigate in the percentage of parishes reporting a drop in numbers:

Table XX: Churching's Decline Reported in Southwark Deaneries, 1951

Deanery	number of parishes	number of parishes reporting decline	percentage of parishes reporting decline
Southwark	67	8	11.9
Lewisham	65	10	15.3
Wandsworth	70	11	15.7
Lambeth	60	12	20
Croydon	28	7	25
Reigate	44	13	29.5

As seen in Chapter Four, the phrases varied. Two vicars made simple statements that no churching went on in the parish. Others told a little more: the practice was 'negligible' at St Andrew, Surbiton [s2/c1]; 'almost extinct' at St John, Coulsdon [s-/c1]; 'not at all' at St Albans, Cheam [s-/c0]; and 'very seldom' in All Saints, Blackheath Park [s2/c1]; though 'a few come' at St Augustine, Bermondsey [s1/c1].

---

³ See Chapter Two, p. 41.
⁴ BRO D/P 143 1B/3, Ss. Peter & Paul, Wantage, Register of Services 1917–1921; DP/ 98 1/B/7, St. Mary, Reading, Register of Services 1918–1921; D/P82 /1/B/2, All Saints, Lockinge, Register of Services Sept. 1936–June 1952; SRO D5676/7/5, Parish Magazines, 1901-5; LMA P78/JNE/006, Register of Churchings 1926-56; Barber, *Christ Church North Brixton*, pp. 73–81.

Some replies were more descriptive: 'nothing like a year ago' at Holy Trinity, Tulse Hill [s2/c1]; and 'declining very fast at the moment, about 4 a month, mostly the poorest' at St Silas, Nunhead [s1/c2]; while some used a variety of measurements in the attempt to estimate 'decline' with: 'once in six months', 'not more than a dozen a year', 'perhaps 10% of mothers'. Only a few offered explanation: 'very seldom as compared with the "inner circle" parishes', 'much less here than in, say, Bermondsey', 'often neglected by the present generation', and 'hardly at all either by church people or others'; though the Reverend Godwin of St Luke's, Reigate [s2/c1] wrote simply: 'nothing like a few years ago ... I can't explain the drop'.[5]

A more precise assessment of periods and rates of decline is possible in the three counties, where regular records show churching numbers diminishing well before mid-century. In Chapter Three proportions of churchings to baptisms have been compared; in the end, though both lines fluctuate in broadly downward directions over time, churching exhibits the greater fall.[6] On the other hand personal testimony, while it offers valuable confirmation that churching did continue into the later twentieth century, at least among church-going families, cannot support estimates of extent or decline. It simply gives clues, a collective impression of churching's survival up to the late 1960s, followed by a serious falling away thereafter.

Putting together the clerical comments, personal impressions and parish statistics, four broad explanations emerge for the decline of the rite of churching. They concern changes within society and the church itself. First is the decline of matriarchal influence over married daughters; second, the major reduction in childbirth's danger; third, a falling away of church membership; and fourth, decisive change in the Church of England's liturgy, which has brought to a final conclusion its commitment to the old churching rite.

The Decline of Matriarchy and the Growth of Young Women's Independence

Women's strong influence within their young families lasted well into the second half of the century. Recalling the 1960s when he was a curate in Lancashire, one distinguished churchman spoke of 'great power in the hands of the matriarchy; very, very powerful'.[7] Peter Willmott and Michael Young emphasised in *Family and Kinship in East London* the close proximity and frequent association that young women still enjoyed with their mothers in the late 1950s. This was in Bethnal Green, where they found a churching rate of 95%. Close and continuous relationships ensured that by insistence, example, powerful expectation, persuasion,

---

[5] See Chapter Four, p. 77.
[6] See London graphs discussed in Chapter Three, pp. 47–9 and Plate 9.
[7] Interview in March, 2002; see Chapter Five, p. 117.

or occasional threats, grandmothers saw to it that the new mothers went along to 'be done'.[8]

Many women in this study's letters, oral testimony and questionnaire replies confirmed that their mothers' advice was the main force driving them to be churched, and that they yielded (though sometimes reluctantly) to such pressure. Of seven who have spoken about being churched since 1970, only two were impelled by their own belief, and as far as is known without the direct participation of their mothers; while the other five spoke of a churching under the persuasive influence of mothers who lived nearby, generally in a close-knit neighbourhood.[9]

Growth of Women's Independence

It is beyond the scope of this study to frame judgements on the reality of these close relationships between mothers and daughters. They will have contained elements of friendship and affection, independence and control, love and ambition, and, on both sides, the negotiation of powerful outside forces. How they worked in each case cannot be known. But it seems certain that, as the normal trajectory of young women's lives changed after mid-century, the once confident, directive influence of their mothers and grandmothers gradually diminished. It was bound to happen as new developments in post-war society brought about widespread physical separation of daughters from their families when schooldays come to an end. Educated to the age of fifteen, later sixteen, girls left home for training, university, joining the labour force and, as they grew less socially confined, taking their place in an increasingly mobile society. They were not always brought back by marriage to live close to their mothers. Though at the time of childbirth grandmothers would travel long distances to be with their daughters,[10] they had often lost the powerful influence of earlier decades when they lived close by and made sure that girls did what they were told. An even more recent pattern was noted by one Staffordshire vicar:

> young people move away ... the girls are not with their mothers, because a lot of them are living with partners.[11]

It seems that by the last quarter of the century, distanced from the traditions of their own families, young women were often living outside the disciplines of religion, and paying little attention to hitherto accepted definitions of respectability, with which churchgoing had once been closely associated.[12] When it came to

---

[8] M. Young and P. Willmott, *Family and Kinship in East London* (London, 1957), Chapter 3, pp. 44–61; see Chapter Five, pp. 106–9, 116–17.
[9] Interview in Walworth, Jan, 2004, about a 1970 churching.
[10] Margaret Stacey, *Tradition and Change: A Study of Banbury* (Oxford, 1960), p. 85.
[11] Interview in Longton, August 2004.
[12] OCRO MSS, Oxf. Dioc. Papers, C300–C389.

their own childbearing, and that of their daughters, the custom of churching after childbirth, if indeed it was known about at all, was seen as belonging to the past.

Several older mothers offering oral testimony of their own churchgoing and childbearing around the time of the Second World War have recalled how they personally defied the command to be churched. Their generation accepted that their own daughters would have little interest in being churched: 'they don't do it now' said one Hammersmith mother: 'they don't bother to get married, let alone get churched' came from the luncheon group at St Chad, Haggerston. None felt that the rite needed to be revived, nor that they as grandmothers had any role to play in perpetuating it.[13]

Richard Sykes in his work on Dudley explains how this gradual detatchment has been laced with indifference, distaste and disbelief. Once more the notion of purification proved a big problem:

> Changes in attitudes to sex and gender stereotyping may have reinforced the weakening hold of the ritual of churching. Some women were not only unclear about the significance of the ritual but also repelled by what was perceived to be the implication of the restrictions on the new-born mother.

This was in the late 1950s and early 1960s. He records two interviewees, one declaring herself 'so disgusted with the service I didn't go for the second one'; the other itemising those attitudes that she had found completely unacceptable:

> You couldn't go into the next door neighbour's house. I've never really fathomed it out. You were classed as unclean or something ... when you had a baby, although it was alright by the church having the baby, because you'd done the [hesitates] deed, you had to be blessed by the vicar to bring you back on the road again. You'd strayed, that's the way I always thought about it. You'd done something like as you'd got to be forgiven or else they'd be punished.[14]

Moral discipline aimed at women rattles out from two rather different pieces of evidence taken from earlier in the century. Infuriated by lapses from obedience and virtue among women parishioners applying for churchings, the Revd W. J. A. Ford, vicar of St Stephen, Barbourne, Worcester kept notes on his decisions made from 1912 to 1931 to punish women by refusal to church: 'I find this woman is a Dissenter'; 'a single woman'; 'Husband an RC so will not church her in future'; 'married at register office August 1930, applied for Churching 6 Jan 1931'; 'obtained churching surreptitiously after adultery'; 'Living with a married man, illegitimate child'; 'child by a married sergeant at Norton Barracks – both seen & neither penitent'; 'very bad case, mar'd May 1920, child born following Aug. the girl

---

[13] Telephone interview, July, 2003; interviews, February and May 2004.
[14] R. Sykes, 'Popular Religion', p. 335; see also Adrian Bingham, 'An Era of Domesticity: Histories of Women and Gender in Interwar Britain', *Cultural and Social History*, Vol. I, No. 2 (2004), pp. 225–33.

= confirmed. Refused to make her confession, refused churching'. A page of these notes and churching application form appear in plates 15–16.

An earlier scene which contains quite ambiguous notions about churching as potentially both reward and reprimand, is in Salford, home of the ever-observant Robert Roberts (born 1905). In his autobiography, *A Ragged Schooling*, he describes two women commenting on Abigail, a landlady whose baby son's red hair proclaims him to be unmistakeably the offspring not of her husband but of her lodger:

> A short time after this affair I overheard two women in the shop giving Abigail a going over. 'She's had the flamin' impudence,' said one, 'to go and get herself churched!'
> The other gasped. 'She wants churchin', that one!' [15]

Roughly when women achieved the independence to reject and shake off such judgmental attitudes has long been a subject of discussion among historians. Its development was undoubtedly slow and uneven. In her studies of working-class women in Preston, Barrow and Lancaster, 1890–1930, Elizabeth Roberts found it beginning between the wars, describing how, at least in respect of childbirth, female views were already altering by nineteen-thirty, even though 'the fatalism, the ignorance, the shame, the stoicism, and the traditionalism are all still very apparent'. In his account of life in Birmingham, *They Worked all Their Lives: Women of the Urban Poor in England, 1880–1939*, Carl Chinn suggests that churching practice, 'still adhered to strongly in the 1950s', and insisted upon by grandmothers in episodes of apparently quite intimidating discipline, manifests a slow rate of social change. Callum Brown considers that women's social liberation began in the nineteen-sixties as 'second-wave feminism and the recrafting of femininity' signalled the end of 'the old discourse of domesticity, separate spheres, limited ambitions':

> The reconstruction of female identity within work, sexual relations and new recreational opportunities from the late 1960s, put not just feminism but female identity in collision with the Christian construction of femininity.

In her later work, *Women and Families: an Oral History, 1940–1970*, Elizabeth Roberts says the same, though still finds tension between old and new, suggesting that much was still left unaltered in family structures and relationships, even as fundamental social change was working to transform and sometimes shatter traditional roles and expectations.

Many people contributing their testimony have named the nineteen-sixties as crucial years of change for women; though two Staffordshire clergy cited changes in the nineteen-eighties, or even nineteen-nineties, as more far-reaching;

---

[15] Worcester Record Office, 850 BA 8450/9: St Stephen, Barbourne, Registers, 1912–31; Robert Roberts, *A Ragged Schooling* (Manchester, 1984), p. 91.

decades when traditional morality in family, school and community fell most rapidly away.[16]

Improvements in the Management of Childbirth

Meanwhile, one of churching's justifications, that it offered comfort after the fearful dread of childbirth's dangers, had been undermined over half a century by improvements in the management of maternity. Once women's fears had been well-grounded: the grim accounts of childbirth in Margaret Llewelyn Davies's *Maternity: Letters from Working Women* depicted in 1915 the pain and physical distress of mothers whose health and environment were desperately poor, sometimes with fatal outcomes for their newly-born infants. Throughout Jennifer Worth's account of midwifery in London's East End, bringing women safely through childbirth even in the nineteen-fifties was clearly a continuing battle. One elderly member of the Cheddleton Knitting Group said:

> You must remember, in the generation before us having a baby was touch and go, not like it is now.

Others in the group nodded agreement as a fellow tricoteuse added: 'most of our grandmothers would have lost a baby'.[17] But from the nineteen-thirties growing numbers of trained midwives and of hospital births gradually made inroads into high maternal and child mortality figures, and mothers' confidence must have gained more ground as fears of pain and death receded. Table XXI, based on figures published in 1977 by Rosalind Mitchison, illustrates the rapid rate of improvement since the first Midwives Act of 1902.[18]

Churching was still to continue, increasingly often in maternity homes and cottage hospitals, where ward sisters and midwives, briefly a parallel matriarchy, saw to it that new mothers were churched before they returned home. But decline of such guidance set in as units closed or moved into general hospitals, and as new generations of nursing staff and chaplains lost touch with the old rite. At the end

---

[16] Elizabeth Roberts, *Working Class Barrow and Lancaster 1890–1930* (Occasional Paper No. 2, Centre for North-West Regional Studies, University of Lancaster, 1976), pp. 62–8; *A Woman's Place: an Oral History of Working-Class Women 1940–1970* (Oxford, 1984), p. 105; *Women and Families: an Oral History, 1940–1970* (Oxford, 1995), p. 99; Carl Chinn, *They Worked All Their Lives: women of the urban poor in England, 1880–1939* (Manchester, 1988), pp. 143–4; Callum Brown, *The Death of Christian Britain*, p. 179; Bernice Martin, 'Declining years', *T.L.S.*, 14 December, 2007, pp. 9–10; interviews with two Staffordshire clergy, August, 2004.

[17] M. Llewelyn Davies (ed.), *Maternity: Letters from Working Women, 1915* (London, 1915; Tiptree, 1978); Jennifer Worth, *Call the Midwife: A True Story of the East End in the 1950s* (London, 2002); interview, August, 2004.

[18] R. Mitchison, *British Population Change Since 1860* (London & Basingstoke, 1977), p. 50; A. Susan Williams, *Women & Childbirth in the Twentieth Century* (Stroud, 1997), Chapters, 8 and 11.

of the twentieth century these thanksgiving routines seem to have disappeared.

Table XXI: Reduction of infant mortality rates in England and Wales, 1900–1972 deaths under one year per 1000 births

1900–2	146
1910–2	110
1920–2	80
1930–2	64
1940–2	55
1950–2	29
1960–2	22
1970–2	18

A General Falling Away of Religious Affiliation

The ending of this once widespread rite of passage is arguably one of the clearest symptoms of the growth of secularism in late-twentieth-century society. In occasional but strongly-felt debate opinions differ over the timing, cause and extent of secularist advance. Some maintain that it has been exaggerated, pointing out that in the 2001 census 72% of people in Britain still described themselves as Christians, and the Church of England remains an established part of the state; each year's calendar continues to be studded with references to the Christian narrative, institutions are still named after saints, and streets after local churches. Problems flare up over access to faith schools, styles of worship and codes of dress. It could be argued that debates about matters of principle and moral purpose are as freely presented and discussed in literature and drama, and in private and public life, as at any time in the last century.

Those who disagree point out that recorded religious affiliation in the form of church membership has been in decline ever since a high point around 1905: is this not unarguable proof of secularism in our society? For support they may point to some recent figures taken from Peter Brierley and Heather Wraight in their *UK Christian Handbook* for 1996/7:[19]

Table XXII: Church membership in the United Kingdom showing decline from 1975 to a projected 2010

	1975	1980	1985	1990	1992	1994	2000	2005	2010
Membership as % of adult population	18.5	16.9	15.5	14.7	14.3	13.9	12.8	12.2	10.8

What explanations are found for such a fall in numbers? Some start early in the century with a widespread loss of confidence in the church's ministry, allegedly connected with its chaplaincy in the First World War. Others point to lack of familiarity,

---

[19] Peter Brierley and Heather Wraight, *UK Christian Handbook*, 96/97 Edition, London Christian Research Association, p. 240.

as religious tradition gradually ceased to be imparted to children by families, schools and Sunday Schools. Oxfordshire clergy in a series of visitations up to 1936 deplored the temptation of alternative secular activities (particularly on Sundays), of affluence, the radio, the motor car. Belief has long been shaken and destroyed by the force of scientific and rational argument, and undermined by society's increasing materialism.[20]

The Churching Rite written out of Liturgical Revision

Undoubtedly the church continued to be treasured by many, and at the very least valued as 'a handy way of marking the rites of life's passage'. But even its members and supporters were allowing the ceremony of churching to fade away. Physical traces were disappearing as churching pews were thrown out and vestry cupboards cleared of old veils and service cards.[21] Some clergy were already re-wording parts of the service to make it less forbidding, as Southwark replies revealed back in 1951; and chaplains were visiting maternity hospitals in order to 'bless' rather than 'church' the new mothers.[22]

As far as the Church of England's liturgy was concerned, the churching of women was not apparently seen as important by the General Synod or House of Laity, the bodies entrusted with voting on liturgical revision after 1965, and which in the end oversaw the changes of 1980 and 2000, replacing the old service with the new thanksgivings. These decisive moves ensured that the rite of churching was to die away, though it is still available in the old Book of Common Prayer.[23]

By all accounts, even during earlier decades when the churching service was still part of current liturgy, clerical commitment to its celebration appears to have been far from wholehearted. It was mentioned in only two of the episcopal visitations examined for this study, both in the diocese of Southwark. The first was in 1919 when clergy were asked to state what fees they charged for a given list of services. This included churching, implying that they were assumed to have been holding this ceremony among many others. A number of clergy answered that one shilling was their regular fee; others said that they made no charge. The second

---

[20] Keith A. Roberts, *Religion in Sociological Perspective* (Wadsworth, Belmont, Canada) 2nd edition, 1990, pp. 77–82, 303–23; Linda Woodhead, Paul Heelas and David Martin (eds), *Peter Berger and the Study of Religion* (Routledge, London & New York, 2001), *passim*; Penny Long Marler: 'Lost in the Fifties: The changing Family and the Nostalgic Church', in Ammerman and Roof (eds), *Work, Family and Religion in Contemporary Society* (New York and London, 1995), pp. 23–60; Brian Appleyard, 'Is it Time to take God out of the State?', *Sunday Times*, 22nd October, 2007.

[21] Appleyard, op. cit.; I am indebted to Robert Sherlock for the card, copied in PLate 2, which he rescued from a vestry clearance at St Mary Magdalene, South Molton in 2002.

[22] LMA, DS VB 12: IIb1, St Mary Magdalene, Bermondsey; interview in London, April, 2005.

[23] See Chapter One, pp. 16–20; the 1662 version is still available.

was in 1951, and the replies that it engendered, seen above in Chapter Four, expressed only occasional engagement or enthusiasm. No mention of churching appeared in visitations in the diocese of Oxford in 1924 and 1928 when comments were invited on pastoral matters (baptisms, confirmations, marriages, confessions and visitations of the sick), and questions of discipline (intemperance, unchastity, betting and gambling, religious indifference and Sunday observance).

It is true that, among individual clergy, there is just a small amount of evidence of late-twentieth-century support for the traditional ceremony. Old-style churchings have been noted at various points between the 1980s and the year 2004: in Oxford; in Walworth, South London; in Berkshire, at Sonning, Wargrave and Lambourn; and in Cheddleton and Longton, Staffordshire. Most took place at the request of the mother. Many other clergy said that they were glad to undertake thanksgivings that put them in touch with newly-arrived children who might be brought soon into church membership through baptism. In 1951 thirty-six of the Southwark clergy had linked churching specifically with baptism, and clearly the two ceremonies were often celebrated together. In recent interviews nostalgia for churching's vanished world was expressed by two clergy. A Reading vicar spoke with a mixture of regret and relief about its demise:

> Churching doesn't happen now; I've only done two in thirty years. Pity it's gone. Weird ladies used to go in for it in Derbyshire, going off into a corner of the church. It's superstitious, grandmothers not allowing anyone into the house: idea that sex is sinful.

He is joined by the chaplain of St Bartholomew's Hospital gladly recollecting the society, now largely lost, in which the church played a central role in the lives of workers and their families, crowded together in poor terraces and tenements, with 'lots of births, all going to be churched', such as he had once known in the Poplar riverside.[24]

But from the rest there were no expressions of regret. In letters and conversations nearly all parish clergy described the churching of women as an old-fashioned ceremony, and were wary, even uneasy, about what they saw as its questionable gender assumptions. In London all those who were invited between 2002 and 2004 to talk about it were sure that the rite had been dying out since the 1960s. They gave a now familiar list of reasons: lack of demand, usually arising from decline in church membership and loss of women's personal belief; reduced apprehension about childbirth and its dangers; and their own admitted reluctance to perform the ceremony. Other incumbents considered that churching had declined to vanishing point due to profound social change: the parish of St Mary, Bow had been transformed by war damage, London County Council development

---

[24] Telephone interview in October 2003. It was not clear what was really meant by 'pity it's gone'; interview in March, 2004

and, by the 1960s, as in Brixton, the arrival of new traditions of worship brought from abroad. But what also deterred several vicars from churching was that they personally recoiled from the implications of purification in the service. They were glad to be finished with the rite.

An ex-vicar, in place from 1989 to 2000 at Christ Church, North Brixton, offered the following very full account of why he did not accept churching: a combination of his own inclinations; his unfamiliarity with, and dislike of, the Anglican ceremony; popular demand for a different rite; and the general shortage of young families in the congregation:

> I am much more conscious of doing 'naming ceremonies' and the like associated with the African community – especially the Nigerian segment, where women would not leave the confines of home until it had happened. It was therefore a good deal less formal and probably not officially recorded in any way ... the issue of the death of the churching of women may therefore at Christ Church be due to the following:
> (a) I had no knowledge of its deep tradition at the church historically (until you have just informed me).
> (b) I was not really brought up on the Prayer Book and so my first port of call liturgically may have been the Roman Rite rather than the Anglican BCP for anything that did not require PCC authority – I would then have adapted and done things informally.
> (c) The church at that time, anyway, was not the first port of call for young Mums and there were next to no young people in the congregation.
> (d) For occasional services I would tend to have responded to local request and need and would never have pro-actively offered a BCP office.[25]

Lack of demand for the ceremony was also the reason given by the rector of All Souls, Langham Place:

> I have been Rector of All Souls Church for the last twenty years, and of course have never taken a churching service here ... the congregation has traditionally been on the young side. Only in the last fifteen years have we been significantly aware of whole families becoming seriously involved – and therefore of young mothers in any great number.

The All Souls Register of Baptisms for 1912–76 shows that indeed it had witnessed a declining annual average of baptisms during these years; though, as churching records have not been preserved in these archives since 1904, it is impossible to discover what choices women's were making in those decades when baptism rates were higher.[26]

---

[25] Letter of 30 June, 2004.
[26] Letter of 31 October, 2003; this recollection was confirmed in LMA D/P89/ALS/82, Register of Baptisms 1894–1930; X095/675, Baptisms 1912–76; P89/ALS/191, Register of Services 1968–91.

Conclusion

The background to churching's decline covers a broad canvas, in which many elements in both church and society that once promoted observation of this ritual may be seen to have altered, dwindled or disappeared. Membership of the church, understanding of its liturgy, and familiarity with its various services have become minority interests. Expectations of relatives, particularly grandmothers, and of neighbours in village and suburb, no longer drive young women even to the obligatory sacraments of confirmation, marriage or baptism, let alone the more optional matter of churching. It is hard to know wherein respectability now resides; but it has surely come to be less dependent on conspicuous religious disciplines and affiliations. Professional skill has replaced the reassurances once offered by the church as women look for safe management of childbirth's uncertainties, though some will also turn to prayer and hope for good luck, and, when it is over, still find themselves giving thanks to God.

Change in the church has also contributed to the abandonment of churching as a regular rite. Though some clergy would still perform it if asked, none display any enthusiasm for promoting its ancient, complex message, as modern ceremonies take its place. And so it seems that in the future the most that grandmothers suggest will be that their daughters go for a thanksgiving, where once there would have been a churching, and the meaning of post-partum ritual will have changed for good. Perhaps the move from the forbidding older service to something more joyful, inclusive and accessible will at least ensure that sometimes during the century ahead this important rite of passage, marking a woman's stupendous achievement of giving birth to a child, is accorded some well-deserved celebration.

CONCLUSION

This piece of research has certainly provided some answers to initial questions about the churching of women. Intrigued by discovering unexpected meanings in this apparently straightforward little service of thanksgiving for the birth of a child, I learned (Chapter One) of its significance as a rite of passage, intent on protecting and controlling women at a critical moment in their lives.

At the outset the extent and duration of churching in the twentieth century was simply not known. Now (in Chapters Two to Four) church records in the three counties and Southwark diocese reveal evidence that it continued for several decades. Some of them run until well after the Second World War. Fascinating detail lay in the registers: lists of women, sometimes named; information about where they lived and so whether it was a long or short walk to the churching gate; what fees they paid out; lapses of time between birth and churching. The Southwark visitations delivered a robust and varied clerical view of the value placed upon this ceremony and the sometimes precarious hold that it was still able to maintain in 1951. Both records agreed that on average between fifty and sixty percent of churchgoing women were choosing to be churched after childbirth.

Oral testimony (in Chapter Five) provided an opportunity to pursue the study into the post-war years, and to examine the experience of this childbirth ritual. Women's words, both written and recorded, recollected a variety of moods. All could remember their own genuine relief at the end of a time of pain and anxiety; but when it came to being churched, generally under maternal direction, their reactions had ranged from willing obedience to indifference, impatience, and sometimes downright hostility. Happy participation in this moment of thanksgiving was balanced by indignation at being pushed around, outrage at suggestions of sin and uncleanness, and indifference to the requirements of the church. From clergy came cautiously positive views of the rite of churching, once an accepted part of the life of a busy parish; but also dismay about its underlying attitude to married women. Several knew nothing about the ritual, and expressed a politely detached interest in its history. All seemed to welcome the new, inclusive post-1980 thanksgivings.

Does this rejection and reluctance tell us that judgments about women and their moral position are now coming to an end? Not quite. For centuries the story of Eve's first disobedience was a potent legacy with which to frame numerous strictures against her inheritors, among them that every new mother needed ritual purification. Echoes of shame, discipline and exclusion are still found in several branches of the Christian church, and linger on in many other fields, replaying a multitude of gender-based prejudices. But with the demise of the churching rite (discussed in Chapter Six) one taboo will surely have been reduced. Its time must have run out by the end of the twentieth century, in which sceptical intellectual climate dismissed the ancient childbirth superstitions, and new ceremonies aimed for enhancement rather than penalty and shame.

APPENDIX

SOURCES AND BIBLIOGRAPHY

Personal Testimony

Below are names of all those who helped with my research, especially those who offered personal testimony, to whom I am indebted for their recollections and comments given in interviews and conversations. As promised at the time, I have not included the names of my 1997 correspondents.

Women's Groups
Blackheath, St. John the Baptist's Fellowship Group; Burton-on-Trent, St Modwen's weekly coffee-morning; Cheddleton, St. Edward's, Knitting Group; Haggerston, St Chad's monthly luncheon group; Lichfield, St Chad's meeting after morning service; Norton-le-Moors, St Bartholomew's church members; Radley, History Club; Reading, Maiden Erleigh Ladies Club; Wantage, Old People's Day Centre; Wednesbury, St Luke's church members.

Individual Women
From Berkshire: Christine Bland; June Brookes; Laura Clark; Ethel Dorsey; Phyllis Evans; June Hunt; Rosemary Jarvis; Alwyne Jeffries; Theo Liffo; Margaret Mayo; Miriam Peck; Anne Radford; Jean Scuse; Edith Swarbrick; Sue Terry; Eva Vause; Winifred.
From Oxfordshire: Helen Willcox; Doris Foster; Mary Pinnock; Suzanne Cooper.
From London: Alfreda Hayes; Jessie Hobbs; Gill Manock; Daphne Potts.
From Staffordshire: Phyllis Barclay; Joan Ely; Elsie Holloway; Irene Gassor; Paula. Mifflin; Jennifer Mulliner; Susan Rout; Magdalena; Joan and Joyce; Gladys Wilkes; Pat Wright.
From other counties: Mary Barsley; E. Dorothy Graham; Margaret Ross; Marinda Rowlandson.

Individual Laymen
From Berkshire: Frank Brooks; William Mitchell; David Baldwin.
From Oxfordshire: John Cooper.
From Staffordshire: Gordon Barclay; Trevor Harvey; Ken Holloway.

Individual Clergy
The Revd Dr Stuart Bell; The Revd Richard Bewes, vicar of All Souls, Langham Place; The Revd Robert Bull, vicar of St Chad, Litchfield; The Revd Dr Terry Burkes,

former chaplain, University of Reading; The Revd. George Bush, vicar of St Mary, Cheapside; The Revd Dr David Chapman; The Revd Canon Christopher Clarke, vicar of St Andrew, Sonning; The Revd Haigh Etches, rector of Bear Wood, Sindlesham; The Revd Paul Farthing, vicar of St Modwen, Burton-upon-Trent; Fr Michael Fisher, clergy team of St Chad and St Mary, Stafford; The Revd John Gawn-Cain, former vicar of Uffington, Fernham and Shellingford; Canon Alan Griffiths, Diocese of Portsmouth; The Revd Nigel Godfrey; The Revd Geoffrey Gorer, vicar of St Mary, Bromley by Bow; The Revd Horace Harper, clergy team of St Chad and St Mary, Stafford; The Revd Elizabeth Jackson, former chaplain of Royal Berkshire Hospital, Reading; The Revd Paul Kingman, vicar of Christ Church, Stone; The Revd Richard Kingsbury, vicar of St Peter, Caversham; The Revd Suzanne Knight, vicar of St Stephen, Reading; The Revd Mark Laynesmith, chaplain of Reading University; The Revd Martin Leigh, vicar of St Edward's, Cheddleton; The Revd Fr Paul Lockett, vicar of Ss; Mary & Chad, Longton; The Revd John Markham, former chaplain of Royal Berkshire Hospital, Reading; The Revd Dr. John Ogden, former chaplain of University of Reading; Bishop Basil Osborne; The Revd John Salter, vicar of Ss Peter & Paul, Wantage; The Revd Dr Jeremy Sheehy, former Principal, St Stephen's House, Oxford; The Revd Brian Shelton, vicar of St Mary the Virgin, Reading; The Revd Michael Stevens, chaplain of St Bartholomew-the-Less, Spitalfields, London; The Revd William Stewart, former vicar of St Michael, Lambourn; The Revd J. P. Townend, vicar of Chaddleworth, Brightwalton and Fawley, Berkshire; The Revd Fr John Walker, vicar of St John the Evangelist, Walworth; Bishop Kallistos Ware; The Revd Jill Warren, vicar of St Paul's, Wednesbury; The Revd Stephan Welch, vicar of St Peter's, Hammersmith; The Revd James Westcott, vicar of St Chad's, Haggerston; The late Ven Frank Weston, Archdeacon of Oxford; 1998 Bishop of Knaresborough; The Revd Alan Wilson, former vicar of St Michael's, Sandhurst; The Revd Michael Wright, vicar of St Barnabas, Jericho, Oxford.

Those who offered help with my research
Berkshire: The late Revd Carole Cull; The Revd Ian Graham; Professor Helen King; Mary Mann; Brigitte Mitchell; Vivien Mosse, Julie Shuttleworth; Karen Sperry; The Revd Jim Payne; Audrey Verdin; Christine Wardingly; The Revd Tom Woodhams;
London: Lucille Barber; Dr Susan Brown; Heather Carson, curator of the Methodist Museum; Samantha Farhall, St Barthlomew's Hospital Archivist.
Oxfordshire: Peter Forsaith and Gareth Lloyd of the Methodist Studies Unit, The Wesley Centre, Oxford Brookes University.
Elsewhere: Ethel Bounds; David Bryer; Joan Foster; Frank and Sheila Himsworth; Hazel Morgan; The Revd Philip Oliver; Robert Sherlock.

SOURCES AND BIBLIOGRAPHY

Bibliography
1. MANUSCRIPT SOURCES

Berkshire
BRO (Berkshire Record Office)
Churching Registers
D/P172B 1A/2, St Stephen, Reading 1919–1942.
D/P1491A/3 on MF8399, St John the Baptist, New Windsor, Register of Churchings and Fees, 1796–1832;
Registers of Services, Preachers' Books and Fee Books
D/P7 1B/2: Register of Services, 1899–1906, Holy Trinity, Ardington; D/P73 1B/1, 1B/3, St Catherine, Bear Wood.
D/P8 1B / 1B / 3: MF 93804/1900–1907, St Nicholas, East Challow.
D/P71 1B/13: St Mary, Newtown, 1902–1931; D/P95 1B/1, St James, Radley.
D/P143 1B/2: 1B/3: Ss Peter & Paul, Wantage, 1898–1912, 1912–1921.
D/P98 1B/7: St Mary the Virgin, Reading, 1916–1921.
D/P102 1B/1–5: St Michael, Sandhurst, 1908–1945.
D/P112 1B/3: St Andrew, Shrivenham, 1907–1928.
D/P109 1 B/1: St Faith, Shellingford, 1887–1926.
D/P 82 1B/1: All Saints, Lockinge, 1927–1950.
D/P75 1B/2: All Saints, West Ilsley, 1902–1909; 1B/3: 1909–1917.
D/P157/1/B/2, /3: St Michael, Wootton 1904–1910, 1910–21; Vestry Minutes for 1913–1926,
D/P 24/1B1–3: All Saints, Brightwalton,1879–1932.
D/P113/1B/1, Register of Fees due to Vicar, Clerk and Sexton of the Parish of Sonning, 1832–50; 1B/2: Register of Fees 1851–1888.
Parish Magazines
D/P97/ 28A/ 9–11: St Lawrence, Reading, 1903 – 1928; BRO D/P96/ 28A/ 17–47, 67, 87: St Giles, Reading, 1900–1920, 1937, 1950, 1960, 1970; BRO D/P98 28A/ 6 (1909), /16 (1918–21, /19 (1930–33), /23 (1947–50): St Mary the Virgin, Reading, 1909–1950.

London
LMA (London Metropolitan Archives)
Churching Registers
P78/JNE/ 006, St John the Evangelist, Blackheath, 1926–1956.
P85/CTC2/ 20, Christ Church, North Brixton, 1907–1971.
P78/EMM/ 1, Emmanuel, West Greenwich, 1888–1906.
P80/PET/ 35/ 1, St Peter's, Hammersmith, 1870–1944.
P81/EMM/ 30, Emmanuel, West Hampstead, 1912–1951.
P83/PAU2/ 22/1, St Paul, Upper Holloway, 1870–1947.
P89/ALS/ 95, All Souls, Langham Place, Marylebone, 1878–1904.
P76/PAU2/37, St Paul, Clerkenwell, Register of Churchings 1878–82.
Registers of Services, Preachers' Books and Fee Books
P91/ANN/12, St Anne, Shoreditch, 1910–16; P 91/CHD/5, St. Chad, Haggerston, 1939–1945.
P 88/MRY2/61/1, St Mary Bromley by Bow, 1901–1913; 2/62, 1913–1919; P/ 91/109, St John

the Baptist, Hoxton, 1927–1930; P 92 / LDM / 36, The Lady Margaret Church, Walworth, 1913–1922.

P92/GEO/372, St George the Martyr, Southwark, Rector's Fee Book, 1777–1783; P95/LEN/81–83, St Leonard, Streatham, Clerk's Register of Fees, 1787–1806; P93/DUN/208, St Dunstan and All Saints, Rector's Fee Book, 1821–30

P90/PET/1, St Peter, Regent Square, St Pancras (Camden), Register of Baptisms, 1829–1841.

P80/STE/62, St Stephen, Hammersmith, Church Attendance Book, 1859–1884

P91/TRI/28, Holy Trinity, Hoxton, Register of Parish Congregational Meetings, 1888–1891.

P95/TRI 1/88, Holy Trinity, Clapham, Account Book of Samuel Symonds, Lecturer 1688–1689.

P82/GEO 1/73, St George, Bloomsbury, Rector's Fee Book, 1765–1772.

Visitation replies

DS/VB 002–13, Diocese of Southwark, Bishops Primary Visitations: 1907; 1915; 1919; 1929; 1936; 1951.

DS/VB/11, 1936 Bishop's Primary Visitation, 1936, St Luke's, Eltham Park; St Clement of Rome, E. Dulwich.

DS/VB/13, Bishop's Primary Visitation, 1951, XV /15, St Chrysostom, Peckham; XV /13, St Silas, Nunhead; VIII /13, St Mary, Beddington.

Parish magazines

P91 / ALL /93–104, All Saints, Haggerston; P94 /AND /203: St Andrew, Newington; P94 /MTS / 08: St Mathias, Stoke Newington.

Oxfordshire

OCRO (Oxford County Record Office)

MSS. Oxf. Dioc. Papers, C300, 1906; C372, 1909; C378, 1918; C383, 1924; C389, 1936.

Staffordshire

SRO (Staffordshire Record Office)

Churching Registers

D729, St Chad, Lichfield, 1845–1883; D834/1/6/1 St Mary, Stafford, 1875–1905; D4242/5 Christ Church, Stone, 1861–1884.

Registers of Services

D1193/5/1, St Luke's Mission, Wednesbury, 1885–1908.

D 5590/1/8, St Edward, Cheddleton, 1899–1904.

D 834/1/6/1, Holy Trinity, Eccleshall, 1931–1952.

Registers of Services, Preachers' Books and Fee Books

F4219/1/8: St Modwen, Burton-on-Trent, Fee Book 1914–1920.

D 497 / 3 / 1 St Edward, Cheddleton, Incumbent's Fee Book, 1920–1972.

Longton, Ss Mary & Chad, Preacher's Book, 1888–1894.

Parish magazines

D4160/6/41 Ss Mary & Chad, Longton, bound volumes of parish magazines, 1897–1905, 1959–1961.

D5676/7/3–5: St James-the-Less, Longton, parish magazines, 1893–1904.

Woking, Surrey

SHC (Surrey History Centre)

SOURCES AND BIBLIOGRAPHY

Churching Register
2397/1/46, St Mary, Mortlake, 1911–36; 3706/4, 1939–1971 (uncatalogued papers in box).

2. PRINTED SOURCES
Primary sources

Church Service books
The Sarum Missal in English, ed. V. Stanley, part II, vol. IX (London, 1911).
The Missal in Latin and English, 2nd edn (London, 1958).
The Book of Common Prayer, and Administration of the Sacraments and other Rites and Ceremonies of the Church, According to the Use of The United Church of England and Ireland (Cambridge, 1862).
The Book of Common Prayer with the Additions and Deviations Proposed in 1928 (Oxford, 1928).
The Alternative Service Book 1980: Services authorized for use in the Church of England in conjunction with the Book of Common Prayer (London, 1980).
Common Worship Pastoral Services (London, 2000).
Methodist *Book of Orders*, 1936.
Methodist *Book of Orders*, 1999.
Service Book of the Holy Orthodox Catholic Apostolic Church, ed., Isabel Florence Hapgood, (New Jersey, 1906, revised 1975).

Histories, Surveys, Commentaries, Diaries
Ayres, J. (ed.), *Paupers & Pig Killers: the Diary of William Holland, A Somerset Parson, 1799–1818* (Stroud, 2000).
Bacon, G. W., *The A–Z of Victorian London* (London, 1887).
Bede, *A History of the English Church and People*, translated Leo Shirley-Price (Harmondsworth, 1962).
Beresford, J. (ed.), *The Diary of a Country Parson: the Reverend James Woodforde 1758–1781*, 5 vols (Oxford, 1924).
Booth, C., *Life and Labour of the People of London*, 17 vols, 3rd Series: *Religious Influence* (London, 1902–1903).
Brightman, *The English Rite*, 2 vols (1915).
Cobbett, W., *Rural Rides* (Harmondsworth, 1975).
Collins, J., *The Revd John Aldworth and his Parish of East Lockinge, 1684–1792* (Wantage, 1989).
Cornish, The Revd J. G., *Reminiscences of a Country Life*, ed. Vaughan Cornish (London, 1936).
Dils, J. (ed.), *An Historical Atlas of Berkshire* (Reading, 2000).
Edelen, Georges (ed), William Harrison, *The Description of England: The Classic Contemporary Account of Tudor Social Life* (Washington and New York, 1968).
Henry, M., *Commentary on the Whole Bible* (London 1960).
Hill, the Revd E., *Diary* (private publication, undated).
Llewellyn-Smith, Sir H. (ed.), *The New Survey of London Life and Labour*, 9 vols (London, 1930–1935).
Methodist *Faith and Order Committee Agenda* (Liverpool, 1975).
Methodist *Church Conference Agenda* (Southampton, 1999).

Methodist *Recorder* (June and July 1999).

Temple Scott (ed.), *The Confessions of St. Augustine, Bishop of Hippo*, vol. X (London, 1911).

Secondary Sources

Abercrombie, N., et al., 'Superstition and Religion: the God of the Gaps,' in Martin, D. and Hill, M. (eds), *A Sociological Year Book of Religion in Britain*, 3 (1970).

Addleshaw, G. W. O., and Etchells, F., *The Architectural Setting of Anglican Worship* (London, 1948).

Anon., *Report on the 1951 Census* (HMSO, 1953).

Barnsby, G. J., *Social Conditions in the Black Country 1800–1900* (Wolverhampton, 1980).

Beresford, J. (ed.), *The Diary of a Country Parson: The Reverend James Woodforde 1758–1802*, 5 vols (Oxford, 1924).

Bingham, Adrian, Review Essay 'An Era of Domesticity? Histories of Women and Gender in Interwar Britain', *Cultural and Social History*; Vol. 1, No. 2 (2004).

Blum, R. and E., *The Dangerous Hour: The Lore of Crisis and Mystery in Rural Greece* (London, 1970).

Brake, G. T., *Policy and Politics in British Methodism, 1932–1982* (London, 1984).

Brierley, P. (ed.), *Prospects for the Nineties: All England Trends and Tables from the English Church Census, with Denominations and Churchmanships*, vols 1–11 (London, 1991).

Brown, C., *The Death of Christian Britain: Understanding Secularization 1800–2000* (London and New York, 2001).

Brown, P., *The Rise of Western Christendom: Triumph and Diversity A. D. 200–1000*, 2nd edn (Oxford, 2003).

Bruce, S., *A House Divided: Protestantism, Schism and Secularization* (London and New York, 1990).

Bruce, S., 'The Demise of Christianity in Britain' in Davie *et al*, *Predicting Religion*.

Carlson, L. H. (ed.), *The Writings of Henry Barrow, 1587–1590* (London, 1966).

Chadwick, O., *The Victorian Church*, Part II (London, 1970).

Chinn, Carl, *They Worked All Their Lives: Women of the Urban Poor in England, 1880–1939* (Manchester, 1988).

S. D. Church, 'Paganism in Conversion-Age Anglo-Saxon England: the Evidence of Bede's *Ecclesiastical History* Reconsidered', *History*, vol. 93, issue 2, no. 310, April, 2008.

Clark, D., *Between Pulpit and Pew: Folk Religion in a North Yorkshire Village* (Cambridge, 1982).

Collins, E. J. T., 'Landholdings and Agriculture c.1900', *An Historical Atlas of Berkshire* (Reading, 2000).

Coster, W., 'Purity, Profanity and Puritanism: The Churching of Women 1500–1700', in *Women in the Church*, W. J. Sheils and D. Wood (eds), *Studies in Church History*, vol. XXVII (Oxford, 1990).

Coster, W., *Family and Kinship in England 1450–1800* (Hong Kong, 2001).

Cox, J., *The English Churches in a Secular Society: Lambeth 1870–1930* (Oxford, 1982).

Crawford, P., 'The Construction and Experience of Maternity in Seventeenth Century England,' in Valerie Fildes (ed.), *Women as Mothers in Pre-Industrial England* (London and New York, 1990).

Crawford, P., 'Attitudes to Menstruation in Seventeenth Century England', *Past & Present*,

(1981).

Cressy, D., 'Purification, Thanksgiving and the Churching of Women in Post-Reformation England', *Past and Present*, XV (1993).

Cressy, D., *Birth, Marriage and Death: Ritual Religions and the Life Cycle in Tudor and Stuart England* (Oxford, 1997).

Cross, F. L. (ed.), *The Oxford Dictionary of the Christian Church* (London, 1958).

Crossick, G., *An Artisan Elite in Victorian Society: Kentish London 1840–1880* (London 1978).

Davie, G., *Religion in Britain since 1945: Believing without Belonging* (Oxford, 1994).

Davie, G., Heelas, P., and Woodhead, L. (eds), *Predicting Religion* (London, 2003).

Davies, D., Watkins, C., and Winter, M., *Church and Religion in Rural England* (Edinburgh, 1991).

Davies, M. L. (ed.), *Maternity: Letters from Working Women, 1915* (London, 1915, Tiptree, 1978).

Douglas, M., *Purity and Danger: an Analysis of the Concepts of Pollution and Taboo* (London, 1994).

Drabble, M., *Arnold Bennett* (London, 1974).

Garbett, C., *The Church of England Today* (London, 1953).

Gennep, A. van, *Rites of Passage* (London, 1960).

Gibson, Bishop E. C. S., *The First and Second Prayer Books of Edward VI* (London, 1910).

Gilbert, A. D., *The Making of Post-Christian Britain* (London & New York, 1980).

Gilbert, A. D., *Religion and Society in Industrial England: church, chapel and social change, 1740–1914* (London, 1976).

Goldin, H. E., *The Jewish Woman and her Home* (New York, 1941).

Green, I. M., *The Re-Establishment of the Church of England* (Oxford, 1978).

Hamilton, M., *The Sociology of Religion: Theoretical and Comparative Perspectives* (London, 1995).

Hartman, T., and Marmon, N., 'Lived Regulations, Systemic Attributions: Menstrual Separation and Ritual Immersion in the Experience of Orthodox Jewish Women', *Gender and Society*, vol. 18, no. 3 (June 2004).

Hastings, A., *A History of English Christianity 1920–1985* (London, 2001).

Havinden, M. A., *Estate Villages: a Study of the Berkshire Villages of Ardington and Lockinge* (London, 1966).

Hays, H. R., *The Dangerous Sex: the Myth of Feminine Evil* (London, 1966).

Hebblethwaite, D., *Liturgical Revision in the Church of England 1984–2004: the Working of the Liturgical Commission* (Cambridge, 2004).

Hinton, M., *The Anglican Parochial Clergy: a Celebration* (London, 1994).

Hirst, R., 'Social Networks and Personal Beliefs: an Example from Modern Britain', in Davie, et al., *Predicting Religion* (London, 2003).

Hyman E. Goldin, *The Jewish Woman and her Home* (New York, 1941).

Inwood, S., *A History of London* (London and Basingstoke, 1998).

Jalland, P., *Women, Marriage and Politics 1860–1914* (Oxford, 1988).

Jephson, A., *My Life in London* (London, 1910).

Kearns, K., *Dublin Tenement Life: an Oral History* (Dublin, 1994).

Kennedy, W. P. M., *Elizabethan Episcopal Administration*, vol. I (London, 1924).

Lee, B. R., 'Men's Recollections of a Women's Rite: Medieval English Men's Recollections Regarding the Rite of the Purification of Women after Childbirth', *Gender & History*, vol.

14, no. 2 (August 2002).
Leyser, H., *Medieval Women: a Social History of Women in England, 450–1500* (London, 1996).
Lowther Clarke, W. K. (ed.), *Liturgy and Worship* (London, 1932).
Lloyd, R., *The Church of England 1900–1965* (London, 1966).
Lloyd, T., *Thanksgiving for the Gift of a Child: A Commentary on the Common Worship Service* (Cambridge, 2001).
Malmgreen, G. (ed.), *Religion in the Lives of English Women 1760–1930* (London and Sidney, 1986).
Meens, R., 'Questioning Ritual Purity: The Influence of Gregory the Great's Answers to Augustine's Queries, about Childbirth, Menstruation and Sexuality', in *St Augustine and the Conversion of England*, ed. Richard Gameson (Stroud 1999); '"A relic of superstition": Bodily Impurity and the Church from Gregory the Great to the Twelfth Century Decretists', in Poorthus and Schwarz, *Purity and Holiness: the Heritage of Leviticus*, vol. II (Brill, Leiden, Boston, Koln, 2000).
McCulloch, D., *Cranmer* (Yale, 1996).
McLeod, H., *Class and Religion in the Late Victorian City* (London, 1974).
McLeod, H., *Religion and the Working Class in Nineteenth-Century Britain* (London and Basingstoke, 1984).
McLeod, H., 'New Perspectives on Victorian Working Class Religion: the Oral Evidence', *Oral History Journal*, vol. 14 (1986).
McLeod, H., 'Religion', in J. Langton and R. J. Morris (eds), *Atlas of Industrializing Britain 1780–1914* (London, 1986).
McLeod, H., *Religion and Society in England 1850–1914* (London and Basingstoke, 1996)
Morris, J. N., *Religion and Urban Change: Croydon 1840–1914* (Woodbridge, 1992).
Newby, H., *Country Life: a Social History of Rural England* (London, 1987).
Newby, H., *Property, Paternalism and Power: Class and Control in Rural England* (London, 1978).
Obelkevich, J., *Religion and Rural Society: South Lindsey 1825–1875* (Oxford, 1976).
Okley, Judith, 'Gipsy Women: Models in Conflict,' in Ardener, Shirley (ed.), *Perceiving Women* (London, 1975).
Palliser, D., *The Staffordshire Landscape* (London, 1976).
Parker, R., *Miasma: Pollution and Purification in Early Greek Religion* (Oxford, 1983).
Pember Reeves, M., *Round About a Pound a Week* (London, 1913, Tiptree, 1979).
Pevsner, N., *The Buildings of England: Berkshire* (Harmondsworth, 1966).
Pevsner, N. and Cherry, B., *The Buildings of England: London 2: South* (Yale, 2002).
Pevsner, N. *The Buildings of England: Staffordshire* (Harmondsworth, 1974).
Pevsner, N., and Nairn, I., *The Buildings of England: Surrey* (Yale, 2002).
Poorthus, M. J. H. M., and Schwarz, J. (eds), *Purity and Holiness: the Heritage of Leviticus*, vol. II (Brill, Leiden, Boston, Koln, 2000).
Porter, R., *London: A Social History* (Harmondsworth, 1996).
Ray, D. E., 'A View from the Childwife's Pew: The Development of Rites around Childbirth in the Anglican Communion', *Anglican and Episcopal History*, vol. LXIX, no. 4 (2000).
Roberts, E. A. M., *A Woman's Place: an Oral History of Working-Class Women 1890–1940* (Oxford 1984).
Roberts, E. A. M., *Women and Families: An Oral History, 1940–1970* (Oxford, 1995).
Roberts, E. A. M., *Working Class Barrow and Lancaster 1890–1930*, Occasional Paper no.

2 (Lancaster, 1976).
Ross, E., 'Survival Networks: Women's Neighbourhood Sharing in London Before World War I', *History Workshop*, issue 15 (Spring 1983).
Ruowhorst, G., 'Leviticus 12 to 15 in Early Christianity', in Poorthus and Schwarz, *Purity and Holiness*.
Sandford, J., *Gypsies* (London, 1975).
Sheppard, F., *London, a History* (Oxford, 1998).
Schmemann, A. *Of Water and the Spirit* (St. Vladimir's Seminary Press, 1974).
Shorter, E., *A History of Women's Bodies* (Penguin, 1982).
Stacey, M., *Tradition and Change: a Study of Banbury* (Oxford, 1960).
Strayer, J., *Dictionary of the Middle Ages*, vol. III (New York, 1982).
Thomas, K. V., *Religion and the Decline of Magic* (Harmondsworth, 1973).
Thomas, K. V., *Man and the Natural World: Changing Attitudes in England, 1500–1800* (Harmondsworth, 1983).
Tindal Hart, A., *The Curate's Lot: the Story of the Unbeneficed English Clergy* (Newton Abbott, 1971).
Wickham, E. R., *Church and People in an Industrial City* (London, 1957).
Williams, W. M., *A West Country Village: Ashworthy: Family, Kinship and Land* (London, 1963).
Williams, S. C., *Religious Belief and Popular Culture in Southwark c.1880–1939* (Oxford, 1999).
Williams, S. C., 'The Problem of Belief: the Place of Oral History in the Study of Popular Religion', *Oral History,* Autumn 1996.
Williams, A. S., *Women & Childbirth in the Twentieth Century: a History of the National Birthday Trust Fund 1928–93* (Stroud, 1997).
Willmott, P. and Young, M., *Family and Kinship in East London* (London, 1957).
Willmott, P., *The Evolution of a Community: A Study of Dagenham after Forty Years* (London, 1963).
Wilson Jones, J., *The History of the Black Country* (Birmingham, 1949).
Woods, R., and Shelton, N., *An Atlas of Victorian Mortality* (Liverpool, 1997).
Worth, J., *Call the Midwife: a True Story of the East End in the 1950s* (London, 2002).

Church and Parish Histories

Barber, L., *Christ Church, North Brixton 1855–1995*, 3 vols (London, 2000).
Bowe, K. and Harvey, T., *Holy Trinity Church, Ecclesball* (undated).
Cheadle, R., *A History of Ss Mary and Chad Church, Longton* (Keele, 2000).
Drysdale, P., Ford, R., Groser, P., Orchard, M., Parkes, A., and Williams, K., *The History of Radley* (Abingdon, 2002).
Holmes, P. J., *St Michael and All Angels, Sandhurst* (undated).
Hudson, R., *Bloomsbury, Fitzrovia & Soho* (Haggerston, 1996).
Lewis, R. A., *Three Stafford Churches* (Stafford, 1980).
Moss, V., *An Illustrated Guide to Shrivenham* (Faringdon, 1995).
Over, L., *The Parish Church of St. Peter, Caversham* (undated).
Perkins, A., *The Book of Sonning* (Wiltshire, 1999).
Philip, K., *Reflected in Wantage*, vols I and II (Tring, 1969–70).
Underhill, C. H. and Pitchford, H. H., *The Parish Church of Burton upon Trent [St Modwen]* (Burton, 1976).

Unpublished Theses
Bartlett, A. B. 'The Churches in Bermondsey 1880–1939' (Unpublished Ph.D. Thesis, University of Birmingham, 1987).
Staton, M. W., 'The Rite of Churching: a Sociological Analysis, with Special Reference to an Urban Area in Newcastle-upon-Tyne' (Unpublished M.A. Thesis, University of Newcastle, 1980).
Sykes, R. P. M. 'Popular Religion in Dudley and the Gornals c.1914–1965' (Unpublished. Ph.D. Thesis, University of Wolverhampton, 1999).

INDEX

attitudes to churching among Anglican clergy 44–5, 91, 94–5, 99–100, 117–23, 134–5. *See also* churching clergy, encouraging/appreciating, and reluctance to celebrate
attitudes to churching among mothers 12–13, 93–4, 104–124, 129
Augustine of Canterbury 3–5
Augustine, St 23

baptism related to churching 17, 19–22, 46–56, 73, 87, 92–4, 107–8, 117–20, 123, 134
Baptist Church 21–2
Barber, Lucille 107
Barrow, Henry 12, 21
Bartlett, Alan 81–2, 95, 97–8
Bede, the Venerable vii, 3
Berkshire's 14 'churching parishes' 26–31, 41–2, 57–9, 66, 121–2, Map 1, Plate 4, p.
– New Windsor, St John the Baptist 15
– Reading, St Lawrence 44
– Reading, St Giles 44
– Sonning, St Andrew 15
Berkshire personal testimony 108–9
Berkshire social landscape 26–31, 56–60, 66–9
Bieler, Ludwig 1
Booth, Charles 36, 62, 78, 81, 120
Brierley, P and Wraight, H 132
Brown, Callum 99, 130
Butler, William 15, 26

Caspers, Charles 8
Census 1951 Report 78–80
chaplains 107, 117, 133, 134
childbirth's pain and danger 5, 9, 13, 19, 22, 44, 111–2, 122, 124, 131–2, 136
Chinn, Carl 130
Church Association 42–3
churched women's lives
– community pressure on 29, 106, 114–5, 122, 124, 136
– considered unclean until churched 4, 6–7, 9, 16, 21–2, 106, 116, 120–129, 134,
– daughters and mothers 86, 95–6, 98, 101–24, 128–31. *See also* matriarchy, maternal pressure
– family networks 54–59, 105–7
– family occupations 63–6
– frequency and regularity of churching 50–4, Plates 9 & 10, p.
– husband 9–10, 15, 24, 63–6, 100, 103–4, 113, 118, 123
– maternal pressure on 55, 95, 103–4, 104–9, 116–7, 119, 127–8
– residence 56–63
– timing of churching after child's birth 66–9, Plates 11a & 11b, pp.
– unmarried 64, 68, 81. *See also* attitudes to churching among mothers
churching after difficult births 111–3, 122
churching after stillbirth 17–8, 68
churching and churchgoing 77, 81, 87,

94, 96, 119
churching and social class 4, 32–4, 38, 63–6, 77, 81–90, 94, 101–4
churching and thanksgiving liturgies
– Sarum Missal 'Blessing' 1, 8–10
– 1549 'Purification' 10
– 1552 'Churching' 10–13
– 1645 abolished 12–3
– 1662 restored 13–4
– 1928 revised 10, 16–7, 133, Plate 2, p.
– 1980 Alternative Version 10, 17–18, 124
– 2000 Common Worship 18–20
  naming ceremonies 81, 135
– thanksgivings in other churches 22
churching ceremony traditions
– cleansing with hyssop 1, 9–10
– fee or offering 1, 11, 15, 17, 63–6, 120, 133–4
– pew 13–14, Plate 1, p.
– public celebration 8–10, 11–13, 20
– no longer a ceremonious rite 104
– veil 12–13
churching clergy
– encouraging / appreciating churching 30, 92, 103–4, 117, 119–20, 122–4, 134
– familiarity with parishioners 40–1
– financial pressure 41
– High Church 26, 35, 38, 42–3, 84, 119–20, 124
– isolation 71
– long service 40
– Low Church 42–3
– parish routine 18, 92, 116, 118
– parish problems 91, 97, 118, 125
– records 24, 26–7, 31–2, 34–5, 38–45, 47, 125–6, Plates 3, 7, 8, 13, pp.
– reluctance to celebrate churchings 92, 95, 118, 134–5

– social background 77, 91–2
– using churching as discipline 14–5, 26, 42, 129–30, Plate 13, p.
– views of parish life 78, 90, 91–6, 119, 134
– views of village life 89–90, 119, 121–2
churching, decline of 89–90, 92–3, 115, 125–36
churching, extent of 81–90, 101–4, Maps 1–4 in Plates 4–6 & 12, pp.
churching no longer obligatory 13
churching, rates of
– affected by powerful clergy 27, 30–1
– affected by dominant local family 28, 56
– among poorer parishioners 14–15, 27, 28, 32–3, 38, 47, 54, 56, 65, 81–6
– among richer parishioners 15, 16, 29, 30, 68–9, 88–9
– compared with baptisms 47–50, Plates 9 & 10, pp.
– estimated in 1951 Southwark visitation 75–90, 126–7
– in inner urban parishes 47, 54, 81–6
– in rural parishes 28, 56
churching, survival of 95, 99, 112–3, 119, 121–3
Cobbett, William 26
Collins, E. J. T. 66
Congregationalists 22
Cornish, J. G. 29, 40
Coster, Will vii, 14
Cottam, S. E. 39, 42
Cox, Jeffrey 95
Cranmer 10
Crawford, Patricia 6
Cressy, David vii, 2, 13–4

Davies, Horton 12–4
Dils, Joan 26
Douglas, Mary 2

INDEX

Eve vii, 3

Fisher, Geoffrey 17

Garbett, Cyril 81, 98
gender assumptions 3, 4, 22–3, 105, 119, 120–1, 129, 134–5
Gennep, Arnold van 2
Gibson, E.C.S. 10–11
Green, Ian 13
Gregory I, Pope 1, 3–4

Harrison, William 11
Havinden, Mark 29
Haw, George 36
Hazzard, Dorothy 12, 21
Hebblethwaite, David 17–18
Hellenic ritual 4–5
Hempton, David 41
Hinton, Michael 45
Holland, William 14–15

Jalland, Pat 16
Jewish ritual 5

Kearns, Kevin 21

Lee, Becky vii, 3, 9,
Levitical Decrees vii
Liturgical Commission 17, 99
Llewelyn Davies, M. 131
Llewelyn Smith, H. 78
Lloyd Lindsay, 28–9
Lloyd, Roger 123
Lloyd, Trevor 18–20
London's 12 'churching parishes' 34–48, 51–3, 61–5, 107, Map 3, Plate 6. p.
London personal testimony 107
London social landscape 34–8
– East End 47, 61–2, 65

– inner urban 35, 61
– suburban 36–7, 47–9
– West End 47, 62, 64–5
London population movement 82–6, 88

maternity hospitals 77, 84–5, 93, 106–8, 115–8, 131–2
McLeod, Hugh 62
matriarchy
– power 96, 99, 106–17, 127–8
– decline 97, 127–8. *See also* daughters and mothers, maternal pressure
Meens, Rob 4
menstruation 3, 5–6, 115, 120
Methodist Church 20–1
Mitchison, Rosalind 131
Moss, Vivien, 28, 39
Mowll, William 39, 43

New Survey of Life and Labour 78, 81–8

Obelkevich, James 5
Okley, Judith 5
Orthodox Church 22–3

paganism 3, 5, 95, 118–9
Palliser, David 32
parish magazines 44, 49
Parker, Robert 4
Parsons, Randall 28
Paul, St 3
Pember Reeves, M., 66
penitentials 1, 8
pollution / uncleanness 4–5, 116, 120–1
popular attitudes to religion
– belief 112–3, 132
– ceremonial, love of 113, 119–20. *See also* churching ceremony tradi-

tions
- conservatism 120–2
- doubt/decline 132–3
- folk religion 119
- indifference 44–5, 81, 83, 84–9, 98
- secularism 45, 132–3. *See also* superstition
Porter, Roy 36
purification 1–6, 10–12, 21, 103, 105–12, 119, 134
- omitted from service title 10–11, 21. *See also* gender assumptions *and* churched women's lives, considered unclean until churched

questionnaires and responses 101–5

Ray, Donna vii, 12, 14, 16, 22
Roberts, Elizabeth 130
Roberts, Robert 130
Roman Catholic Church 21, 109
Ross, Ellen, 54
Ruowhorst, Gerald 4

Sanders, Henry 31, 39, 40, 42
Southwark's visitations
- 1936 33, 73–4, 91
- 1951 33, 73, 91
- clergy replies 72–89
- database 75
Southwark's social landscape 72–4, 84–90, 96–7
- analysed in Census Report 1951 78, 80
- analysed in New Survey 78–9

Staffordshire's 10 'churching parishes' 31–4, 42–53, 60, 63–4, 106
- Norton-in-the-Moor, St Bartholomew 106, 112, 118
Staffordshire personal testimony 106–7, 116
- Cheddleton knitting group 55, 106, 118
- Wednesbury group 114–6
Staffordshire social landscape 31–8, 63–4
Staley, Vernon 8
Staton, M. W. 6–7
superstition 2, 5–7, 73, 84–5, 87, 94–7, 106–7, 111, 114, 116, 123–4, 134
- fear of ill-luck / the devil 2, 5, 12, 21–2, 95, 111–2, 114–6, 119, 124
Sykes, Richard. vii, 7, 129

taboo vii, 34–5, 116
thanksgivings
- celebrated beyond England 22
- replace churching 16–22

Thomas, Keith 5–6

Vasey, Michael 20

Young, M. and Willmott, P., 127

Walter, Sir John 29
Williams, Sarah C. 81, 95
Williams, A. Susan 131
Woodforde, James 14
Worth, Jennifer 131

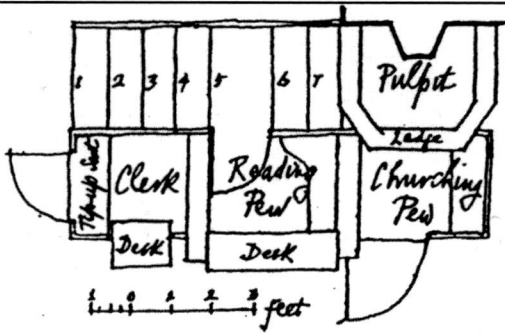

ROMALDKIRK, Yorkshire. *The component parts of this interesting three-decker, with its churching pew, dating from 1728, were dismembered in 1926 and only the pulpit now remains in position. The remaining fragments are unhappily stored at the back of the church. There were originally crimson velvet hangings.*

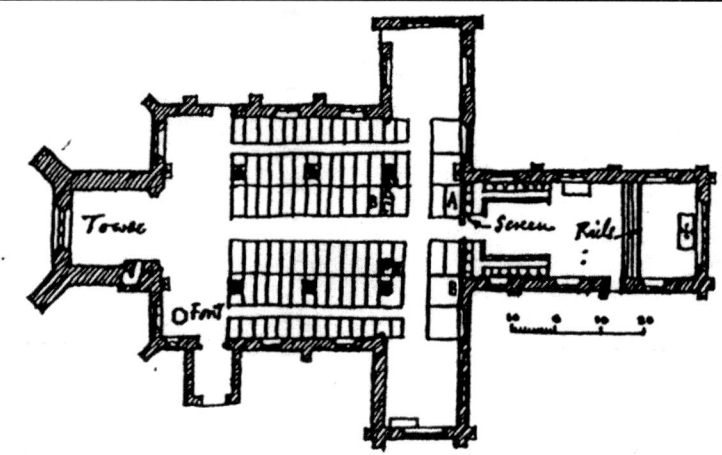

SEDGEFIELD, Co. Durham. *A medieval fabric refurnished in the late seventeenth century. The stalls and rails in the chancel remain, but the church was repewed in the nineteenth century. The plan shows the nave fittings as in 1663; the screen was erected c. 1638. The pew marked A was for the 'parson's wife' and that marked B was 'the sick wife's stall', i.e. a churching pew.*

1. *The churching pew:* these plans show the placing of the large churching pew in Romaldkirk, Yorkshire, dating from 1728, and the mid-seventeenth-century fittings in Sedgefield, Co. Durham, which included a 'sick-wife's stall' next to the screen. From Addleshaw, G. W. O., and Etchells, F., *The Architectural Setting of Anglican Worship* (London, 1948), pp. 85, 94.

This Service is a copy of the Service in the Deposited Book referred to in the Prayer Book Measure of 1927 as amended in accordance with the provisions of the Prayer Book Measure 1928. Publication of this Service does not directly or indirectly imply that it can be regarded as authorized for use in Churches.

THE THANKSGIVING OF WOMEN AFTER CHILD-BIRTH
COMMONLY CALLED
THE CHURCHING OF WOMEN

¶ *The woman, at the usual time after her delivery, accompanied by her husband, if he so desire, shall come into the church, and there shall kneel down in some convenient place, as hath been accustomed, or as the Ordinary shall direct: And then the Minister shall say unto her,*

FORASMUCH as it hath pleased Almighty God of his goodness to give you safe deliverance, and to preserve you in the great danger of child-birth; you shall therefore give hearty thanks unto God, and say,

¶ *Then shall the Minister say the 116th Psalm,*
Dilexi quoniam.

I AM well pleased : that the Lord hath heard the voice of my prayer;
2 That he hath inclined his ear unto me : therefore will I call upon him as long as I live.
3 The snares of death compassed me round about : and the pains of hell gat hold upon me.
4 I found trouble and heaviness, and I called upon the name of the Lord : O Lord, I beseech thee, deliver my soul.
5 Gracious is the Lord, and righteous : yea, our God is merciful.
6 The Lord preserveth the simple : I was in misery, and he helped me.
7 Turn again then unto thy rest, O my soul : for the Lord hath rewarded thee.
8 And why? thou hast delivered my soul from death : mine eyes from tears, and my feet from falling.
9 I will walk before the Lord : in the land of the living.
[10 I believed, and therefore will I speak : but I was sore troubled : I said in my haste, All men are liars.*]
* *The tenth verse may be omitted.*
11 What reward shall I give unto the Lord : for all the benefits that he hath done unto me?
12 I will receive the cup of salvation : and call upon the name of the Lord.
13 I will pay my vows now in the presence of all his people : in the courts of the Lord's house, even in the midst of thee, O Jerusalem. Praise the Lord.

Glory be to the Father, and to the Son : and to the Holy Ghost;
As it was in the beginning, is now, and ever shall be : world without end. Amen.

Or,
Psalm 127. *Nisi Dominus.*

EXCEPT the Lord build the house : their labour is but lost that build it.
2 Except the Lord keep the city : the watchman waketh but in vain.
3 It is but lost labour that ye haste to rise up early, and so late take rest, and eat the bread of carefulness : for so he giveth his beloved sleep.
4 Lo, children and the fruit of the womb : are an heritage and gift that cometh of the Lord.
5 Like as the arrows in the hand of the giant : even so are the young children.
6 Happy is the man that hath his quiver full of them : they shall not be ashamed when they speak with their enemies in the gate.

Glory be to the Father, and to the Son : and to the Holy Ghost;
As it was in the beginning, is now, and ever shall be : world without end. Amen.

¶ *Then the Minister shall say,*
Let us pray.
Lord, have mercy upon us.
Christ, have mercy upon us.
Lord, have mercy upon us.

OUR Father, which art in heaven, Hallowed be thy name; Thy kingdom come; Thy will be done; In earth as it is in heaven. Give us this day our daily bread. And forgive us our trespasses, As we forgive them that trespass against us. And lead us not into temptation; But deliver us from evil : For thine is the kingdom, The power, and the glory, For ever and ever. Amen.

Minister. O Lord, save this woman thy servant;
Answer. Who putteth her trust in thee.
Minister. Be thou to her a strong tower;
Answer. From the face of her enemy.
Minister. Lord, hear our prayer;
Answer. And let our cry come unto thee.

Minister. Let us pray.

O ALMIGHTY God, we give thee humble thanks for that thou hast vouchsafed to deliver this woman thy servant from the great pain and peril of child-birth; Grant, we beseech thee, most merciful Father, that she, through thy help, may both faithfully live, and walk according to thy will, in this life present; and also may be partaker of everlasting glory in the life to come; through Jesus Christ our Lord. Amen.

¶ *Then, if there be no Communion at the time of the Churching, shall the Minister say to the Woman,*

UNTO God's gracious mercy and protection we commit you. The Lord bless you, and keep you : the Lord make his face to shine upon you, and be gracious unto you : the Lord lift up his countenance upon you, and give you peace, both now and evermore. *Amen.*

¶ *Prayers which may be used at the discretion of the Minister before the Blessing.*

O GOD, our heavenly Father, we thank thee and praise thy glorious name, that thou hast been pleased to bless this woman thy servant, and to bestow upon her the gift of a child : Grant, we beseech thee, most merciful Father, that she [with her husband] may diligently lead her child in the way of righteousness, to their own great blessing and the glory of thy name; through Jesus Christ our Lord. Amen.

O GOD, whose ways are hidden and thy works most wonderful, who makest nothing in vain, and lovest all that thou hast made : Comfort this thy servant whose heart is sore smitten and oppressed; and grant that she may so love and serve thee in this life, that she may obtain the fulness of thy promises in the world to come; through Jesus Christ our Lord. Amen.

¶ *The woman, that cometh to give her thanks, must offer accustomed offerings; and, if there be a Communion, it is convenient that she receive the Holy Communion.*

SIDE LINES CALL ATTENTION TO MODIFICATIONS OF THE BOOK OF COMMON PRAYER EITHER IN TEXT OR RUBRIC, OR TO NEW MATERIAL.

Published in London by the OXFORD UNIVERSITY PRESS, the CAMBRIDGE UNIVERSITY PRESS, and EYRE AND SPOTTISWOODE (PUBLISHERS) LIMITED.
Copyright. Printed by Eyre and Spottiswoode Limited, London.

2. 1928 Churching card from the Church of St Mary Magdalen, South Molton. This shows the text of the proposed revision of the *Book of Common Prayer*, 1928.

3. Samples taken from three churching registers in the records of Metropolitan London.

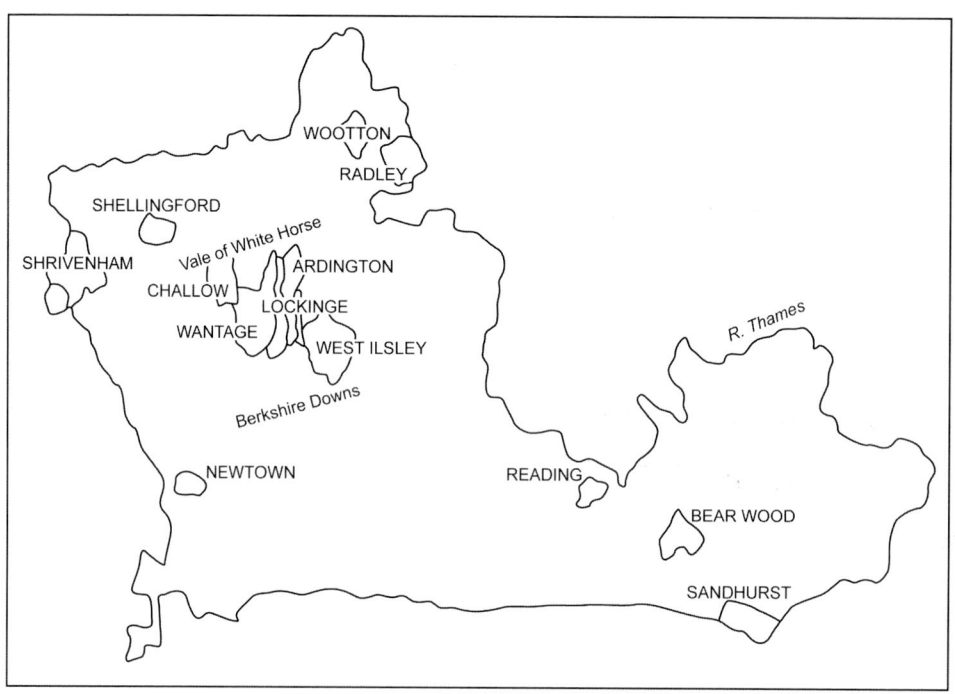

4. Map (1) showing the location of parishes holding the fullest twentieth-century churching records in Berkshire.

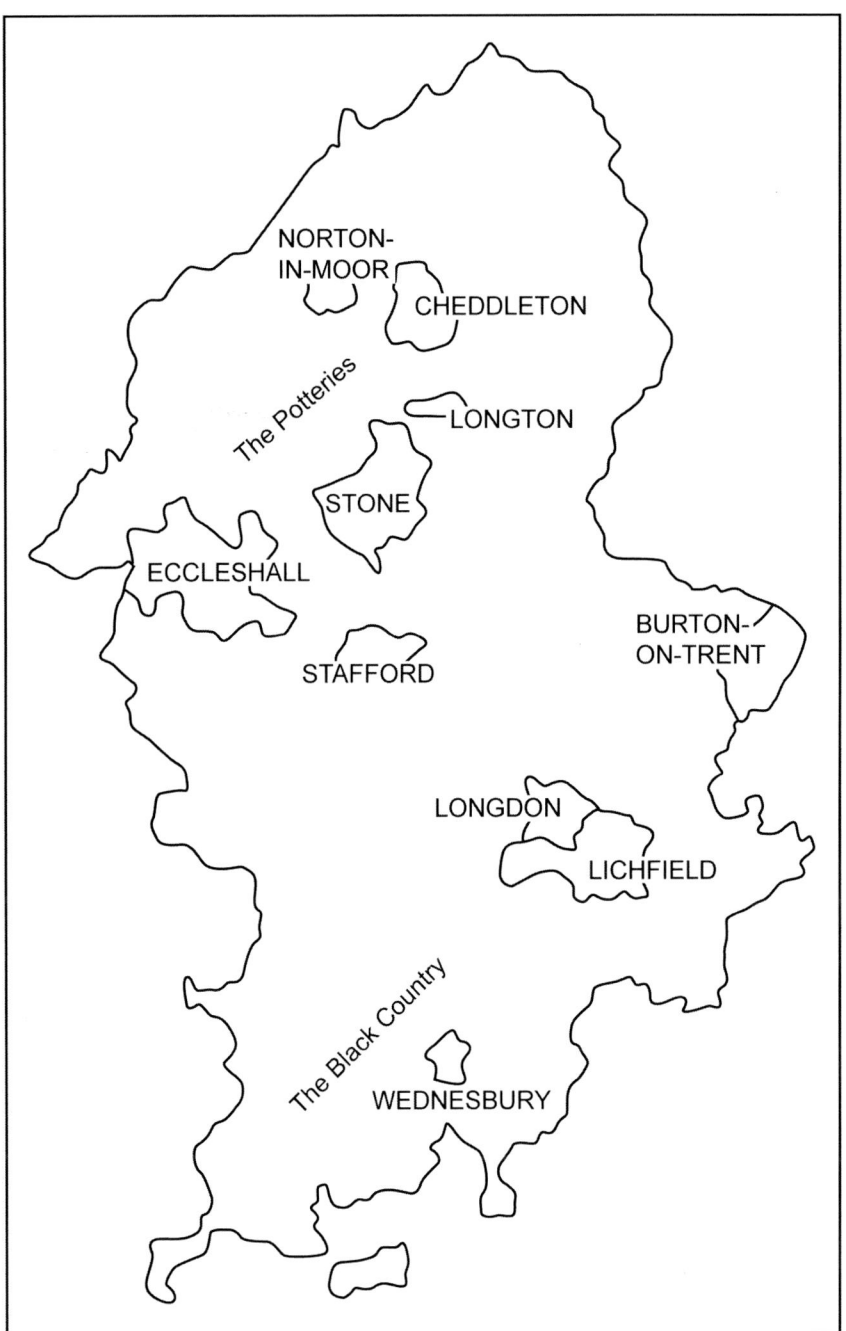

5. Map (2) showing the location of parishes holding the fullest twentieth-century churching records in Staffordshire.

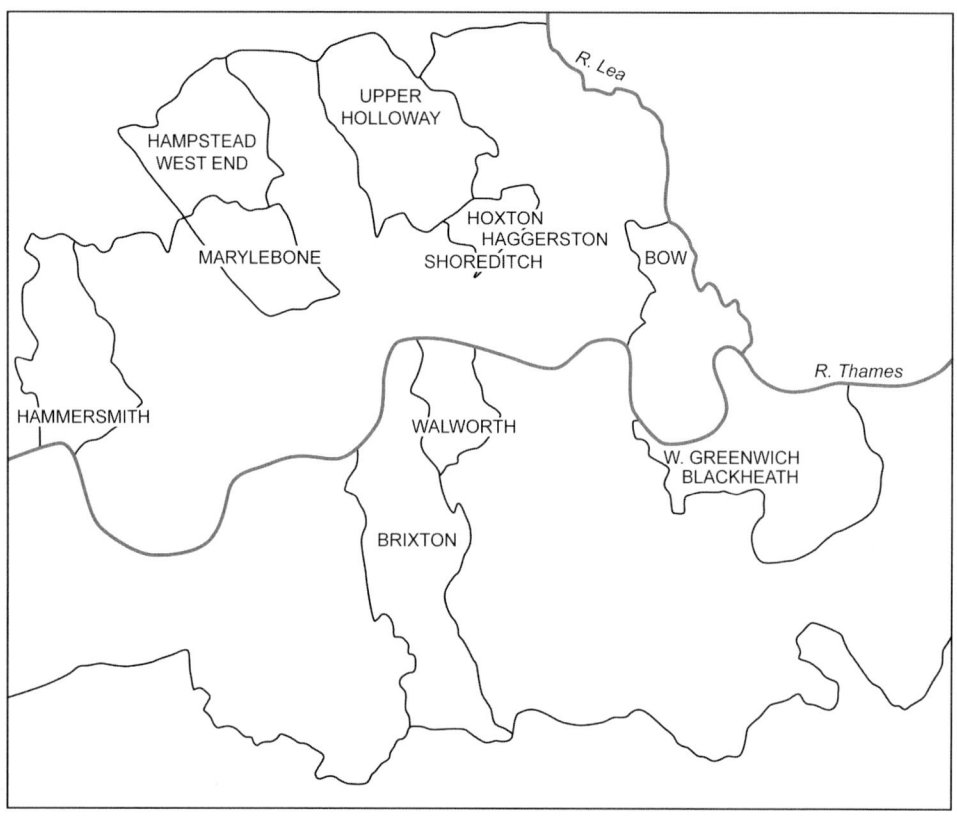

6. Map (3) location of parishes holding the fullest twentieth-century churching records in Metropolitan London (1948 borough boundaries).

7. Page from the Churching register of St Mary, Stafford, 1900.

8. Page from the service register of St Anne's, Shoreditch, July 1910.

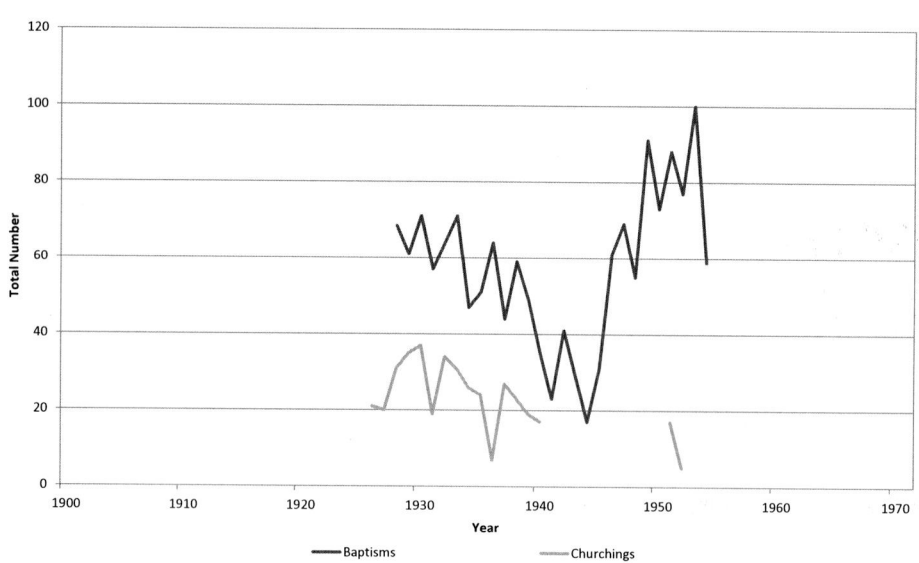

9. Figure showing churching and baptism in five London parishes: (i) Blackheath

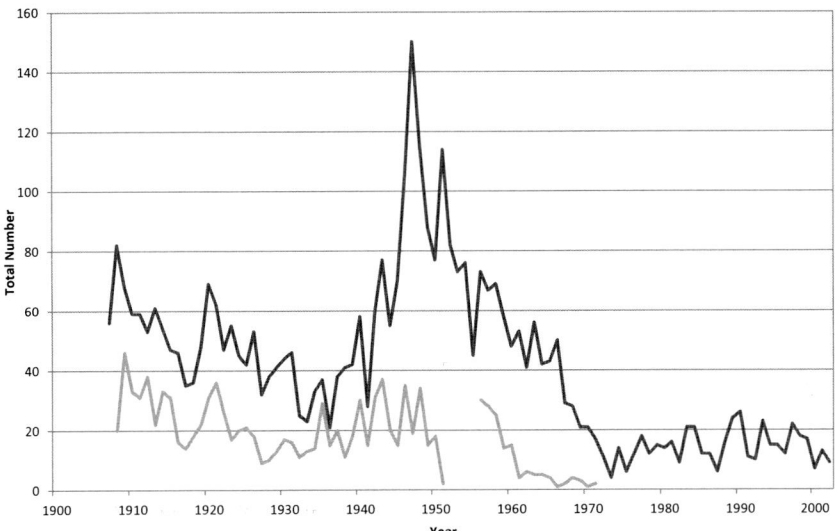

9. Figure showing churching and baptism in five London parishes: (ii) North Brixton.

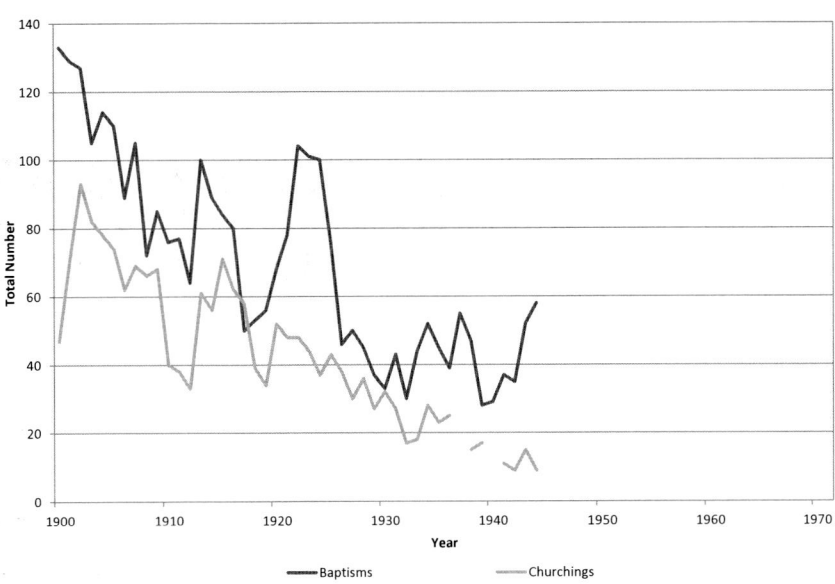

9. Figure showing churching and baptism in five London parishes: (iii) Hammersmith

9. Figure showing churching and baptism in five London parishes: (iv) Upper Holloway

9. Figure showing churching and baptism in five London parishes: (v) West Hampstead

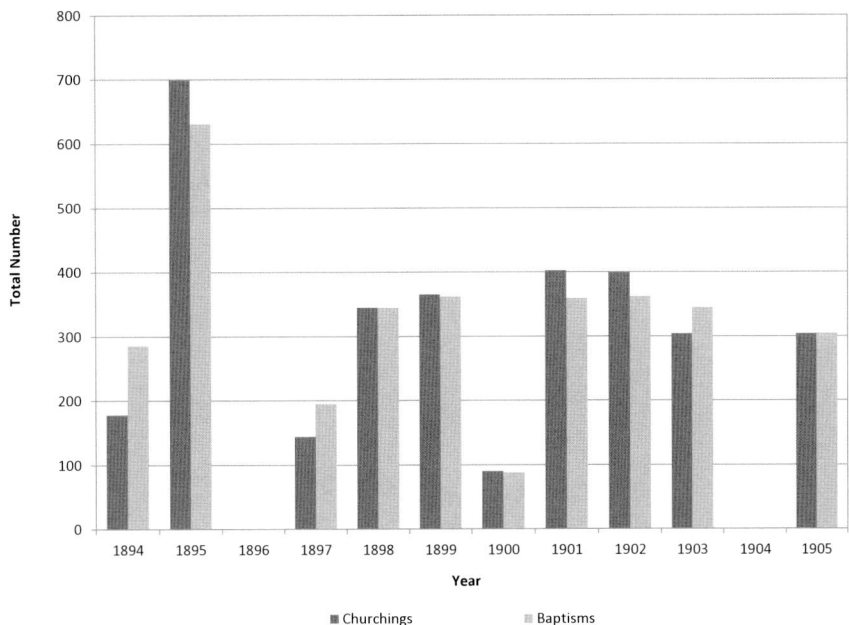

10. Churching and baptism in the parish of St. James-the-Less, Longton, 1894–1905

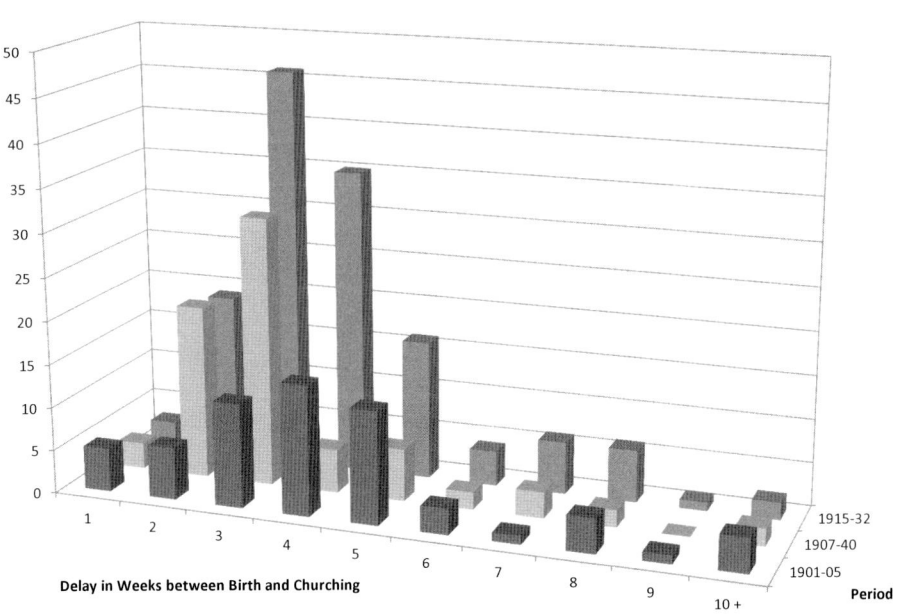

11. Distribution of churching and interval between birth and churching.

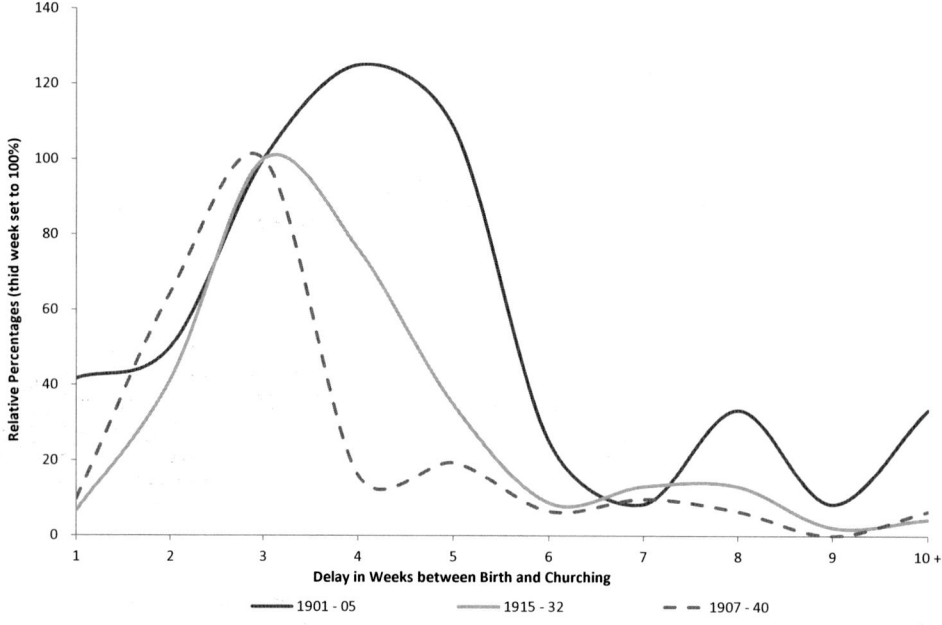

12. Variation in interval between birth and churching between 1901 and 1940.

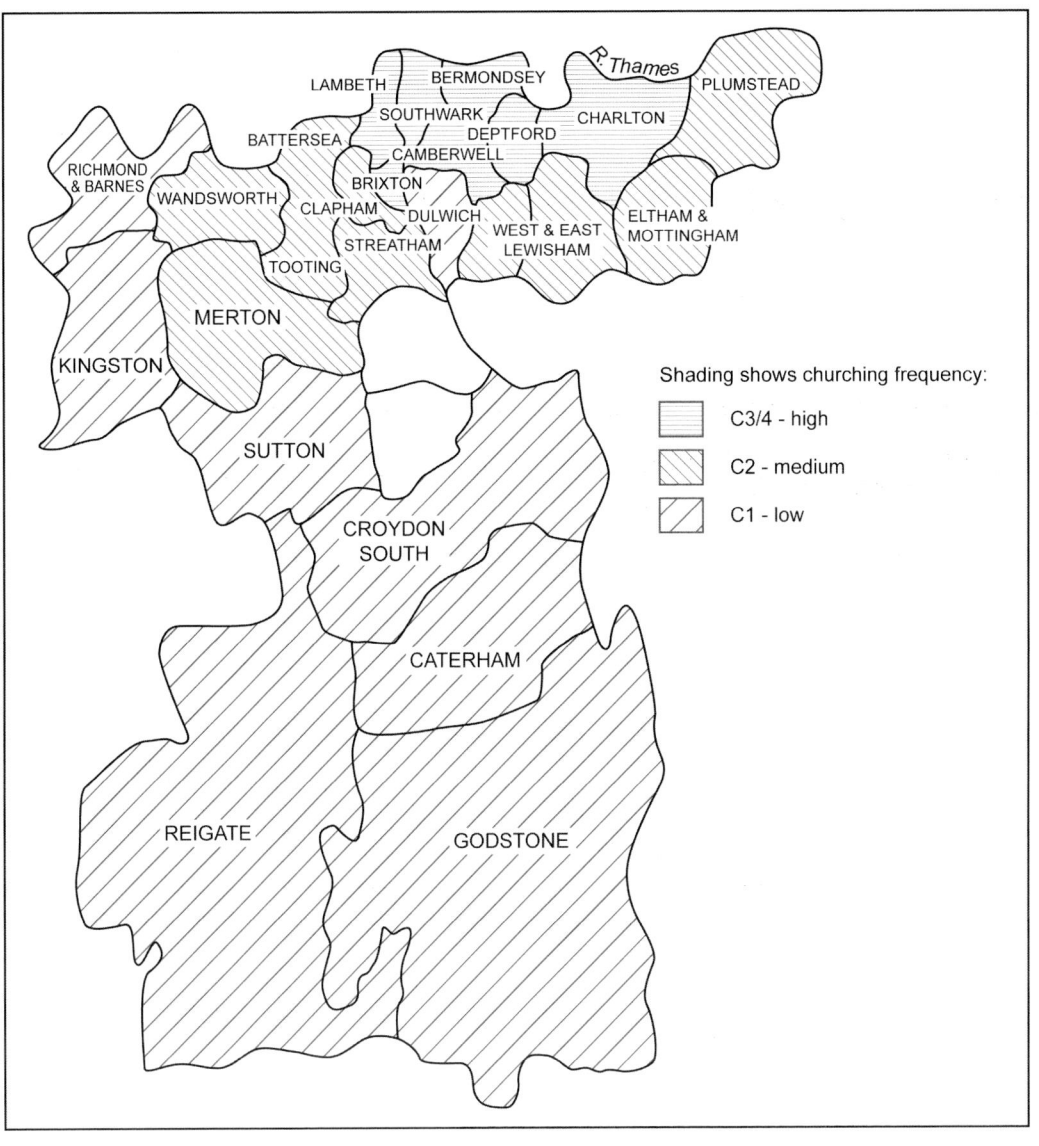

13. Map (4) Location of deaneries in the Diocese of Southwark, showing varied levels of churching frequency

List of ~~refusals~~ of Churching ~ Bad moral Cases.

1. ~~[struck through]~~ ~~[struck through]~~
2. Fletcher — Vine St. · Oct. 13.
3. Chance — New Bank St. -13.
4. Sinclair — Pickett St.
5. Thomas — Northwick Hall Cottage — Aug 18.
6. Cole (Mrs) — 4 Bromsgrove St.
   Obtained Churching surreptitiously after adultery. Aug '18. Has been told that she is excommunicate from all Church privileges including burial except absolution has been sought for & received. [Has received Absolute[?]

7. Lily Jones — 7 Pardiswell St. Living with a married man. ~~[struck]~~ another child, Aug '18. & others.

8. Jervas (née Smith): Pickett St. very bad case, [annotations in margin] mar'd Aug 1920. Child born following Aug. The girl = confirmed. Refused to make her confession: refused Churching.

9. Carter (Ada) 45 Pardiswell St., child by a married Sergeant in Norton Barracks. [annotations in margin: Now Barraca / living in Albany Terrace?] Both communicants, & neither penitent. 1921 The house is 'excommunicate' Another child 1923. Now married & living same house.

14. Notes and comments on churchings by the vicar of St Stephen, Barbourne, Worcestershire, 1931.

Note marriage of Edwin Brewer 6 Jan 1923
girl named Hampton.
o Saunders 39 Perriman St   Dec 29
1 Draper   24   "   "   Jan. 30 (lodger

X Afterwards made Confession at S. Geo.
Tore children there for H. B. is now to
at Butchers Shop, Amberley Rd

Married at Congregational Meeting House.

S. Stephen's, ✝ Barbourne.

FORM OF APPLICATION FOR THE CHURCHING OF WOMEN.

Please arrange to Church

Name, Mrs. B. Hodgkins

Address 4 Checketts Lane

to-morrow, at 5 - 45 p.m. o'clock.

This form is to be detached from the page opposite and left at the Vicarage <u>the day before</u> Churching is desired.

15. Form of application for churching, St Stephen, Barbourne, Worcestershire, 1931.